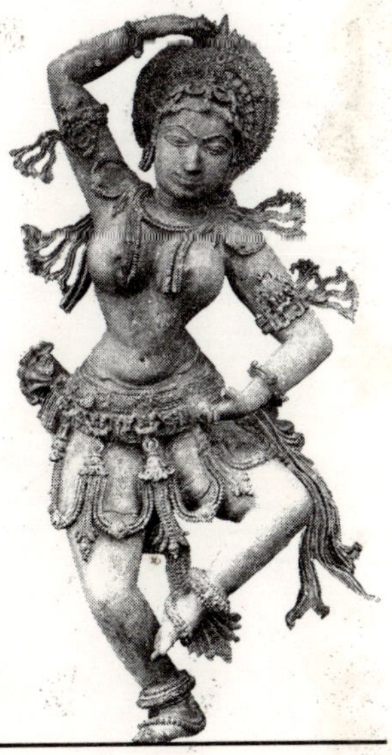

APSARAS IN HOYSALA ART
A NEW DIMENSION

APSARAS IN HOYSALA ART

A NEW DIMENSION

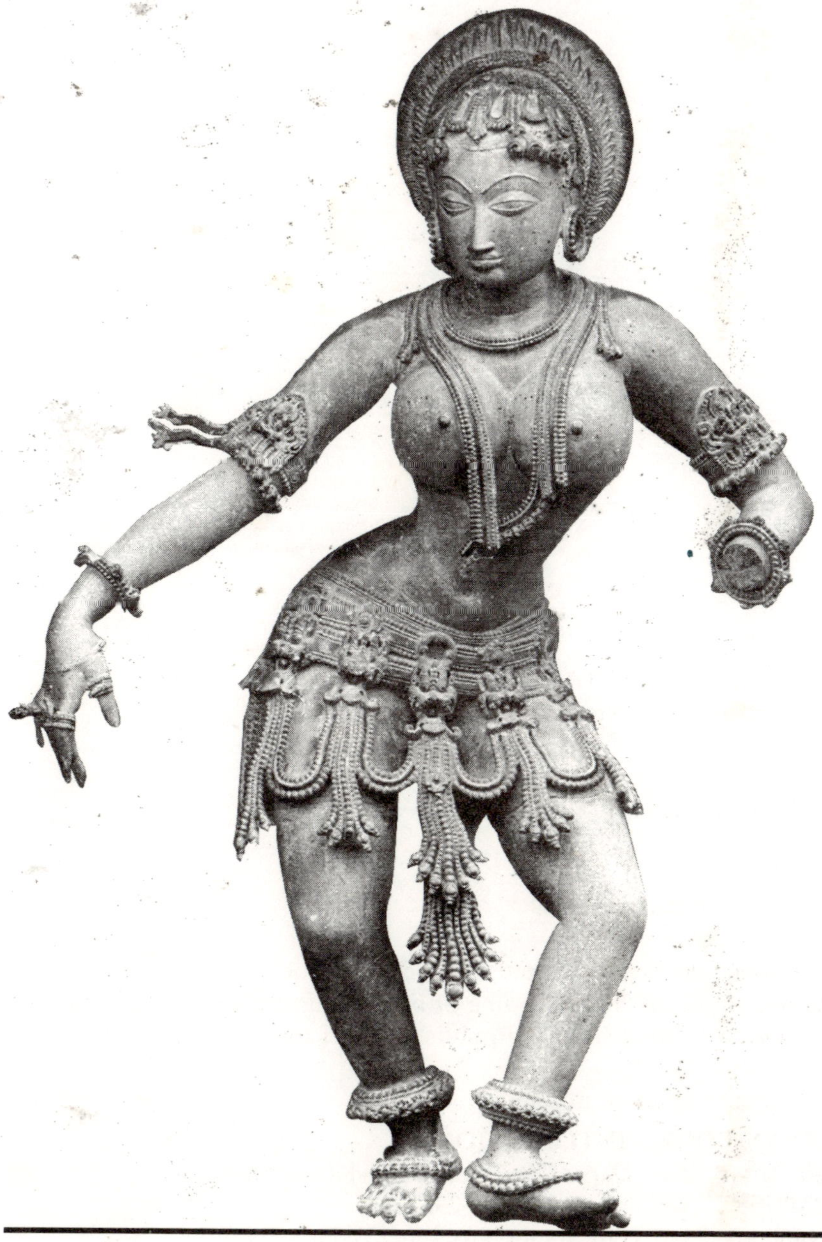

REKHA RAO

ARYAN BOOKS INTERNATIONAL
New Delhi

APSARAS IN HOYSALA ART
A New Dimension

ISBN: 978-81-7305-379-5

First Published in **2009** by:

ARYAN BOOKS INTERNATIONAL

Pooja Apartments, 4B, Ansari Road, Darya Ganj, New Delhi-110 002 (India)
Tel.: 23287589, 23255799; Fax: 91-11-23270385
E-mail: aryanbooks@vsnl.com, aryanbooks@gmail.com

Printed in India at
Mudrak, 30-A, Patparganj, Delhi-110091

Foreword

I have great pleasure in writing a foreword to the book *Apsaras in Hoysala Art: A New Dimension* with reference to Belur Cennakēśava temple authored by the reputed dancer and scholar Mrs. Rekha Rao. She has taken great pains to study the physical, spiritual and emotional aspects of the dancing figures in Belur Cennakēśava temple with special reference to the ancient texts on dance.

Before referring to the special features of Rekha Rao's monograph, I deem it fit to trace the role of Hoysala art in the general context of Indian art and architecture.

The Hindu ideal of art was to give expression to the inner self or *Ātmā*, purified and exalted, holding communion with the Universal Soul, *Paramātmā*. Hence details of the physical body were not of much importance to the Indian artist so long as he could bring out the spiritual greatness of his subject. But the emphasis on spiritualism did not hinder the artist from maintaining standards of art with an eye for proportions, depth, curve and lines. For instance, the dancing couple of Karla, the *mithuna* figures of Badami caves and Virupaksha temple, Pattadakal, the bracket figures of Mallikarjuna temple, Kuruvatti, the *Apsara* figures of Kēśava temple, Belur, and the folk dancers in the Vijayanagar monuments are excellent examples of realism in Indian art. So far as the representation of divine and semi-divine beings is concerned, the Indian artist tried to depict the subtle body. While the Greeks had the athletic physical body as their ideal, the Indians had the subtle body pulsating with energy (sap of life) and serving as a vehicle for realization of a state higher than the physical state. The *Sarnath* Buddha, the Vishnu on *Ananta* in Badami caves, the *Yogiśvara Śiva* of Ellora and the *Gomateśvara* of Srvanabelagoḷa are striking examples of this subtle body.

The Chalukyas of Badami who carried out major experiments in temple building were influenced to a very limited extent by the Gupta and Pallava traditions. While there are a few missing links in the evolution of temple architecture of the post-Gupta period in the north, there is no such missing link in the experiments of temple construction and embellishment carried out by the Karnataka dynasties beginning from the Badami Chalukyas (6th-8th century) and ending with the Vijayanagar rulers (14th-16th century) and their feudatories, Nayakas of Keladi, Tanjore, Madurai and Wodeyars of Mysore (16th-18th century). The archetypes evolved in the 8th century became the models for temple construction in Eastern India.

Similarly, certain experiments in Indo-Islamic architecture carried out by the Bahmani kings and their successors resulted in a new school of Islamic architecture in Karnataka.

One may wonder how such a long tradition of art and architecture was fostered in Karnataka. The reason is not far to seek. Karnataka has a long tradition of royal patronage for art and literature and shared the common heritage of monumental culture with the Indian subcontinent. According to *Kāvyamīmāṃsā* of Rājasekhara, the king was himself expected to be a poet, artist, not for parading his intellect or aesthetic qualities, but for adjudging the literary equipment and artistic skill of his subjects and the need for preserving and enriching the monumental culture of the kingdom. He should convene the assembly of poets and artists as was done by Bhūlokamalla Someśvara (AD 1126-38) the Kalyani Chalukyan king who refers to the *Sabhā* or assembly of lovers of art in his famous work *Abhilashitārtha Chintāmaṇi* or *Rāja Mānasollāsa*. Besides this monumental work on art, Karnataka has to its credit two more major works on art, namely, *Śivatattvaratnākara* of Basava Bhūpāla of Keladi (17th century) published by Keladi Museum and *Sritattvanidhi* produced under the patronage of Sri Krishnaraja Wodeyar III of Mysore (1799-1868). With so much of encouragement it was but natural that even poets could speak of the technique of painting and sculpture, as for instance, in *Kavirājamārga* of *Ārcvijaya* and *Mallināthа Puraṇa* of Ranna.

An outstanding royal patron of fine arts was Someśa or Someśvara (AD 1126-28), the author of *Abhilashitārtha Chintāmaṇi*, which contains details of fine arts and pastimes besides throwing light on social and cultural life of the times. This work has five parts (*prakaraṇas*), each divided into 20 chapters. The first and second *prakaraṇas* deal respectively with ethics and polity. The third *prakaraṇa* deals with architecture and painting. The fourth *prakaraṇa* deals with amusements and the fifth with sports and pastimes. The attainments expected of a cultured person (*nāgarika*) in those days were very high. It is interesting to find that *Nṛttaratnāvali* of Jayapa (1253-4), the Kakatiya General refers to the fact that during the *Bhālu Mātṛdēvatā*, Someśa witnessed with curiosity a girl singing and dancing in *Bhilla Veśā* and was so pleased that he arranged the dance into proper sequences and brought it into use. In some of the Kalyani Chalukyan and Hoysala sculptures, dancing damsels are in the costume of *Bhils* or *Gondals*. Someśvara was not only an exponent in dance but also in music. The minute details of music, dance and architecture are discussed by the author in three chapters. He refers to the assembly or court of art lovers and the musical instruments *Vīṇā* and *Kinnara*. His treatment of the subjects is practical. The *Jaina* poet Ranna's *Gadāyuddha* (AD 990) based on *Pampa-Bhārata* was a very popular *Champu*, the *Karuṇā* and *Raudra* sentiments of which seem to have caught the imagination of the Chalukyan and Hoysala sculptors. They have chiselled beautiful narratives in stone. During the Kalyani Chalukyan period Chandrarāja wrote in AD 1030 *Madanatilaka*, a work on erotic, which was relied upon by sculptors for carving erotic scenes, with some exaggeration, on the temples of Amriteśvara at Amritapura and Kalleśvara at Bagali. But Vatsyayana's *Kāmasūtra* too had abundant material for eroticism in Indian art.

HOYSALA ARCHITECTURE

Hoysala rulers evolved a new style of temple architecture in which sculptural art played as important a role as architecture itself. The evolution of the Hoysala style from a simple to a sophisticated one becomes apparent when the Late Chalukyan temple at Doddagaddavalli is compared with the Cennakēśava temple at Belur and the latter with the Kēśava temple of Sōmanāthapura. In the early stage, the *Vimāna* (shrine and *sukanāsi*) was attached to the *navaraṅga* through a vestibule and finally to a large pillared hall, which is often uniform in plan. In later Hoysala style, the pillared hall is small and directly connected to the shrine. But in both the phases the unity of the structure is not disturbed; the pillared hall also formed a part of an organic whole, which is further emphasized by the friezes running continuously on the plinth (*adhishthāna*) and lower part of the external face of the walls of the halls and shrine. Unlike the Kalyana Chalukyan temples wherein the hall was separated from the *Vimāna*, the Hoysalas integrated the two.

In plan and elevation, the Hoysala temples show a departure from the Kalyana Chalukyan temples. The ground plan of the *Vimāna* is laid out in a series of points to produce a star shape obtained as if by rotating the square on its common centre, the number of angular displacements depending upon the number of points needed in the star. The platform on which the temple is built closely follows the stellate plan. The high plinth is ornamented with successive bands of floral designs and figure sculptures. The treatment of the wall surface is horizontal with three bands of figures running around the *Vimāna* and two round the hall (*navaraṅga*). The upper tendency of the superstructure is indicated by the fluting effect of the tower produced by carrying the stellate plan through the eave up to the finial (*Kalaśa*), but the introduction of the horizontal courses in the *śikhara* makes it less northern in style. Some Hoysala temples are single-celled, but there are others in which two, or even three cells, each with a *śikhara* are attached to a common hall. The Keśava temple at Sōmanāthapura is the most complete, while the Cennakēśava temple at Belur is the most ornate. The latter is unparalleled for its enchanting bracket figures and minute details of carving in the ceiling and doorways.

The moulded courses of the plinth are embellished with successive friezes of elephants, scrollwork, dancers, musicians and rows of female figures standing under bowers. Some ladies in the act of dressing evoke admiration for details and delicacy of carving.

Rekha Rao's new approach to Hoysala art in general and *Apsara* figures in particular lies in explaining the various emotions (*rasas*) underlying the charming physical beauty of the dancing figures and also the role of the attendants generally ignored by art historians.

According to the author, the *Pātras* (exclusive dancers) who took part in a ballet (dance drama), are represented as *Apsaras*. They were held in high regard as servants of God and therefore first to receive the *prasādu*.

I congratulate Mrs. Rekha Rao for a thought-provoking interpretation of the concept of *Apsara* as a dancer. I am sure that both experts and general art lovers will benefit from reading this book.

Bangalore

S.R. Rao
Former Deputy Director General
Archaeological Survey of India
New Delhi

Appreciation

The author Smt. Rekha Rao is a Bharatnatyam and Kuchipudi dancer, scholar, teacher and choreographer. She has been teaching for many years and some of her students are now accomplished performers.

She has delved deep into the study of temple sculpture, architecture, yoga, philosophy, *mudra vigyan*, *nadayoga* and the *Natyashastra*. Her theories are based on a careful study of the sculptures of the dancing *apsaras* of the Belur temple of the Hoysala period. She has interpreted her observations both from the point of view of the physical character and features of the figurines as well as the inner spiritual dimension that they represent, describing it as an experience of *nadayoga*.

The first part is devoted to the physical attributes of the dancing sculptures. She examines facial features, costume, ornamentation, etc., identifying the *rasas* expressed. While in the second part she examines the sculptures according to the *gunas* from *rajas* to *sattva* and explores the dimension of *chakras*, *koshas* states of *jeeva* and *nadayoga*. And to strengthen her arguments she has also examined the plan of the temple architecture in relation to *yantras* and *mandalas*.

Rekha Rao deserves praise for enlightening us with a comprehensive, holistic approach to the subject, an outcome of her in-depth study, understanding and complete involvement in the subject. I am sure scholars and readers will understand her point of view and welcome her work.

Padmashri Darshana Jhaveri
Director, Manipuri Nartanalaya
Ex. President, Manipuri Nritya Kendra

Preface

The *Apsara* sculptures at the Belur Cennakēśava temple, have been a source of inspiration for lovers of art, ever since they adorned the walls of this temple. Even to this day dancers are motivated to imitate the postures of these *Apsaras* in their recitals. Artists have been sculpting the replicas of these figures in all mediums like wood, stone, metal, paper mache, etc. and innumerable poets have given their imagination, based on the beauty and themes of these *Apsaras*. Born and brought up in Mysore, situated 155 km away from Belur, this temple was the monument which I frequented often on vacations, as the *Apsaras* had caught my fancy. Belur is a small town, in Hassan district of Karnataka which is around 224 km away from the city of Bangalore.

As a young girl undergoing training in *Bharata Nāṭya* style of classical dance, I always wondered whether there exists a linkage between the present form of *Bharata Nāṭya* and the *Apsara* sculptures at Belur. In pursuit of this mission, I studied Indology at post-graduate level with specialization in Hoysala art and architecture. Establishing linkages still continued to be a mirage. I continued this journey through further studies of dance related texts like *Nāṭyaśāstra* and *Daśarūpaka* to have a deeper understanding of dance. During this period I tried to analyze as to which form of present classical style has the closest resemblance to the dance sculptures at Belur temple. Through many years of continued studies of these sculptures, I could understand that these sculptures are more interpretative of a theme and only some of them depict the techniques of pure dance movements. They closely relate to the personality of *Nartakīs* as described in the *Nāṭyaśāstra*. In my approach to understand the dance of *Apsaras*, I gained some clarity of thought when I first classified the 42 *Apsara* figures into recital and thematic based figures, focusing my observations on the dwarf figures present on either side of the *Apsara* scultpure.

Apsara Figures
(42 Nos.)

Pure Dance and Music (24) (Attendants hold instruments)	Dramaturgy (18) (Attendants play different roles)
• String • Percussion • Wind • Metallic • Pure dance	• Interpretative dance (Thematic representation of sentiments – *Rasas*)

Twenty-four figures depict her recitals, either music or dance, in which the dwarf attendants are the accompanying artists, playing instruments. The 18 thematic figures has dwarf attendants playing different roles, in support of the theme that the *Apsara* depicts. When the photographs of *Apsaras* with the same theme were placed in a sequence and compared, like the *Apsaras* with bow and arrow or the sculptures associated with a parrot were segregated, I could trace the theme that they are projecting. With my in-depth observation of these sculptures, aided by the magnified photographs, I realized that the alternate or inner thoughts of the *Apsara* are expressed in some sculptures through the attendant sculptures. The position of the limbs and the facial features like head, eyes, eyelids, cheeks, chin, lip, etc. in sculptures, are according to the mode of expression as described in *Nāṭyaśāstra.* The external accessories which these figures are holding like weapons, objects, animal representation and costumes, are in accordance with the *Āhārya* (Chapter 23) of *Nāṭyaśāstra.* The dwarf attendants which are present at the base of each figure, are according to the explanations of 'Dūtīlakṣaṇa', that is described in *Nāṭyaśāstra* (Ch. 25, Sl. 9-11) and *Daśarūpaka* (Part 2; 46).

With this background I tried to relate the classical dance interpretation of *Apsara* to the fourfold art of *abhinaya*, the *āṅgika* (physical expression), the *vācika* (verbal), *āhārya* (external accessories used) and *sāttvika* (internal and natural).

My observation of *rasas* in *Apsaras* is based mainly on four texts: *Nāṭyaśāstra, Daśarūpaka, Abhinaya Darpaṇa* and *Mānasōllāsa*. *Nāṭyaśāstra* is a treatise on Indian theatre arts, which was compiled during 2000 BC to 500 BC (the date is however controversial), by Bharata Muni. It deals in detail through 36 chapters about the stage, dance, music, drama, jewellery and other accessories, which are meticulously followed by every classical artist, even to this day. *Daśarūpaka* is a commentary on certain chapters of *Nāṭyaśāstra* which was written by Dhanañjaya in the 10th century AD. It gives a detailed knowledge about the various types of sentiments, the mode of expressing sentiments, types of heroes, heroines, villains, their attendants, etc. Nandikeśava's *Abhinaya Darpaṇa* was written in AD 1000. It is a text after Bharata's *Nāṭyaśāstra*, explaining the gestures that are used in dance and theatre. *Mānasōllāsa* is also encyclopaedic in nature, written by the Kalyana Chalukya King Someśvara during AD 1126 to 1138. It is written in five parts, dealing with the political set-up, medicines, architecture, cultural and social entertainment which existed in that particular period. A study of *Mānasōllāsa* gives a clear picture of the royal hunting game *Dīpamṛgaja* that is depicted in some of the bracket figures. It also tells us about the instruments used in *Apsara* dancing sculptures.

Going through the texts of *Mānasōllāsa*, *Nāṭyaśāstra* and Holy *Geeta* – a commentary on *Bhagavadgita* by Swamy Chinmayananda, I could visualise *Apsaras* from three different perspectives as detailed below:

1. *Apsaras*, when viewed on the basis of *Mānasōllāsa*, it appears that queens of Chalukya and Hoysala dynasties were portrayed as role models through these sculptures, displaying their status, skills, hobbies, and insight in the fine arts.
2. *Apsaras* when viewed on the basis of *Nāṭyaśāstra*, represent dance postures and the expression of moods – the sentiments detailing most of the elements of *Nāṭyaśāstra*, such as postures, accessories, costumes, jewellery, attendants, and the categories of *abhinaya*.
3. When viewed from the philosophical perspective of getting into the inner world, the sculptures depict various stages of mind through 'guṇas' such as *sāttvik*, *rājasik* and *tāmasik*.

Just to illustrate the above through examples, the three Bracket figures (referred in this book as B.F.), B.F. - 6, 17 and 23, are related to the act of bow and arrow.

According to *Mānasōllāsa*, these sculptures depict the royal hunting game 'Dīpamriga' and 'Paniyaja' (for details ref. ch 3/4, of part I).

According to *Nāṭyaśāstra*, they demonstrate the mode of depicting the sentiment of heroism and the four acts that are to be followed while using bow and arrow in dramatics.

From a philosophical perspective, the bow and arrow stand for weapons to clear the veils of *māyā* illusion. (All Hindu gods and godesses hold weapons like a sword, bow and arrow or a spinning wheel which symbolise powerful weapons used for the destruction of ignorance and illusion, that are personified as demons.)

To quote another example, B.F. 7 has a lady holding her long tress of hair. This can be interpreted as sqeezing of water after playing the water game 'Sechana krida' (for details ref. ch 3/ 4 of part I). It is also viewed as the depiction of the sentiment of *śriṅgāra*, and examining the neatness pearly hairnet 'Śikhā jāla' that is worn by dancers which is described in ch. 23 of *Nāṭyaśāstra* under the category of jewellery. When viewed as a personality, from a psychological perspective, it is the display of one's possession vanity, the long and thick hair that she is proud of – a typical of *Rajoguṇa*. All the three views look convincing.

Similarly, B.F. 9 and 22 depict *Apsara* in the form of Bhairavī (a form of Goddess Durgā). It can be interpreted as 'Kathāvinoda', of *Mānasōllāsa*, where the queen entertained the king by a dramatic narration of Purāṇic episodes, adopting the costumes and execution of the sentiment 'raudra' or anger, as described in *Nāṭyaśāstra*, or it may also hint the stage of 'Śivahood' – the oneness with Śiva – the ultimate truth, an ultimate stage of awareness, when analysed what a Bhairavī stands for.

The various activities of royal women appear to be the theme of these *Apsara* sculptures, which are executed in dancing mode following the description of *Nāṭyaśāstra*, and concealing the essence of eternal philosophical truths within, in a subtle way, the revelation of which unveils with an in-depth analysis. From the description, through examples, it is clear that one has to have a holistic approach in the analysis of sculptures and not limit to any one theme.

These sculptures are refered as *Apsaras* in this book, seeing them from the location of sculptures, in the temple, as they are mounted on an oval-shaped pedestal – the *padmāsana* which is the seat used to invoke the demi-gods and they are on pilasters to symbolise that they are in a higher abode. They are also into the *Gandharva kalā* – the art loved and performed by the celestial dancers, which adds logic in calling them as *Apsaras*.

Even to this day I am awestruck to discover the thorough knowledge the sculptors had during those days regarding the intricacies associated with dance, instruments, sentiments, etc. precisely as they are prescribed in *Nāṭyaśāstra*, and in the field of Hindu philosophy. In my attempt to trace the sentiments that the *Apsaras* are depicting, I noticed the absence of two of the nine *rasas*, the pathos or *karuṇa* and disgust or *bībhatsa*, which dampen the moods of the spectators.

The material is distributed in Part I, over 13 chapters. The first two chapters are about the historical background, the general description and the plan of the temple. The third chapter is dedicated to *Apsara*, as she is described in literary, inscriptional and sculptural evidences. Further, the 4th, 5th and 6th chapters deal in brief with the attendants of *Apsara*, the basic leg postures, observed in *Apsara* sculptures, and the nine sentiments (*rasas*). Seventh chapter onwards it is about the various sentiments (*rasas*) as depicted in *Apsaras*. Each *rasa* is dealt with its components like, the depiction - (*Vibhāva*), the root cause of the *rasa* - (*Ālambana*), the promoting aspect of *rasa* (*Uddīpana*), the mode of presentation (*Anubhāva*), and, lastly, the durable effect of *rasa* and human personality (*Sthāyibhāva*). Her standing postures are also mentioned, as it is a supporting aspect in the depiction of *rasa*.

The bracket figures of *Apsara* sculptures, which are 42 in number, are numbered according to the sequence as they are located in the temple (ref. pl. I, fig. 3.). I have tried to establish a rational linkage by grouping the *Apsara* sculpture with the same theme, but located with different bracket figure numbers. Such group of bracket figures in which I could trace a continuity of movement are attached along with the text. I have no reasons to explain why they are not placed sequentially, according to the themes that they are depicting. Beyond Plate No. VII, where each *Apsara* sculpture is analysed individually, the reference to *Apsaras* in this book go by the bracket figure numbers. They are called bracket figures, as the figures are enclosed in intricate decoration of creepers on the top and sides, and fixed between the capital and entablature of the external wall.

The translation of Sanskrit words used in the text are given at the end in the Glossary.

Rekha Rao

Contents

Part - II
APSARA – THE PHILOSOPHER

Acknowledgements

I express my heartfelt thanks to Dr. S.R. Rao, Former Deputy Director General, Archaeological Survey of India; Former Advisor, Marine Archaeology Centre, National Institute of Oceanography, Goa; Member, UNESCO-Sponsored International Committee for Underwater Cultural Heritage, who has been an inspiring source in bringing out this book. I am indebted to him for his guidance and for having consented to write a Foreword for this book.

I recall with reverence Shri H.V. Nagaraja Rao, Honorary Dy. Director, International Sanskrit Research Centre, J.S.S.R.S, Mysore, for guiding me in the use of Sanskrit words that are used in this book.

My very sincere thanks to Dr. Sharada Ajit, H.O.D. of English, The Oxford College of Science, Bangalore, for going through the manuscript.

My sincere thanks to Mr. Harikumar K. from Nashik for typing the manuscript.

I am thankful to Aryan Books International, and to Mr. Vikas Arya in particular for printing and publishing this book.

PHOTOGRAPHIC CREDITS

(1) Courtesy American Institute of Indian Studies, Gurgaon, Plate No. II (Fig. 1) and Bracket Figure Nos. 1, 2, 3, 6, 7, 9, 12, 14, 19, 20, 21, 22, 23, 24, 25, 27, 28, 30, 31, 33, & 38.

(2) Courtesy Archaeological Survey of India, Bangalore – Bracket Figure Nos. 4, 9, 39, 40, 41, & 42. Plate No. III, fig. 3, Plate No. IV, figs. 1, 2, 3.

(3) Courtesy Archaeological Survey of India, Dharwad, Plate No. III and Plate No. IV.

(4) Other Photographs – Personal collection of Mr. Rohit Eswer, Lecturer in Archaeology, Maharajas College, Mysore, and a performing artist of Classical dance.

Abbreviations

B.F.	Bracket Figures (as seen in temple)
D.R.	*Daśarūpaka* by Dhanañjaya – Kannada translation by K.V. Subbanna
E.I.	*Epigraphia Indica*
E.K.	*Epigraphia Karnataka*
N.Ś.	*Nāṭyaśāstra*
Ref.	Reference
S.I.Ins.	South Indian Inscriptions
Ch.	Chapter
Sl.	Sloka

List of Illustrations

Plate & Figure Nos. **Illustration**

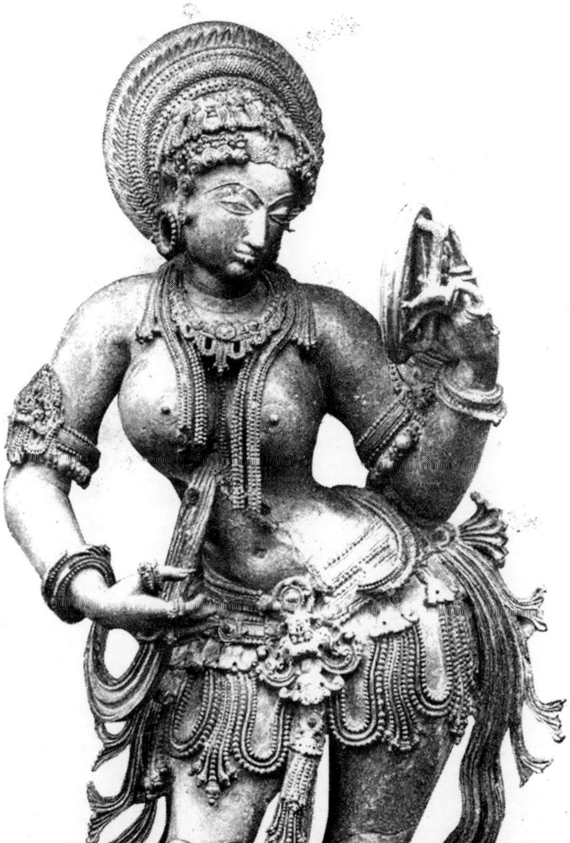

PART - I

APSARA – The Dancer

I
Introduction

The vast area of Deccan between the Tungabhadra and Kaveri river basins saw the rise and fall of great dynasties of early Chalukyas of Badami, Rastrakutas, Gangas, late Chalukyas of Kalyana, Hoysalas, Vijayanagara rulers and Wodeyars. Each dynasty made significant contribution to the field of architecture, which immortalised their name and work. These architectural monuments have given Karnataka a place of distinction in the cultural heritage map of India. The rock-cut temples of early Chalukyas of Badami in Bijapur district, datable to 6th-7th century AD, give an idea of early sculptural representation of Hindu gods. The Ladkhan temple of Aihole which was built in AD 550 and the Durgā temple in the same area built in 6th century AD were some of the earliest representations of structural temple architecture in Karnataka.

The Rastrakutas who succeeded the Badami Chalukyas were responsible for further development in the art of temple construction as evinced at Pattadakal. During this period from AD 753 to 972, they gave a final shape through experiments to the northern Rekhā nāgara and the southern Dravida vimāna styles of temple architecture. The former is represented by Mallikārjuna, Sangameśvara and Virupakṣa temples and the latter by Galaganatha, Jambuliṅga and Kāśī Viśveśvara temples. Their feudatories, the Gangas, could carve out the monolithic statue of Gomaṭeśvara at Sravana belagola in 10th century AD. The late Chalukyas of Kalyana who ousted the Rastrakutas in AD 973 built a large number of temples noted for their fusion of both northern and southern styles, as well as richness of sculptural details on walls and doorframes. Some of the best examples of this phase are the temples of Kāśī Viśveśvara at Lakkundi, Mahādeva temple at Ittagi and Mallikārjuna temple at Kuruvatti. Chalukyas were succeeded by the Hoysalas who were in power for more than 300 years from AD 1022 to AD 1310. This was the golden age of cultural activity, when the rulers patronized not only construction of temples, but also other fine arts such as dance and music. Even though Nripakama (AD 1006 to 1046) and his son Vinayaditya were the first rulers of Hoysala dynasty, gaining independence from their Ganga overlords, it was Ballala (AD 1108) and his brother Viśnuvardhana (1108-1142) who were considered as the great rulers of Hoysala dynasty for having captured Talkad from Cholas and liberated themselves from the clutches of the Chalukyas of Kalyana. Later, the Hoysalas expanded the territory and ruled over the fertile basin between Tungabhadra and Kaveri rivers and built innumerable temples, big and small, in almost every village. Among them the most noteworthy temples are the Cennakēśava temple at Belur, Keśava temple at Somnathpura, Hoysaleśwara temple at Halebid. Hoysalas were defeated by the commander of Delhi Sultanate Mallikaufer in AD 1310. It is only under Vijayanagara rulers that Karnataka regained its glory for high cultural activity.

It is interesting to know why and how the Chalukyan and the Hoysala dynasties could build so many temples and embellish them with intricate carvings. The political, economic, social and religious conditions were conducive for the development of art and architecture. The Chalukyan temples no doubt were the models for Hoysalas both in conception and design, but the art got polished in the Hoysala era. Other contributing factors for the fineness, delicacy and exuberance of sculptures in the Hoysala temples are the

1. Technological advancement,
2. Dynastic greatness, and
3. Religious and social developments.

1. TECHNOLOGICAL ADVANCEMENT

The primary technical advantage enjoyed by the Hoysala artists lay in cutting and transporting of rock. It became possible for them to build larger, more ornate temples and more often. The early Chalukyas, who used coarse-grained sandstone as medium for temple construction had their own limitations. Late Chalukyas and Hoysalas brought into usage chloritic schist, a greenish or blue-black soap stone, which was softer than sandstone. The soapstone of volcanic origin, quarried in the neighbourhood, was soft when first dug and hardened on exposure to atmosphere. As this change of material was easier to carve and polish, it resulted in a revolutionary change in the sculptural art of Hoysala period. Chalukyas of Kalyana evolved a cruciform plan of temple, which the Hoysalas developed into a stellate plan. The single cell (*garbhagṛha*) became multicelled, each cell with a vestibule leading to a large and common pillared hall. The pillars were lathe- turned, profusely ornate, highly polished and each of them had a different design. The square ground plan, modified later into a simple star plan, further got developed, with the angular displacements to sixteen and more points. The more the number of angular offsets, more the space for embellishment, which made the Hoysala temple look like a jewel box full of intricate carvings. The Chalukyan shrine motif of niche and solitary sculptures, was replaced by bands of figures and sculptures, which were protected by the huge projecting and curved eaves running all through the exterior wall of the temple, thereby separating the *śikhara* or the tower from the *vimāna* walls.

The tower or *śikhara* also observed the stellate plan formed by a series of closely set horizontal tiers, rising one above the other and each tier decorated by a grouping of miniature shrines. The height of the *śikhara* thus became dwarfed. It was topped by a lower parasol- shaped finial, the cupola. The temple stood on a spacious platform called *Jagati*, which followed the stellate body of the temple. It provided a spacious *pradakṣiṇa patha*, an open circumambulatory passage to view the ornamental facade at close proximity. With these technological advancements in the total anatomy of temple parts, the Hoysala temples got a unique identity.

2. DYNASTIC GREATNESS

The Hoysala dynasty rulers felt the need to demonstrate their own greatness and royal status by overshadowing the temples of the past, whether it was starting a new temple or adding to what was already built. The more wealth a dynasty had for its building projects the more powerful it appeared. The new land, which they acquired by conquest, was highly fertile with major rivers – Tungabhadra, Kaveri and Krishna – and helped production of abundant agricultural outputs. This gave them access to trade and market their produce, resulting in vast financial reserves. Hoysala Kings Viśnuvardhana and Vira Ballala II, were keen to promote themselves as ideal kings. Many inscriptions describe in idyllic terms, the abundant wealth and well being of the people in the kingdom. This prosperity was used to build innumerable temples and maintain the vast number of artists and other staff who were in the service of God. Hoysala kings believed in the ideal thought of *Matsya pūraṇa* that, one who rejoices in making temples gets everlasting riches and he is worshipped in heaven. This concept motivated not only the king, but the generals, ministers, merchants and commoners to extend outstanding support to temple building. The idea which the king cherished born out of deep devotion to God, that the excess wealth should be used solely for religious institutions, got deep-rooted in the minds of his subjects. Temples and tanks were built in the major cities, in trade routes, and banks of rivers, which attracted a large number of devotees. The lavishness of labour and the elaboration of detail of the Hoysala temple pattern attracted the skilled sculptors. The master sculptors and artists from other places got attracted to the material gains, and considered it a prestige to work for Hoysala kings and ministers. The Hoysala architects used the emblem of a young man slaying the lion as the motif to give a separate dynastic identity, which was positioned on the entrance door of the temple. The Hoysala kings believed in the power of knowledge. The lion signified a beast, a demon or darkness. Under the threat of a lion, the courageous king drew the sword of knowledge and protected himself (and the people) from *māyā*, with the help of a shield, signifying dispassion.

3. RELIGIOUS AND SOCIAL DEVELOPMENTS

Jainism reached its zenith during the Hoysala period and the two Hindu sects – Vaiṣṇavism and Śaivism – also saw rapid growth and increased popularity among the masses. Jainism was a well-established religion in the territory conquered by the Hoysalas and was patronized by their predecessors like Gangas, western Chalukyas and Rastrakutas. King Viśnuvardhana was raised as a Jain. His queen Śāntalatādevi and his greatest generals were devout Jains, who actively advanced the repair and construction of Basadis, the Jain temples. King Viśnuvardhana, after his accession, was influenced by the philosophy of Vaiṣṇavite teacher Ramanuja – who propagated Vaiṣṇavism in Hoysala territory and the King got himself converted into a Vaiṣṇavite and dedicated the Belur temple to Vaiṣṇavite God Vijayanārāyaṇa who was also called Keśava. Thus, Vaiṣṇavism enjoyed a royal support.

Like Jainism, Śaivism also was an established sect in the territory ruled by the Hoysalas. Kalamukhas and Kapalikas were the two subsects of Śaivism. Halebid, the capital of Hoysalas, Shimoga, Gadag and Dharwar districts were centres of Śaivite sects. Many priests of the Kalamukha sect, resided in these centres, building temples and educating the masses in *Śaiva āgamas*. Majority of sculptors and artists who hailed from these places were Śaivites.

The active Bhakti movement in conjunction with the royal patronage resulted in vast temple building campaign. Hoysala rulers emphasized on the oneness of God and practised religious tolerance, which was meticulously followed by commoners. King Viśnuvardhana was a Vaiṣṇavite, his elder brother Ballala I, was a devout Śaivite and his queen Śāntalatādevi was a Jain devout, and the broad-minded patrons promoted all sects with equal support. King Viśnuvardhana further emphasized his unbiased outlook by carving Śaivite sculptures on the walls of Vaiṣṇavite temple or vice versa and Basadi was erected in the campus of a temple.

In South India, temple worship became a glorious tradition and the Bhakti movement reshaped the culture of medieval India. The vast number of temples built served a utilitarian purpose. Religion-based social activities, which accounted for the boom of temple activity in Chalukyan and Hoysala periods, can be classified as:

1. Religious discourses (*Dharma prasaṅga*)
2. Donating the acquired wealth for a good cause (*Dāna*)
3. Dedication of temple to loved ones *(Paroksha vinaya)*
4. Special occasions and annual festivals *(Parva)*

The Kalyana Chalukyas promoted the values of donations for a religious cause through religious discourses exemplified by Purāṇic stories. People were influenced and inspired to donate their wealth for the construction and maintenance of a temple. There are many inscriptions dating back to 11th and 12th centuries, which give an account of the donations made for temples. The discourses that were conducted in temple premises were sometimes audio-visual in nature, which brought about an awareness of the moral values among people. The new awareness resulted in a prolific construction of temples and Basadis dedicated to immortalise the names of loved ones like teacher, father, mother, husband, wife and so on. Hoysala rulers maintained this order which was laid out by their Chalukyan overlords. Belur temple inscription states that huge donations were given by the queen Śāntalatādevi and other rich people, towards the maintenance of temple or construction of a Basadi. Temples were also centres where annual festivals like *Sankranti* (harvest season rituals), *Ugadi* (new year), and *Deepavalī* (festival of lights) were celebrated. Large gatherings were fed and images of gods were taken on a procession called *utsava*.

With bigger temples, the responsibilities also increased. Every temple had a caretaker called *Sthānapati*, who looked after the maintenance of the temple, its finance, and the priest, who performed the worshipping rituals. Some Śaivite temples got associated with the monastic college called *Maṭha*, where learned men of high esteem trained the younger generations in Vedic lessons and it also arranged the boarding and lodging of students and travellers, through the donations that were received. Gradually two types of temples evolved –

1. The ones, which gave services of *Aṅgabhoga*, the worshipping rituals, and
2. Temples that offered *Raṅgabhoga*, a service through dance and music.

Aṅga in Sanskrit means a part of the body. *Aṅgabhoga* was the service rendered to comfort the body of the main deity, like bathing, change of clothes and sacred thread, offering food and lighting the lamps. *Raṅga* means a stage, a place of public amusement. The *Raṅgabhoga* rituals involved great expenditure as the responsibility of hiring and maintaining artists like singers, musicians, flutists, percussionists and dancers came under temple maintenance. Such temples had raised dancing platform inside the temple called *Navaraṅga* and a large pillared hall for audience to assemble. Besides this, the temple also had an associated place called *Sūḷēgēri*, a place where all these artists resided under the care of a teacher called *Sūḷēvaḷa,* who taught dance to girls. The *Raṅgabhoga* temple service became a popular form of worship during the late Chalukyan and Hoysala periods, attracting a large number of devotees, as it gave them an opportunity to see and enjoy fine arts.

The dancers and sculptors became familiar with *Nāṭyaśāstra*, the traditional text on dance and dramaturgy. The dancers who were called *pātra,* had to know the intricacies of expressive dance, otherwise called *abhinaya,* as they had to enact lead roles in episodes of Purāṇic stories. These dancers were moulded into the versatility of *nartakīs,* as described in *Nāṭyaśāstra*. The *Apsaras* of Belur temple are probably the sculptural representation of *pātras*, the temple dancers, who rendered dance services everyday in a temple. Sculptors were enthusiastic to carve dancing sculptures as they looked more artistic and gave them ample scope to exhibit their skill, which served like permanent records.

Thus, temples which were mere worshipping places evolved as an indispensable part of the society with various types of responsibilities. They served as centres of religion, education and fine arts, thus promoting the mass and younger generations in the field of education and cultural heritage. It gave employment to teachers, sculptors, priests, dancers, musicians and attendants, through whom the cultural heritage was carried over from generation to generation.

With the prolific temple building activities during the Hoysala period, temple art reached the zenith of its glory under the leadership of Kings Viśnuvardhana, Narasimha and Ballala, who were great patrons of art. Even though Hoysala temple came out with its own unique style and identity, there were stylistic differences in the various workshops in the Hoysala period. The Cennakēśava temple at Belur built by King Viśnuvardhana in AD 1117, was the earliest structure constructed in a fully evolved Hoysala style. The temple, which was dedicated to God Vijayanārāyaṇa, in celebration of his victory over Cholas, reflected his faith in religion and his love for art. His queen Śāntalatādevi who was also a temple dancer before her marriage, probably inspired the sculptors to carve out sculptures in dancing postures. Of the many temples built during that period, Cennakēśava temple at Belur enjoys a special place because of the dancing sculptures of the celestial beauties – the *Apsaras* – who are on the outer walls of the temple, entertaining gods forever, and are a sensual reward of the king who fought bravely. These *Apsaras* are like permanent records of the unique sculptural style, reflecting the in-depth knowledge of dance and music, which both the dancers and sculptors had in that period.

This book is devoted for a deeper understanding of the versatility of the *Apsara* as an artist, and the various sentiments (*rasas*) that are expressed in these figures. With their hypnotic beauty, the *Apsaras* have charmed the spectators ever since they adorned this temple. They are the majestic example of the art of Hoysla civilization. These figures still reveal their devotional qualities, which existed during the height of Hoysala civilization. Even after about 850 years, these graceful dancing *Apsaras* still display their warmth and beauty.

II

General Description of the Belur Cennakēśava Temple

The Cennakēśava temple at Belur is a typical and the first statement of Hoysala School of Architecture, which branched off from Chalukyan style after the 11th century AD. Hoysala rulers traced their descent to the moon as belonging to Yaduvaṃśa. The Belur inscription confirms this. The E.P.C. VI, CK 20 and 137 states that Sala, an ornament of Yaduvaṃśa, had an encounter with a lion in a forest of Sosevur. An ascetic gave an alert call to Sala 'Poy' (Hoy) meaning to attack. Sala followed the command and was celebrated for his heroic courage that led to his becoming the founder of the Hoysala dynasty. Henceforth, the symbol of Sala attacking the lion, served as the emblem of Hoysala dynasty. Lion is symbolic of great and terrible in nature. It is also used as a battle emblem, military victory and royal power. The Hoysala emblem indicates the military victory over the powerful Chalukyas.

A stellate plan, the sanctum built on a raised terrace, and profuse sculptural detail with jewel-like delicacy carved on soapstone, are the highlights of this temple (Plate I, Fig. 2). The temple consists of a *Mūkhamaṇḍapa* pillared hall, a *Navaraṅga* with a dancing platform, a vestibule (*Antarāla*) and the sanctum sanctorum (*garbhagṛha*), all set in an axial strike. The *Śikhara* of this temple was structurally unsound indicating the basic weakness of the stellate form of tower and hence is missing. The temple has three entrances led by a flight of steps to the *Navaraṅga*. The steps are flanked by miniature shrines of *śikhara* moulding, embellished with different forms of Viṣṇu in it. The eastern entrance door has a pair of Hoysala symbol, a man attacking a lion. The *makara tōraṇa,* an elaborately carved arch, gives an exciting welcome.

In the moulded course of the plinth, the lower portion has (1) a row of elephants, (2) string course of garland of beads and lion heads, (3) a delicate scrollwork of creepers with birds and animals, (4) frieze of pearl garlands, (5) male and female figures standing in the small projecting ornamental niches, interspersed with figures of *Yakṣa*, and (6) female figures in the act of dressing or dancing between miniature lathe-turned pillars. Railings have a projecting course, ornamented with leaf and bud motif, surmounted by miniature towers, between which are seen lions forming a canopy over archers, dancers, etc. From the creepers and flowers spring the sculptures, illustrating the *Rāmāyaṇa* and 51 *Mahābhārata* legends. Above the railings are the bell-shaped pillars, which support the roof. In-between the perforated screen and the pillars, stories of *Mahābhārata* or Purāṇa are carved. Above the perforated screens, on the pilasters and the entablature are fixed at an angle of 35°, the graceful bracket figures of *Apsaras* popularly known as *śīlabālikās* (the images of young ladies engaged in various activities). These beautiful and graceful dancers gave flash to the stone representation of the voluptuous *Apsaras* that are found on the exterior wall of the Belur temple. All the above-mentioned decorated motif runs all through the external walls of the temple. The southern and northern doorways are also highly decorated.

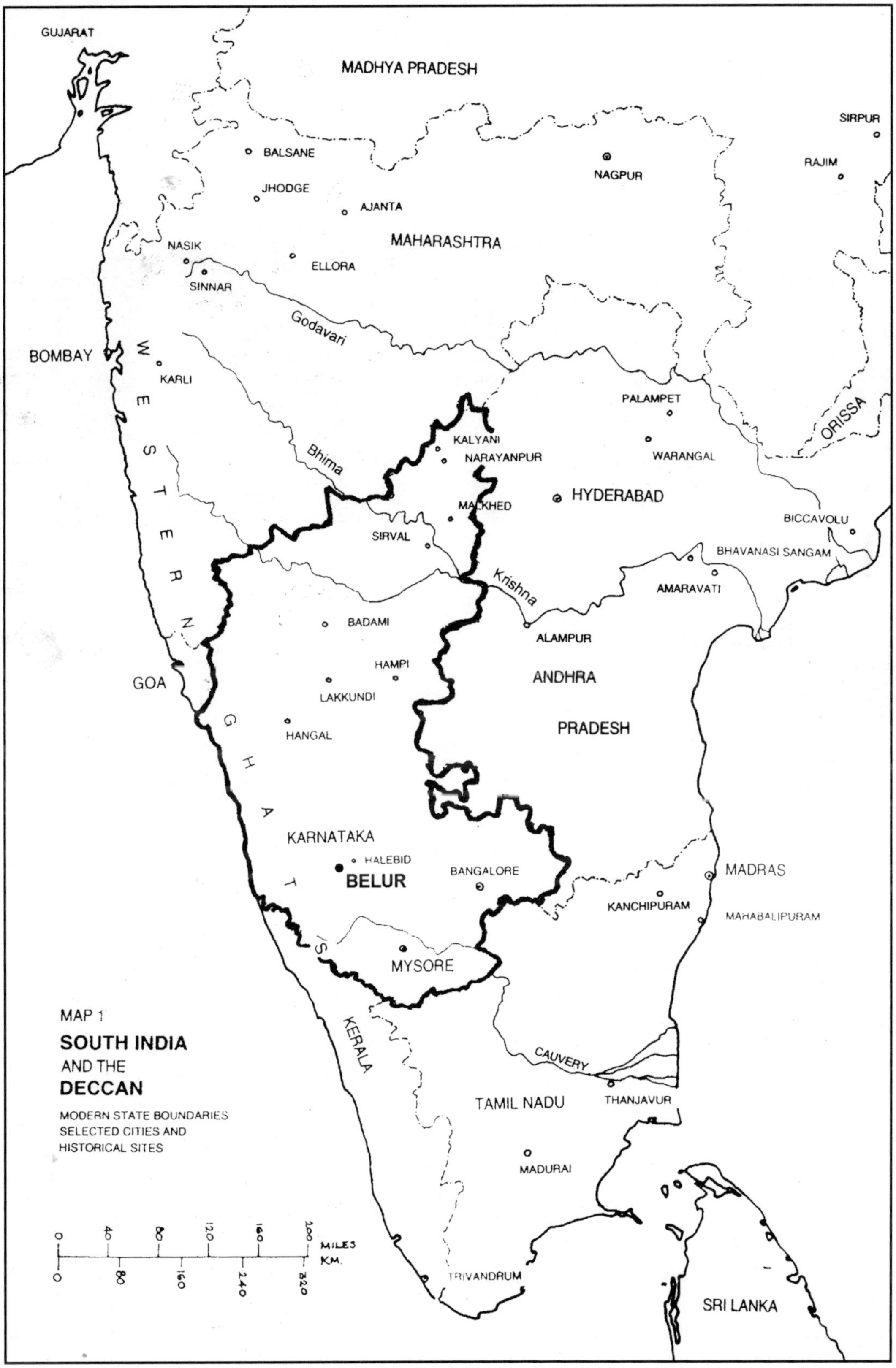

Pl. I. Fig. 1. Karnataka State and Belur

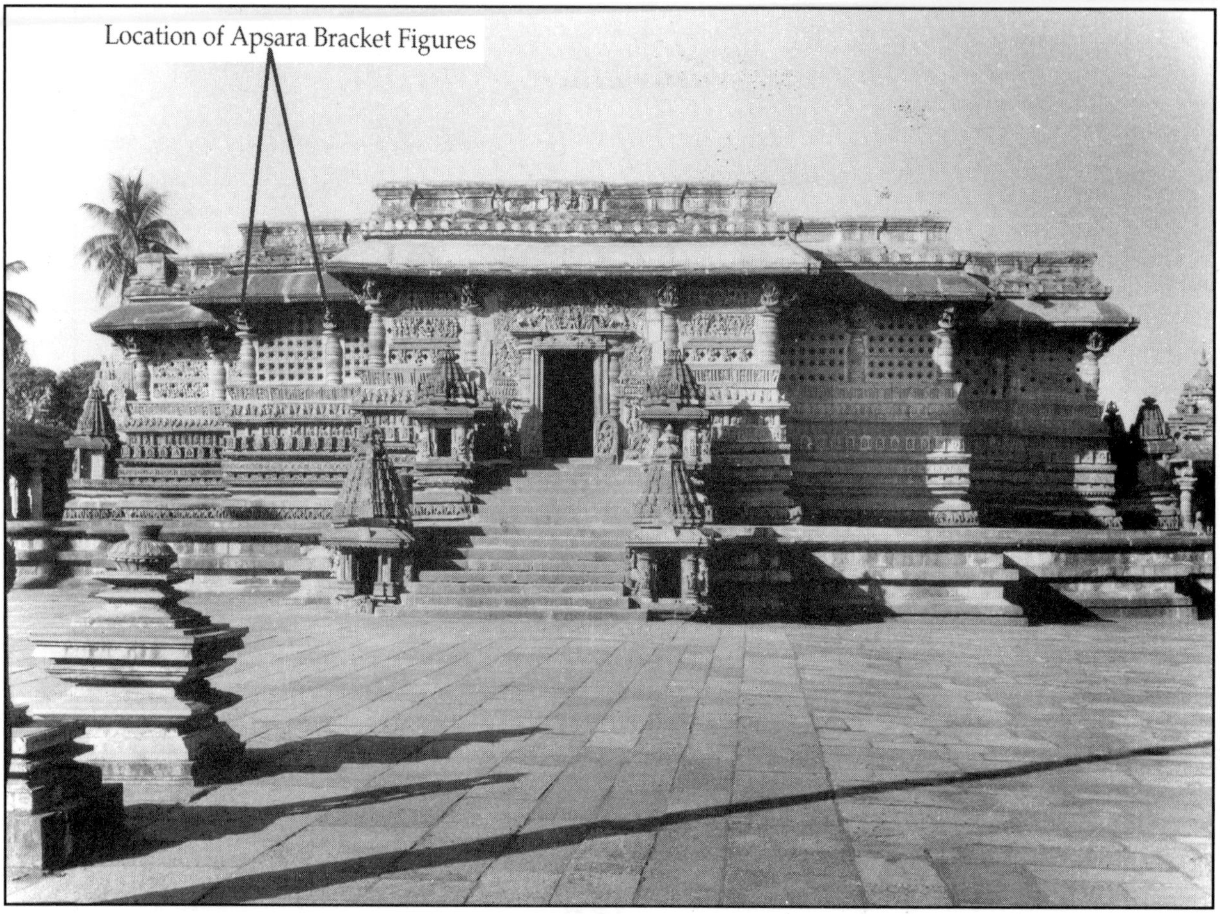

Pl. I. Fig. 2. General view of the temple

The stellate plan has increased the number of offsets enabling the sculptors to carve a large number of figures. The spacious platform (*Jagati*) on which the temple stands, provides an open circumambulatory (*Pradakṣiṇa Patha*), providing enough space for the devotees to see the ornamental facade and permitting large congregational worship, while the pillared hall with delicately carved pillars and sculptures served as a *sadas* for devotees to assemble. Temples of Belur hold the attention of visitors with their sculptural art that is so exquisite and intricate, that one cannot dream of cloning it.

THE STRUCTURE OF BELUR CENNAKĒŚAVA TEMPLE AND ITS RELATION TO THE *MAṆḌALA*

The Belur Cennakēśava temple in its original form with the *śikhara* (which is not existing now) would have looked like a 3-dimensional version of a *yantra* or a *maṇḍala*. The basic diagram of a *maṇḍala* or a *yantra* and the basic plan of this temple can be compared at microcosmic and the macrocosmic levels in its abstract configurations.[1]

*Yantra*s and *maṇḍala*s are power diagrams of a particular configuration with the elementary geometrical designs that function as thought forms about the inherent forces and nature of the cosmos. Even though structurally both *yantra*s and *maṇḍala*s resemble, the basic differences between them is that *yantra*s are small in size, made of permanent material, and are worshipped or worn on the body where as *maṇḍala*s are big and benefitial when viewed. Architectural

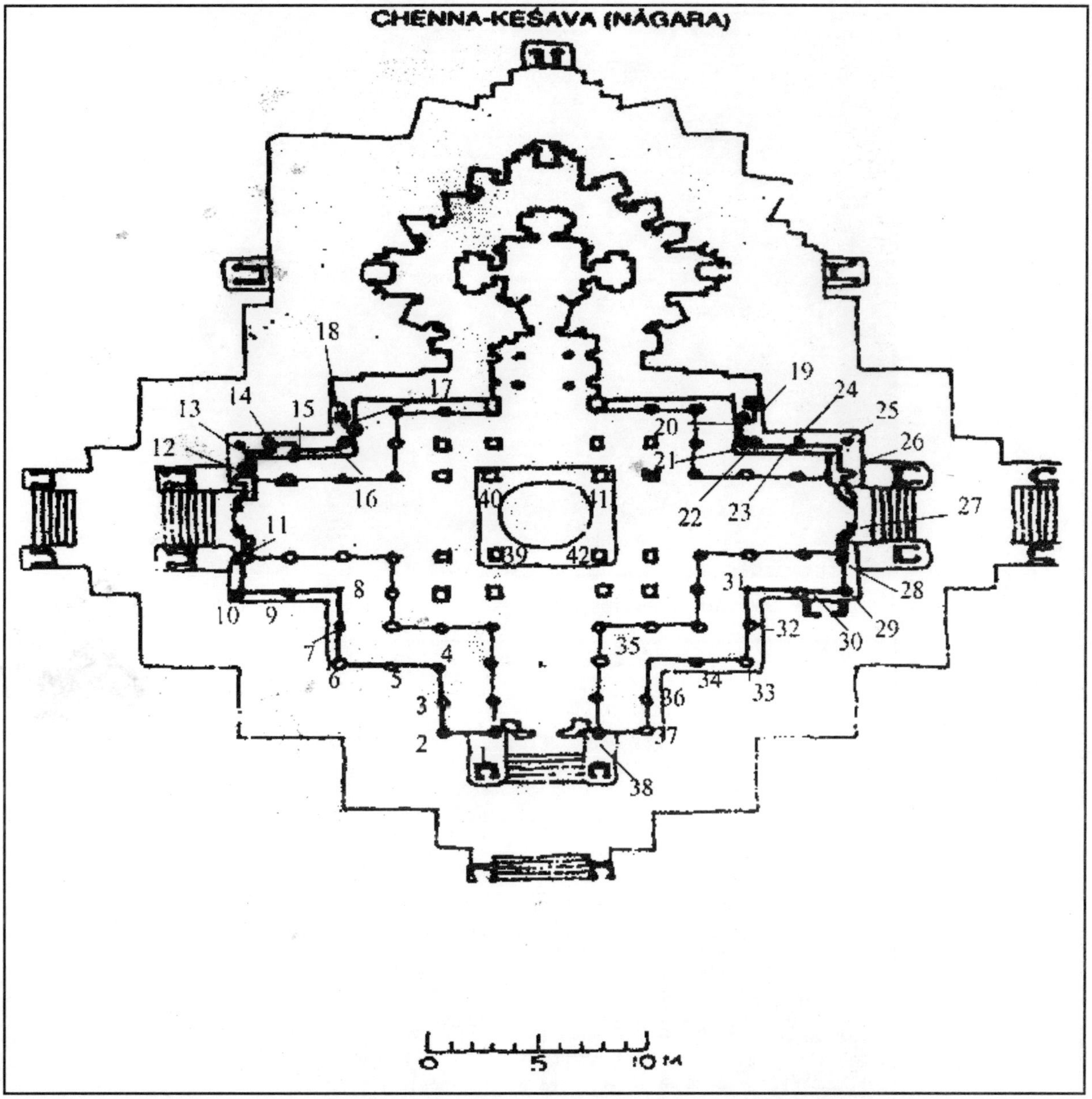

Pl. I. Fig. 3. Indication of *Apsara* bracket figure numbers, as they appear on the outer wall of the temple

*yantra*s are not the ground plans for the temple but temples are schematized on the principles of a *yantra* or a *maṇḍala*.

In general the diagram of a *yantra* or a *maṇḍala* has three components – the central point or the *bindu*, the concentric circles around the point constituting the body of the *maṇḍala*, and a protective square boundary called *Bhupura* around it, with four gate openings on all the four sides. The central point represents the unmanifested state of the chosen deity, which is the source of positive energy and perpetual bliss. The concentric circles around this constitutes the body of the *maṇḍala*, which represents the entire cosmos, and the abode of supporting deities. It is always shown as circles, hinting the everchanging cycles of time and realms of spirits. An architectural image of this concept is in the dome, the central ceilling of the temple hall. This is

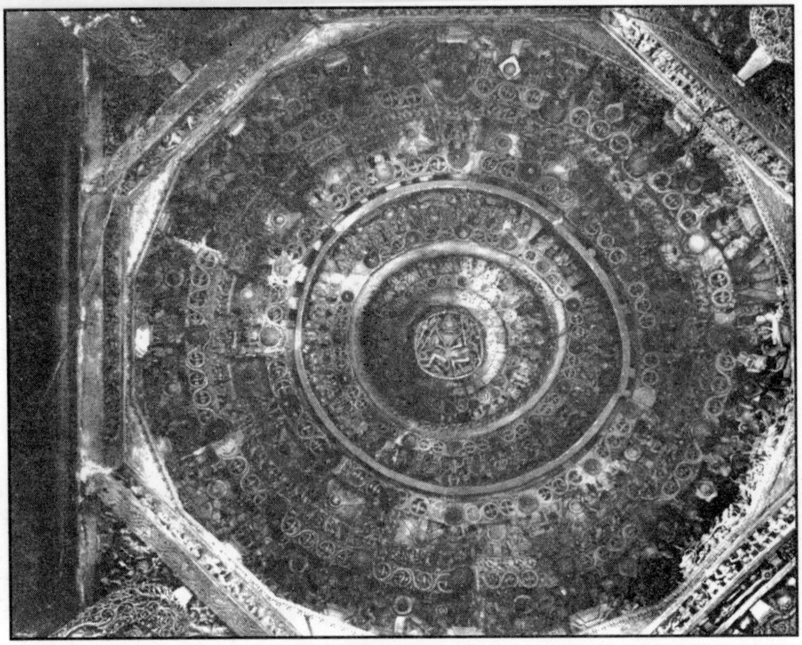

Fig. 1. Bhuvaneśvarī – the ceiling of the *Navaraṅga* hall, with the *maṇḍala*

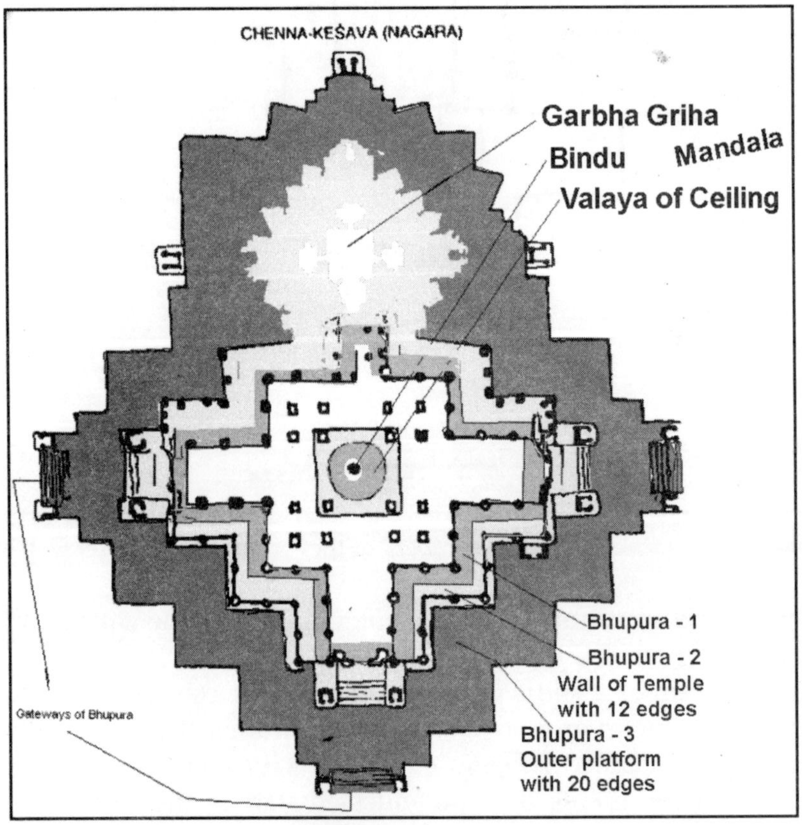

Fig. 2. Plan of the temple showing the *Bhupura* – the courtyard of the *yantra* and the *maṇḍala* in the centre

Pl. II.

housed in a square boundary, called the *Bhupura* to protect the deities that are invoked in the *maṇḍala*. The *Bhupura*, along with the openings, symbolic of the four gates of knowledge, may be represented in an expanding way.

In the Belur Cennakēśava temple, the circular design of the *maṇḍala* is placed in the central dome of the *Navaraṅga* hall – called the Bhuvaneśvarī, which is huge and measures 13 feet in square and 6 feet in depth. The wall of the temple corresponds to the square boudary of the *yantra*.

The association of the power of *śakti* or forces of the cosmos to *yantras*, can be traced as far back as the days of *Atharvaveda*, *Upaniṣads*, *tantras* and *Purāṇas*. *Yantras* are known to be most auspicious and powerful which transform the spiritual status of the worshipper. It purifies and energizes the environment by driving away all the negative vibrations and bestows through its cosmic power, peace, happiness, health, wealth, prosperity, power and success to the worshipper. King Viśnuvardhana had chosen the figure and content of the *yantra* (probably the *Sudarśana yantra*, as the central deity is Lord Narasiṃha) for the design and construction of the temple, placing the circular *maṇḍala* in the ceiling of the *Navaraṅga* hall (Plate II, Fig. 1). Constructing a temple on the plan of a *yantra* was followed in the time of late Chalukyas. Early Chalukyas had mostly a square plan for the temple which got transformed into a stellate looking plan later, as (they followed) the *Bhupura* part of the diagram of *yantra* was adopted while planning the walls of the temple in consecutive stages. A *yantra* which is in a 3-dimensional form, made of stone or crystal, is very sacred and auspicious for the possessors. The temple of Belur, no doubt transforms all the devotees to a spiritual plane, as per the qualities of a *yantra*.

The central point – the *bindu* of the *maṇḍala* – in the Bhuvaneśvarī of the Belur temple, looks like a pendant. It symbolizes bliss, *turīya avastha* and the *sarva ānandāmayī chakra*. At this point resides the chosen deity. The *bindu* is symbolic of the force of positive energy within all of us (at a microcosmic level), that continues to expand, enrich and unfold its radiance to ultimately merge in the all- enveloping cosmic force. The Belur temple has the figure of Viṣṇu in the incarnation of Narasiṃha who is the destroyer of negative aspects like pride, vanity and *māyā*. It symbolizes victory. According to the *Ahirbudnya saṃhitā*, a king who is desirous of kingship or the one who is deprived of kingship and overpowered by other kings, should install the *yantra* of Lord Viṣṇu in a temple and worship it regularly to enjoy a sound kingship, attaining all the wealth that was aspired for. King Viśnuvardhana adopted Vaiṣṇavism and built this temple to celeberate his victory over the Chalukyas of Kalyana.

This point or *bindu* of the *maṇḍala* is encircled by three concentric circles, suggesting the concept of expansion of positive energies, which are extensively decorated with scrollwork and are pictorial with the figures of the episodes of Lord Kṛṣṇa, in this temple. These circles are enclosed in an octogonal structure, which again hints the expansion of positive energy in all the eight directions. The octagonal design of the ceiling is placed in a square geometric boundary, which is supported by four pillars, with *apsara* sculptures of different themes. The theme of these *Apsaras* can be compared to the four states of the awareness, like *Jāgrut*, *Svapna*, *Suṣupti* and *Turīya avasthā*. The pillar in the north-east represents an *Apsara* in *Jāgrut avasthā* (B.F. 42), hinting an attachment for the physical body. The south-east pillar corresponds to *Svapna avasthā* (B.F. 39), where detachment from the physical body is hinted. The *Apsara* in *Suṣupti avasthā* on the south-west pillar (B.F. 40) indicates a state of meditation, and the *Apsara* on the north-west pillar (B.F. 41) denotes the *Turīya avasthā*, a state of oneness with the ultimate reality, which has elevated her to the state of Goddess. (For details ref. Ch. 1, Part II of this book)

The square outline which is common to all *maṇḍalas* symbolizes the royal palace in which the deities reside. This area of the *maṇḍala*, or the sacred space is revered and protected from the disintegrating forces of chaos. The *maṇḍala* which is purified after the installation, becomes useless, if damaged or touched by magical practitioners. Hence it is placed high, at an inaccessible place.

The circular *maṇḍala* – the inner part of the *yantra* – is on the ceiling, while the square courtyard is at the floor of the temple hall. This is called the *Bhupura* or the *Trilokya mohana chakra* identified with the earthly sphere. It has four gateways in four directions – symbolic of esoteric knowledge (or vedas) to be transmitted.

The *Bhupura* – the boundary is constructed by three parallel lines in this temple, and is the outermost part of the *yantra*. The first periphery of the temple is the first line of the *Bhupura* part, which is basically square, but with four gateways which makes it appear a twelve-angled structure. The outer enclosure which follows the twelve-angled body of the temple with the four gateways gives the twenty angles of the temple plan, which makes it look stellate in shape (Plate II, Fig. 2).

The contents of the *maṇḍala* or *yantra* varies according to the deity who is installed in the temple. It was a common practice to install *yantras* in temples from ancient times, by the kings and political leaders for attaining fame, power, financial success and attainment of happiness. All *Vāstu* deficiencies were negated by the installation of the sacred *yantra*. Hindu temples, which are a three-dimensional version of *yantra* in stone, are truly centres of cosmic and divine powers, which transform all humans to a spiritual strata.

The *garbhagṛha* or the sanctum sanctorum is to the west of the *Navaraṅga* hall, that is based on the *Bhupura* plan of the *yantra*. The *garbhagṛha* is connected to the main hall by a small vestibule called *Antarāla*. The *garbhagṛha* has the image of the main deity Cennakēśava, with his consorts on either side.

Architecturally, the temple is symbolic of the three worlds, *Bhurloka*, *Bhuvarloka* and *Svarloka*. The base of the temple wall, which has horizontal mouldings, with the figure of animals, human beings, and geometric pattern of floral designs correspond to the world of mortals – the *Bhurloka*.

The upper part of the wall is in contrast to the basal designs, which represent *Bhuvarloka*, the world of the purified, where the figures of *Gandharvas*, *Vidyādharas*, celestial beings, *Apsaras*, figures of various divinities are carved, which are indicative of the upper strata.

At the highest level (*śikhara* is now missing) is representation of *Svarloka*, the world of gods. The temple was a representation of the three *lokas* that are believed to make the universe.

The temple, which was completed in AD 1117, was provided with a compound wall, kitchen, granary and a temple pond, in the reign of Ballala II. But, the main gateway was burnt down by the Muslim King Mohamad Bin Tughlak and the temple got raided and damaged. It was renovated during the time of Vijayanagara rulers who built a lofty brick *Gopura*. The front pavilion or the *maṇḍapa* was also constructed in the Vijayanagara period, out of the materials obtained from the ruined Hoysala temples in the neighbourhood. The temple constructed over centuries boasts of sculptures that exhibit Indian artisans' talent, and their depth of knowledge in the art of dance, music and spirituality.

NOTE

1. According to Indonesian heritage – Ancient history, an inscription at the Indonesian temple, where Hindu and Buddhist monuments emerged simultaneously during 8th-9th century AD, refers to *maṇḍalas* as a simple circle. In religious sense, it means a symmetrical arrangement of deities in concentric circle, surrounded by a square-shaped enclosing wall. *Maṇḍalas* drawn on ground were believed to create spaces, within which religious devotees could meditate, free from the danger of disurbance by evil spirit. Temples were designed as three-dimensional *maṇḍalas*.

III

Apsaras

The concept of *Apṣara*, is a representation of a highly talented artist, ranked as semi-divines, as evident by their location in the temple, at a higher level on a lotus pedestal. It is therefore essential to have a clear understanding of the history and the evolution of *Apsaras* since vedic times.

In general, the *Divyāṅganās* or the *Apsaras* as they are called, represent the celestial beauties. *Apsaras* are symbolic of youthful charm, with a capacity to draw the attention of the viewers for centuries to many centuries more. They are immortal beauties, standing with a purpose as seen in the temples of India. They are like permanent guides, teaching about the aspects of *Gandharva Kalā*, the science of dance, music and dramaturgy.

Apsaras are considered as semi-divine, celestial beauties as *Divyāṅganās*, with superhuman powers. They are represented in different forms with different capacities and hence are seen in different families. Even though the concept of an *Apsara* was maintained uniformly, their representation in Indian art history is different at different historical periods. They may be projected as beauties in water, or as courtesans in service of Indra residing in the sky or as *Gandharva strī*, wife of *Gandharvas*, who were fond of music, dance and physically ever youthful.

They enjoyed a higher status in social life for their knowledge in art. Hence, they are represented as residing in the sky, which is symbolically indicated by placing them on a *padmāsana*, a pedestal that is used for gods and demi-gods, or on a pilaster, to indicate an elevated status.

Apsaras were believed to take away the stress of humans, for which purpose they are placed in Indian temples.

1. *APSARAS* IN ANCIENT INDIAN LITERATURE

In a few passages of the *Ṛgveda*, mention is made of celestial water nymph called *Apsara* (moving in the pool of water), who was regarded as the spouse of a corresponding male genius residing in the sky, called *Gandharva*. *Apsaras* of many varieties are spoken of in the *Ṛgveda*. The rare mention of *Apsaras* in *Ṛgveda* became more prominent in *Yajurveda*, where they were addressed by individual names. In *Atharvaveda*, these water deities came out as wives of *Gandharvas*, with a mystic touch, as *śaktis*. Their abode, in later Vedic period, was extended to earth, where they frequented trees, which resound the music of their lute and cymbals. The Brāhmaṇas describe them as distinguished by great beauty, devoted to dance, song and play.

The fifth Veda, the *Nāṭyaveda* was created by Lord Brahmā, where he used recitation from *Ṛgveda*, song from *Samaveda*, *abhinaya* (histrionics) from *Yajurveda* and *rasas* (sentiments) from *Atharvaveda*. For this *Gandharva veda* (a *Upaveda*) was used in the preliminaries and techniques related to the ballet, dance, music and dramaturgy and was performed by Sage Bharata with his sons. Even though it was energetic and grand with verbal aspects, the aspect of grace was lacking. Lord Brahmā created a class of *Apsaras* who were experts in the aspects of grace and beauty and handed over them to Bharata to use them in the production of *Nāṭya* for graceful style and embellishment. The dramatic art then became full-fledged.

In the post-Vedic period *Apsaras* became the courtesans of Indra's heaven. Later, *Apsaras* were occasionally loved by men also. In the late Vedic period, *Gandharvas* were associated with *Apsaras* frequently, as celestial singers, residing in the realm of air or ākāśa. In the post-Vedic mythology, *Apsaras* were spoken as a class of celestial nymphs, endowed with seductive charms of female beauty and occupied a very important place in post-Vedic mythology.

Regarding the social life of Ṛgvedic people (Ref. *History of Sanskrit Literature* by Arthur A. Macdonell); dancing was a source of great amusment, indulged by both men and women. The goddess of dawn, Uṣās, was personified and compared to a dancer, who danced in the open air. *Ṛgveda* X 76, 6 refers to the line which describes that thick dust arose from men who danced *nṛtyatam*. Various references in *Ṛgveda* show that Indians in that early age, were acquainted with different kinds of music. Three types of percussion instruments and *dundubhi*, flute (*vana*), the lute (*vīṇā*) are mentioned, which indicate that Vedic Indians were fond of instrumental music.

The *Sūtras* also mention that instrumental music was performed as religious rites, especially the *vīṇā*. By the time of *Yajurveda*, several kinds of professional musicians appear as lute players, flute players, drummers, conch blowers and so on. Singing is mentioned in *Ṛgveda*, which got into a complicated method of chanting *Samaveda* in musical notes. The mention of *Apsaras* as water nymphs in *Ṛgveda*, were represented in post-Vedic period and mythology as a class of celestial beauties, who were experts in the art of music and dance, with a notion of their home being in the realm of air – the city of the *Gandharvas* and *Apsaras*. The dance and music of *Apsaras* was regarded as auspecious, the mention of which is there in *Rāmāyaṇa* and *Mahābhārata*. *Apsaras* danced when the sons of King Dasaratha were born, they danced in the celebration of Lord Rama's marriage and later his coronation. Even in *Mahābhārata* it is said that Arjuna learnt the art of dance and music from a *Gandharva* named Chitrasena and taught dance to King Virata's daughter. Dance of *Apsaras* was considered auspecious, probably because they elevated the state of mind of the gathering through their art, and they were thus promoters of classical art.

Apsaras continued to be a favourite theme in later literary and architectural works of India. *Apsaras* in sculptural form, were seen as early as first century BC, in the gateways of Sāñcī Stūpa. A continued tradition was represented in Hoysala period also. Dancers, who were called as *pātra* in Chalukyan inscriptions, who belonged to a separate class in service of God, were represented as *Apsaras*, on the outer walls of the Chalukyan and Hoysala temples. Dancers enjoyed a good social status, and even the queens of Chalukyan and Hoysala rulers were well trained in the art of dance and music. The popular opinion about these sculptures in Belur temple, is that they represent Queen Śāntalatadevi, wife of the Hoysala ruler, who was a pātra before her marriage (E.K. V, Belur, 58. AD 1117).

2. HISTORICAL AND SOCIO-RELIGIOUS ASPECTS OF DANCERS – THE *PĀTRAS*

As per the inscriptional evidences, God is live and He is to be revered with different types of rituals and offerings. The same reverence was extended to the king, as he represented God on earth as *Naradevatā*. The worship rituals that were offered to God and kings were of two types, namely, *Aṅgabhoga* and *Raṅgabhoga*. *Aṅgabhoga* was a service rendered to the main deity, which included bathing, change of cloth, change of the sacred thread, application of sandal paste, lighting oil lamps and offering food. These services, which comforted the body of the deity, were performed in privacy. The *Raṅgabhoga* which included the offering of *Gīta* and *Vādya* through music, dance and recitation of Purāṇas was meant to please the God. It was open to the public. The devotees who offered *Raṅgabhoga* belonged to the educated class. Temples which offered *Raṅgabhoga* had to be large enough with a dancing platform and a pillared hall to accommodate the audience. It had to have an attached place called *Sūḷēgēri,* where dancers and other artists could reside and it involved huge money as these artists could not do other types of jobs for their livelihood. Chalukyan rulers believed that the dance rendered by young and beautiful girls attracted large number of devotees, which probably helped in maintaining harmony in cultural and religious heritage. King Vikramāditya the VI, built the Cennakēśava temple at Ittagi and donated a modest place and money to take care of the dancers who were employed (E.I., XIII, page 56).

Girls who were young, beautiful and talented were brought either locally or from outside; they were looked after well in *Sūḷēgēri,* a special residential place for these artists. Each Sūḷēgēri had a male dance teacher and a caretaker called *Sūlēvāḷa* or *Naṭuva,* who was well versed in *Nāṭyaśāstra* and who trained girls in dancing.

These artists were in general called *Dēvaditi,* meaning an ardent servant of God. The *Dēvaditis* who were exclusive dancers were called *pātras*. *Pātra* means 'role' that is played in a ballet (dance drama). The lady who was a *pātra* had to perform the main roles of a dance drama, and she had to know the rules of the art of communication to express the *abhinaya* (expressive part of dance), and the episodes related to the mythologies and the Purāṇas. *Pātras* had to be young, beautiful, exponent of music and had to undergo vigorous training in dance lessons. The other artists who assisted *pātras* were *Vaṃśikā* (flutist), two *Maddalekara* (percussionists), *Gāyaka* (a singer) and *Parekara* (an instrumentalist) and so on, who were called *Kuśīlava* according to *Nāṭyaśāstra*. These *pātras* or dancers performed dance everyday in front the main deity, on a raised dancing platform called the *Navaraṅga*. Dancers and musicians thus played a very important role in the temple rituals of *Raṅgabhoga* and so we see them in temple architecture of Chalukyan and Hoysala era. The position of the main dancer *pātra* was not always hierarchical. Anybody could learn the art of dancing and become a *pātra*, as it was a prestigious and respected position and she was the first one to receive *Prasāda* – the blessings of God.

The Sulegeri Govindeśwara temple inscription (S.I. Ins., IX-1-101, AD 1018) gives detailed descriptions of twelve ladies who were employed for dancing in the temple along with a teacher and caretaker *Naṭuva*. One of the Belur temple inscriptions (E.K., V, Belur 58, AD 1117) mentions about the queen *Śāntalatādevi*, wife of King Viśnuvardhana, who herself was a *pātra*, well versed in music and dance. She donated very liberally to the livelihood of *pātra* and other artists, rendering the service of *Raṅgabhoga*. Among the other servants of God, the lady who stood by the side of a pillar was called *Kambasūḷē* and the lady who fanned with the *cāmara* was called *Cāmarasūḷē*. They were next to a *pātra* in status and we see them as dwarf attendants in some of the *Apsara* sculptures of Belur temple.

The *pātras* were presented as dancing sculptures in the temple and probably they were called *Apsaras*, the everlasting youthful dancers. *Apsaras* mainly depict the cultural and social heritage and thus invite the attention of pilgrims to holy shrines. Their main role was confined to herald the art and architecture, with special emphasis on dance and music. It can be inferred that *Nartakīs* and *Naṭīs* according to *Nāṭyaśāstra* were the role models for the performing artist, *pātra*, of the Chalukyan and Hoysala era. The rulers, through the media of *pātra*, enjoyed the essence of art and provided the unique opportunity to a large section of pilgrims to watch the performance and thus indirectly educated the public about our rich cultural heritage.

The *Nartakīs* of *Nāṭyaśāstra* were the fitting models, on which the *pātras* of Chalukyan and Hoysala era evolved, and who were in later years denigrated to *Dēvadāsīs* due to exploitation by the rulers.

The permanent sculptural record of *pātras* are now seen as *Apsaras* in Belur temple. These sculptures are perennially attracting devotees and propagating our art form. The concept that was conceived by Chalukyan and Hoysala rulers has stood the test of time and are still attracting people from all over the world. Many forts and palaces built by the same rulers are seen in a ruined state, but the temples have remained intact because of the aspect of fine art that was involved.

3. SCULPTURAL EVIDENCES IN KARNATAKA

According to sculptural evidences, the concept of carving *Apsaras* as bracket figures in Indian temple architecture can be traced as far back as 1st century AD, in the famous *toraṇa* (gateways) of the Sāñcī Stūpa. They bracketed the *toraṇa* pillar to the lowermost band of *toraṇa*, with the figure of a young maiden amidst the branches of a mango tree. The youthfulness of the girl was probably viewed to inspire freshness and enthusiasm in life. She stands under a mango tree with one arm and one leg wrapped around the tree's trunk, while the other hand draws the branch towards her. She supports the Indian belief that the figure of a woman was auspicious, as she is associated with fertility, growth, abundance and prosperity. Hence *sālabhañjikās* were always conceived as a symbol of auspiciousness. These bracket figures were part of many temples all over India as Indian temples were basically religious and cultural centres, and these auspicious figures were emphasized by repetitions. Most of these figures are in dancing postures because *Śilpaśāstra* was a main chapter of *Gandharva Veda*, and dancers have always been successful in capturing the public attention and interest.

Tracing back the history of *Apsara* sculpture in Karnataka region, in the early Chalukyan period (6th cent. AD), the bracket figures were seen as *mithuna* sculptures. As seen in the Badami cave no. 3 bracket figure (Plate III, Fig. 1), the figure of couple is on the entablature, but not on the shaft of the pillar. The Kalyana Chalukya rulers brought out distinctive changes from their predecessors in 8th cent. AD in the mode and medium of sculpture tradition. The huge sculptures in rock-cut caves were replaced by delicate and smaller sculptures placed on the outer walls of the temple.

In the later period of Chalukyan rule (AD 973-1126), the decorative sculptures were on the outer walls, as *Ālasakanyā*, *mithuna* or *Apsaras*, seen on high relief. The sculptures were tall with longish limbs, with a medium built. The *Apsaras* had an oval and smiling face with soft body contours. Ornamentation was not heavy. A distinctive waistband, a Chalukyan feature with hanging pearl strands, is seen in all figures. *Apsaras* were in various activities of dressing up or dancing posture with instruments in their hand. These figures came with attendants who were short and stout. The bracket figure from Mahādeva temple at Ittagi, shows a superstructural slab, where a creeper runs as a frame around the female bracket figure. It looks like one of the earlier concepts of a bracket figure in Karnataka temple (Plate III, Fig. 2).

The Kuruvatti Mallikārjuna temple's right and left entrance pilasters have female bracket figures (Plate III & IV) which have slim and long body frame with a smiling face; bracket figures are mounted on a dwarf demon-like figure called *Bhāravāhakas*, lifting the whole slab. In the bracket figure, on the right side entrance pillar, the lady appears as though she is beating cymbals (the hands are damaged, pl. III, fig. 3) and the male attendant accompanying her is playing the flute. On the left entrance pillar, the *Apsara* is dancing in a brisk movement, twisting her waist and playing a percussion instrument (pl. IV, fig. 1). Another sculpture also shows a lady in a

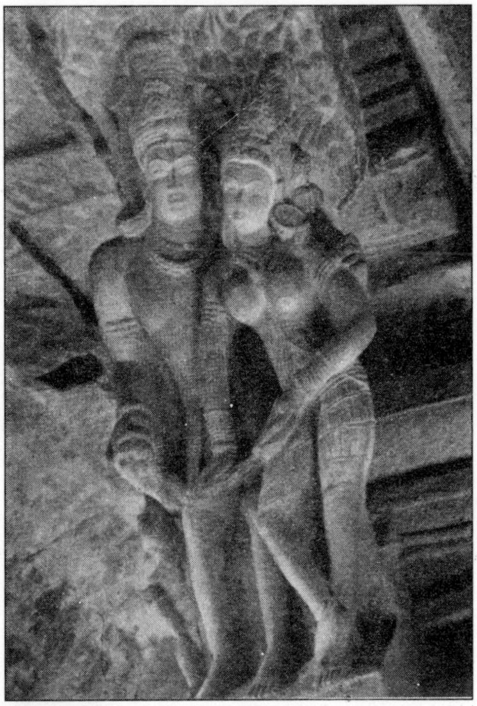

Fig. 1. *Apsara* and *Gandharva* in the Cave number 3, Bracket figure of Badami Caves – Early Chalukyan period

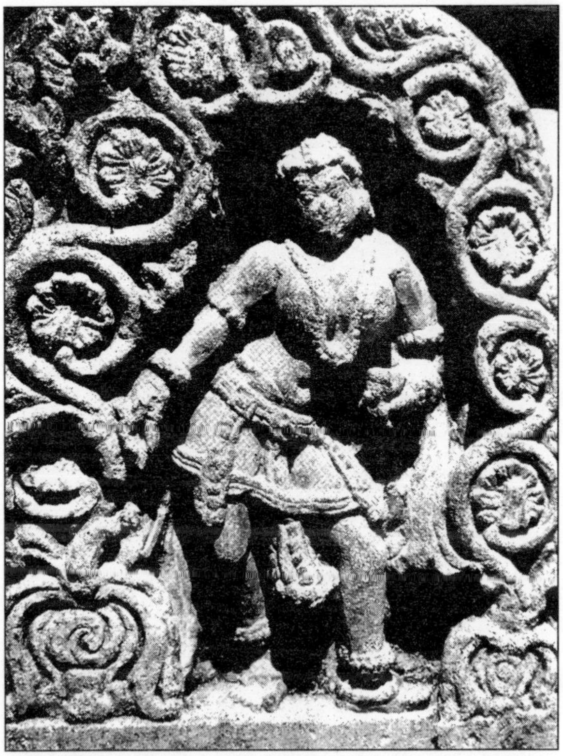

Fig. 2. Ittagi temple, superstructural decorative slab *Apsara* sculpture, Late Chalukyan period

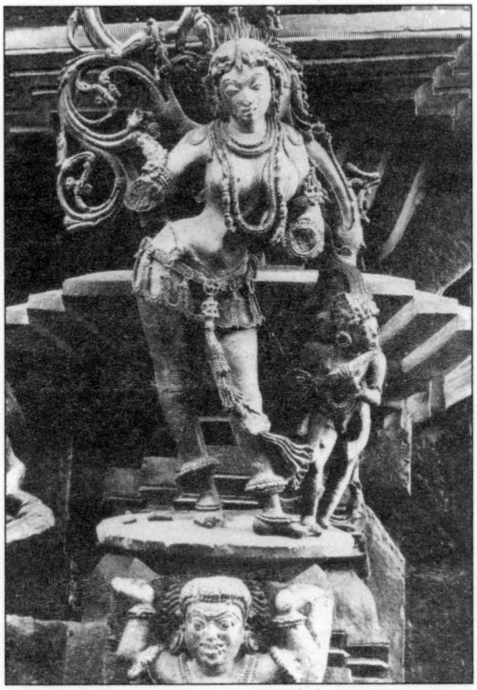

Fig. 3. *Apsara* on the right entrance pilaster at the Kuruvatti Mallikārjuna temple, Late Chalukyan period

Pl. III. Tracing the history of *Apsaras* in Karnataka

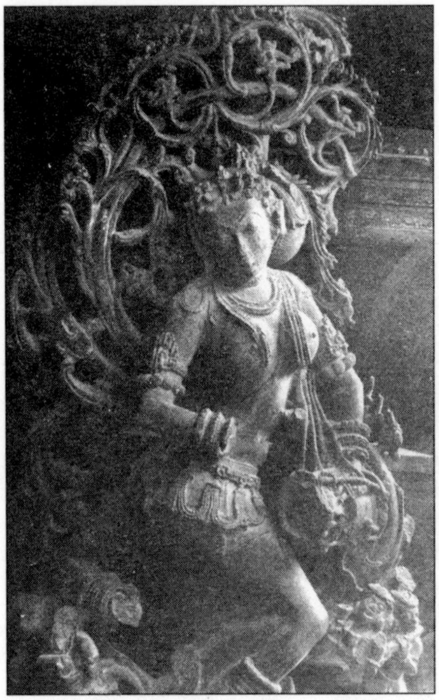

Fig. 1. *Apsara* on the left entrance pilaster at the Kuruvatti Mallikārjuna temple

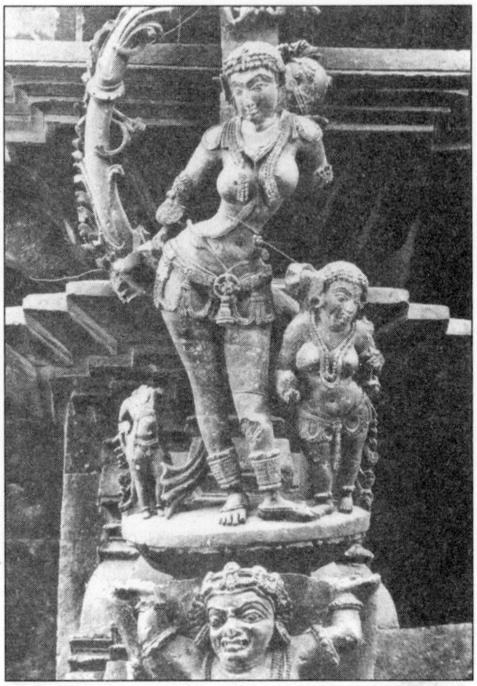

Fig. 2. *Apsara* placed on a *Bharavahaka*, at the Kuruvatti Mallikārjuna temple

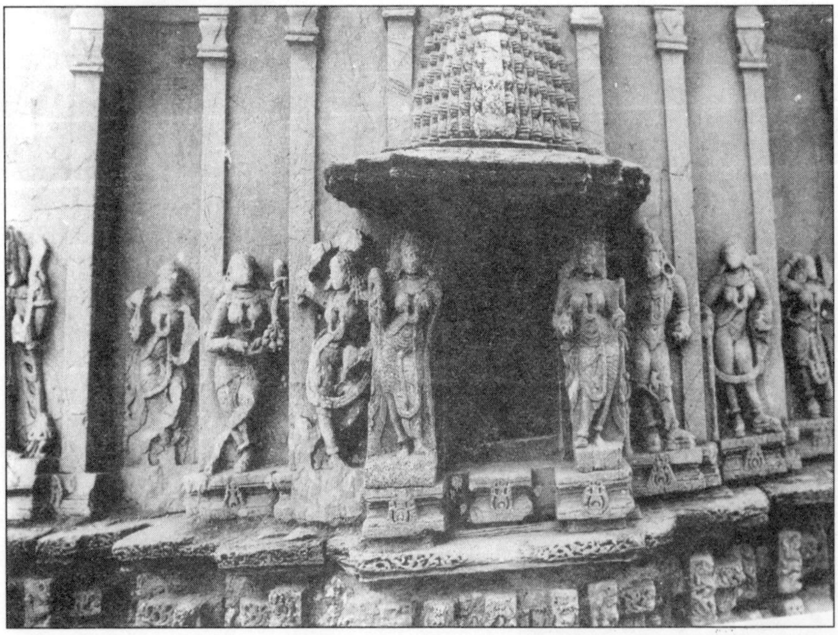

Fig. 3. A group of *Apsaras* on the west wall of Amrutaliṅga Maṇikeśwara temple at Nanditāvare, Late Chalukyan period

Pl. IV. Tracing the history of *Apsaras* in Karnataka

standing dancing posture but the hands are badly damaged. The fat and stout female attendant holds a fruit and probably a *chouri* in her left hand. All these figures have delicate work of creepers around them, as though the *Apsara* is in front of a creeper bush.

The Śiva temple as *jalasanghavi* depicts a bracket figure, writing a letter to her beloved. In the Amrutaliṅga and Maṇikeśvara temples at Nanditāvare (dating to early 11th century), the temple's west wall has many *Apsara* figures (ref. pl. IV, fig. 3) which are again slim and tall in standing and dancing postures, with themes like enjoying a bunch of berries, driving away a monkey, admiring oneself in a mirror, etc. But these figures are without any creepers or scrolls around them.

Late Chalukyas brought into usage chlorotic schist, a softer stone which was more suitable for intricate carving. Inscriptions in these temples indicate that women from royal families and noble class were highly interested in music and dance. Many dancers were appointed in temples, for prayer rituals, and these dancers probably modelled for the sculptors. These inscriptions also mention about the grants given by the queen to musicians, actors, and actresses in temples. Hoysala sculptors maintained the thematic concept of *Apsaras* in some aspects like the late Chalukyan figures. But they used their skill in adorning the figures with intricate jewellery and scrollwork in intricate designs too. Hoysalas also adopted a half sitting leg posture to depict dancing movements. The depiction of various attendants and musicians who are at the base of main figures as dwarf images, appear better in the Hoysala sculptures than the late Chalukyan figures. Most of the Hoysala temples had bracket figures, but unfortunately many of them were destroyed. It is only in Belur Cennakēśava temple that out of original 44 sculptures, 42 of them are intact. This is the only temple where the gallery of *Apsaras* are preserved the best and thus offer scope to study *Apsaras* in their original setting.

In Belur Cennakēśava temple, *Apsaras* are fixed between the capital and the entablature of the external wall of temple as bracket figures with purely decorative significance. The Hoysala sculptors have used various themes to express themselves freely, highlighting the beauty and grace of a young maiden. These elegant female figures were truly conceived as an abode of beauty and were created by sculptors and artists whose genius has never been equalled. These sculptors had a magical affinity with dancing maidens whose grace is captured in stone, that it appears the world stopped, time frozen, with heat and humidity being forgotten.

Several gods of the Hindu pantheon, namely, Lakṣmī, Gaṇeśa, Saraswatī, Pārvatī and Kṛṣṇa are sculptured as dancing gods around the main deity. Next in the rank are *Apsaras, Gandharvas, Kinnaris* and *Gaṇas* as minor gods. The figures of *Ṛṣis* and *Apsaras* are required to be placed in Hindu temples according to the *Āgamaśāstras,* and as such are not mere mythological curiosities having theoretical existence and possessing imaginary descriptions. We come across their representations here and there in temples and it is not to be considered out of place in temples. Embodying the physical and psychological elements of an adolescent female, the *pātras* as *Apsaras* are considered no less than celestial beings endowed, as they work in art and physical grace. The classical dance, which was performed daily as prayer, obviously attracted the sculptors to carve the figures in movement as *Apsaras* or enchantress, on the outer walls of the temple. Dance was an irresistible source of inspiration to a sculptor, and no doubt these sculptures are like a permanent guide to generations of dancers.

The *Apsara* figures at Belur depict young women who are slim, and proportionate with a slender waist, and appear to be in the prime of their youth. The face is either oval or in the shape of a sesamum seed with a sharp nose and sharp chin. Lips are thin but well defined and most of them give a peaceful smile. Eyes are large but mostly downward looking. The hair is neatly groomed with one or two curls near the forehead. They wore tight fitting short costumes, called *dvipadis* (as mentioned in *Mānasōllāsa*), on which they tied the decorative hip belt to hold the garments in position. Girdle was also an emblem of chastity (In B.F. 1, 4, 25 and 39, the lower seam of the underpants 'dvipadi' can be seen above the knee level.) They all stand in a graceful *tribhaṅga* posture to enhance the natural grace and curves of a woman. The description of *Apsaras* in literary and sculptural evidence, prove that they danced, fully attired, adorned with a lot of ornaments, like varieties of anklets, bangles, girdle band of several string, heavy head-dress, which might have been the costume of the contemporary professional dancers.

Nāṭyaśāstra, a treatise on Indian dramaturgy, describes various types of *Divyāṅganā* or the celestial beauties with particular dress code (Ch. 23-Sl 49 to 59).

Vidyādhārī - A celestial beauty who is well versed in the fourteen types of *vidyās* (knowledge). She has her hair tied into a knot and she is decorated with lot of ornaments.

Yakṣiṇī - One who has the capacity to change her form and abode at will. They have their hair tied into a topknot called *śikha.*

Apsara - A celestial courtesan and Madanikā; one who can exhilarate and delight and is decorated with precious stone ornaments and pearls.

Nāga kanyā - Ornaments in pearls but should have snake-hoods over their heads.

Muni kanyā - The sacred ones living in the forest. They wear single braid of hair, not decorated with too many ornaments and are in the dress of ascetic's wife.

Yoginī - The celestial one, who is in practice of *Yoga* and is in the service of Goddess Durgā. They wear ornaments of pearls and emeralds.

Siddha strī - One who is endowed with supernatural powers and magical skills. They wear ornaments of pearls and emeralds.

Gandharva strī - Celestial ones who are well-versed in the art of music and dance. They wear ornaments of rubies and hold a flute or any other instrument in hand.

Sālabhañjikā is another category of *Divyāṅganā,* who resides in trees. They appear as an *Apsara* holding the branch of a tree, indicating that they are tree spirits.

The *Apsaras* at Belur belong to the category of *Gandharva strī. Gandharvas* are the celestial musicians – a class of demi-gods – regarded as the singers or musicians of gods. *Gandharvas* and their consorts, *Gandharva strī,* reside in the imaginary city in the sky, and are exponents of *Gandharva kalā* – the science of music, dance and dramaturgy. *Apsaras* are dancers of heavenly abode, who were exquisitely beautiful, perfect in their appearance, and decorated with elaborate jewellery. They decorate many temples in India. When in a standing posture, they are considered as *Devatās* and if they are represented in dancing postures, or are seen as flying, they are termed *Apsaras.* Dance is a spontaneous physical expression of joy, when the body, mind and spirit are in harmony, and one with the *nāda* or the music. This aspect of harmony is considered as an evolved and divine state of mind according to Hindu philosophy, for which reason gods and semi-divine gods are depicted in dancing postures. At Belur temple, *Apsaras* are in dance postures, depicting either the mode of expressing a particular *rasa* (sentiment) or the frozen dance postures of the pure dance movements. They are also depicted with stringed, percussion and metallic instruments to project their mastery and love for instrumental music. For the sake of convenience, they are referred here as *Apsaras,* considering the value of the broader spectrum that this terminology is used for in Indian sculptural art.

Even though they are popularly called *sālabhañjikās* – the *Apsaras* who appear amidst the *Sāla* tree holding a branch – the representation of a lady holding the branch of a tree is not very precise. The Hoysala sculptors have used the intricate tendrilar motif as background for these sculptures, the purpose of which appear more to enhance the scope for projecting the architectural skills and grandeur, than bearing a relation to the theme that is projected in each

Apsara's sculptural unit. Because of this analysis, they are not referred here as *sālabhañjikās*, as the tendrilar leafy decorations are like a decorative backdrop or a frame, in front of which *Apsara* is exhibiting her talent, or it may also be interpreted as *Apsara* in a 'latā gṛha'. The symbolism of loose, inter-woven knot patterns of creepers can represent infinity and longevity also.

All the *Apsara* sculptures are placed on *Padmāsana*; as the name suggests, it is the lotus base on which the figures are fixed and they are oval in shape. In Indian iconography, divine or semi-divine sculptures are placed on these types of seats or *āsanas*.

Belur Cennakēśava temple has 42 *Apsara* sculptures. 38 of them adorn the pilasters on the outer wall and four on the central pillars of *Navaraṅga*. These sculptures stand mostly in a gently curved *tribhaṅga* pose, a posture where the bodyline is deflected at three places like hips, the torso and the neck, and are bent in alternating angles. The face has the characteristic arched eyebrows, big eyes of the shape of a fish, downcast eyelids and a slender long nose – with all aspects of perfect feminine grace, according to the ancient Hindu thought. Figures are dressed traditionally according to the *Āhārya* (extra accessories), the jewellery and ornaments prescribed in *Nāṭyaśāstra* (N.S., Ch. 23, Sl. 21 to 41) for women. The various types of head decorations were *Śikhāpāśa, Śikhāvyāla, Śikhājāla* (B.F. 7 & 42) – the types of nets used to trap the length of hair; *Śikhāvyāla* gave the image of a serpent with the hood, *Śikhājāla* gave the image of a long cylindrical hairdo, with pearly decoration in the bottom. On this was given *piṇḍīpatra* – a decoration with circular leaves looking like petals above the forehead. *Cūḍāmaṇi* was to be worn at the centre of the head (as in B.F. 25) and *makarapatra* or the pearl net was used to decorate the front part of the head (B.F. 19). The hair was also decorated with *vēṇīguccha*, a flowering ornament to be tied on braided hair (as seen in B.F. 7, held by a *dāsi*).

Most of the figures have *Kuṇḍalas* (large ear-rings) worn on the lower lobe of the ear. *Mocaka* (ear pendant) is seen in some figures.

On the neck various types of *muktāvali* (pearl necklace), *harṣaka* (snake-shaped chain), *ratnāvali* and *ratnamālā* (neck ornaments with precious stones), *Sūtraka* (the necklace with 2-3-4 strings) are used. All *Apsaras* are with *yajñopavīta*. On fingers, *vetika* (golden ring), and *mudrāṅgulya* (rings with design like lotus or bird) are worn.

On the upper arm are seen *aṅgada* (arm band) and *valaya* (arm ring).

On the lower arm are seen *kharjūraka* and *sochitika kadaga* (various types of bracelets and large bangles).

On the hips, *tālaka* (network of pearls), *mēkhalā* (girdle with 8 strings), *kāñcī* (girdle with 1 string for *dāsīs*), and *raśanā* (girdle with 16 strings) are tied.

Anklets or *nūpura* with *kiṅkiṇī* (belts on the foot and above the ankle) and *ratnajālaka* (broader anklets) are tied.

Various toe rings and *tilaka* for the big toe are seen. Silk robes are seen around the thigh region. These jewellery are prescribed for *Apsaras* and *Yakṣis* (N.S., Ch. 23, Sl. 49 to 61). She also has a special type of hair dress in most of the dancing figures called *vidyādhārī* where the hair is tied in top knot and decorated profusely with ornaments (as seen in B.F. 25). All the *Apsara* images are adorned with the above-mentioned ornaments. Variation can be seen only in the hairstyles. *Nāṭyaśāstra* mentions that women on earth should be represented according to regions (N.S., Ch. 23, Sl. 62 to 71). This variation in hairstyles is observed in the *Apsara* sculptures that are discussed in this book which may reinforce the view that *pātras* are represented as *Apsara* sculptures. Women in the northern region have a hairstyle called *śikhanda*, where the hair is held up and tied which looks like peacock feathers and is covered by a garment. This is seen in the *sālabhañjikā* of Sāñcī Stūpa gateway. Women in east and northeastern region tie their hair tight, making a bun, decorate it and cover it with a veil (the veil can be seen dropping at the back of the figure or resting on the hands like in B.F. 12). Women from the western region have curly hair with a long braid (B.F. 7) decorated with *śikhapāśa*. Women from southern region have a style called *kumbhi bandhaka* where hair is tied into a small jar-like shape, as seen in B.F. 32, 5 and 34. The representation of nose ring is not observed in these figures, as it is not mentioned in the *abharana* (chapter 23) of *Nāṭyaśāstra*. The hair-dress and jewellery demonstrate different disposition and moral qualities of typical characters of Indian interpretative art, so the viewers can distinguish from one another easily. It is also like a demonstration of the art of stage performance, closely integrating with body movements, dialogue recitation, singing and dancing, thus, possessing a unique artistic style of the national characterstics.

Some sculptures exhibit the height of conscious bliss (*cittānanda*). Some embody within themselves the force and grace of different *rasas* and exhibit them in different arts. They display them in rhythms and gestures and by their attributes, which they have in common with *Yogins. Yogins* are angels having transcendental power. By their attraction in the outer circle, they satisfy the devotee's response to them so that the devotee can proceed to the inner sanctum with devotion. They are grouped also as *Āvaraṇa Devatās*, surrounding divinities who are endowed with more intellect which is expressed in concrete by their art forms.

As *Apsaras*, these images are embodiments of movement in atmosphere signifying the female spirit of nature. In sculptures they are represented as having slender waist, large gluteals and well-developed busts. They should look very pretty, smiling and adorned with all ornaments and draped in silk garments. As *Yakṣi* she is associated with the trees and flowering vines, suggesting the forest spirits. As *Nāṭaka* she is shown as a dancing figure or as an artist by the name *Apsara* and may appear in the body of a man as a dancer. As *Devatā*, she is a vibrant power, resembling the great goddess who bends over the *Ahaṅkāra*, the ego of the person, who tries to meet her power. In all forms, these enduring beauties are considered very artistic and talented. *Apsaras* loved to dance and they always performed for gods, while serving as inspiration for lovers of art.

In the *Nāṭaka* group of *sālabhañjikās*, *Apsara* sculptures of Belur Cennakēśava temple are carved according to the *Lakṣaṇas* of *Nartakī*, as per the *Nāṭyaśāstra* (Ch. 34, Sl. 50-54). A *Nartakī* should be delicate and pleasant in looks, should have inborn qualities of a dancer like good voice, beautiful physique, thorough knowledge of various instruments and music, proficiency in 64 types of arts. She has to be intelligent, polite and modest, a lady without any physical deformity, always active without getting tired, proficient in dance, music and singing. She should catch the attention of public by her looks and qualities. Belur temple *Apsara* sculptures appear to be the exact representations of *Nartakīs*, according to the *Nāṭyaśāstra*. Hence, Belur sculptures are *Apsaras* with the personality of a *Nartakī*.

The *Apsara* images were added after the completion of the main temple in AD 1117. Hence they obscure the original brackets. They also depict stylistic development of sculptures over the other sculptures of Belur temple. They bear closer resemblance to the images of gods and godesses around the upper walls of Halebid temple than the other sculptures at Belur. The sculptors have not revealed anywhere about the scriptures of *Śilpaśāstra* or the style and text of dance and music followed. But they have left their signatures under each sculpture, indicating self-praise and their pride in these accomplishments. The figures are carved at *7 talas* as 9 and 8 *talas* were the measurements of gods and goddesses on the outer walls of the temple and 10 *talas* was the measurement of the main deity. *Tala* is the distance between the tip of the thumb and the middle finger when they are fully extended. It comes to about 9 *angulas* approximately. The sculptors have adhered to the measurement of body parts, according to the *Śilpaśāstra* or the ancient art manuals. *Apsara* figures look a bit plump, short and robust, with heavy breasts and a very small waist, which appears a bit unnatural in body proportions. Indian iconoplastic art has to be judged from the standpoint of its motive, to grasp soul of the art and appreciate the hidden worth. The causes that had affected the iconoplastic art, were the hard and fast rules laid down in the *Āgamas*, in making the images, which were based on the idealised form of feminine beauty and grace. The sculptors were not free to disregard these rules, and thus their imaginary skills took a second place.

Each main bracket figure of *Apsara* has attendants shown as dwarf figures at the base who are assisting her in her activities. It is only because of a strict adherence to the rules of *Śāstramāna* that even the dwarf sculptures look most delectable and artistic, in bringing out the buoyant spirit of music or dance, thus depicting the oneness of Indian sculptors with dance and music.

4. TEXTUAL REFERENCE

Mānasōllāsa is an ancient treatise, an encyclopedic work in Sanskrit dealing with the political, social, cultural and religious aspects written by the Chalukyan King Someśwara III, son of King Vikramāditya, in AD 1128-1136. *Mānasasōllāsa* is also called 'Abhilashitārtha chintāmaṇi'. *Chintāmaṇi* means a fabulous gem, that is supposed to yield its possessors all that is desired and *Abhilashitārtha* is from the root word *Abhilāṣā* which means desired or longing for. Probably Chalukyan King Someśwara intended to give information sought about the royal families in his encyclopedic work. This exhaustive work is divided into five books or *Vimsatis*, each further containing 20 chapters, in total presenting 100 chapters. Each chapter has a varying number of *ślokas*. The 5th *Vimsati* deal with amusements, sports and pastimes of royal people. The data documented in *Manasollāsa* is in general a study of the lifestyle of the Chalukya, the Hoysala, the Kalachuris and the Yadava royal dynasties, who ruled the southern part of India during AD 1000 - AD 1400. The social life pattern is a progressive phenomenon evolving over a period of time. The information regarding the lifestyles can be viewed as that which existed in and around that period with the preceding and succeeding dynasties, and not restricted to the limited period of AD 1126-AD 1138, the compilation period of the text. All the 100 chapters throw light on the life of various sections of the society, with emphasis on royal families. The leisure and pleasure of royal women, their costumes, the fashion of the elite, their amusements and pastimes, are discussed in the 5th part of *Mānasōllāsa*. The visual proof of this written document in *Mānasōllāsa* can be seen in the female sculptures – *Apsaras* as they are popularly called in the innumerable temples, that were built during 11th, 12th and 13th centuries. In some temples these sculptures are coarse but in some they are exclusive and fine. But the *Apsaras* of Belur Cennakēśava temple are the ones, which exclusively depict the theme of social life in the contemporary period of *Mānasōllāsa*. The social aspects that are hidden in the *Apsaras* sculptures stand out, when observed keenly, keeping the 4th and 5th parts of *Mānasōllāsa* as the background. There are many miniature figures depicting the everyday chorus of commoners in the lower bands of the temple's outer walls. The *Apsaras* stand out as individual figures with attendants and with different levels of activities, which hint that the royal women enjoyed a better upbringing, calibre, and hence they are placed in the upper bands, that are categorized as *Apsaras* popularly.

The Chalukyan and the Hoysala dynasties were very wealthy. The queens came from rich families, where the girls were groomed and learned in all branches of fine arts like music, dance, drama and literature. Women took part in debates and discussions and were well versed in adventurous sports activities also. The Chalukyan kings like King Someśwara III, were mostly lovers of art, great musicologists, well versed in *Nāṭyaśāstra* and other texts related to music, and knew the intricacies of the art of dancing and music. The Belur Cennakēśava temple was consecrated in AD 1117 and the period of Someśwara was AD 1126. A difference of nine years can be viewed as a short period, when aspects of cultural and social heritage are considered. The literary data of *Mānasōllāsa* text, and the archaeological proof of it can be seen as a parallel thought process, emanating from two dynasties, as Hoysalas were feudators of Chalukyan rulers.

The question arises why these social themes projected-are in dancing postures. The answer to this query is that the creators of both *Mānasōllāsa* and the Belur temple, were all well versed in the *Nāṭyaśāstra*, and knew the intricacies of dance and music. Sculptures were used as a media to express the thought process, be it in the field of fine arts or in the field of philosophy. *Nāṭyaśāstra* was used as a 'sūtra', a base or foundation, on which social, mythological and philosophical aspects manifested as structure. The result of the influence of *Nāṭyaśāstra* is reflected in the projection of Hindu gods, mythological personalities and the *Apsaras* – all represented in dancing modes. Even the social theme of a queen's enthusiasm in archery, or her joyous moments are depicted in a dance mode, in stone, meticulously observing the leg, hand and head positions, costumes and accessories that can be used, as laid out in *Nāṭyaśāstra*.

The queens relaxed by engaging themselves in various outdoor and indoor activities depending on the season and climatic condition, besides their involvement in the field of music and dance.

1. Archery

Archery, the outdoor game which the women enjoyed, is beautifully described in *Mānasōllāsa*. Women specialized in archery – a heroic sport that developed heroic spirit. The science of archery was inevitable in warfare. Women of royal families were also trained to play with bow and arrow, as they often accompanied the king in the game of archery. A woman shooting arrows was a favourite theme of sculptors in Chalukyan and Hoysala era. The skill in archery the queen accomplished was depicted in stone, through a lady shooting arrows at bull's eye, or a lady shooting an arrow from a mobile platform. One of the *Apsara* sculptures at the Belur temple (Ref. B.F. 17) depicts a lady in a heroic posture, shooting arrows at birds. These sculptures indicate the interest women had in archery. The lady is seen with an assistant, who is carrying a bundle of arrows.

2. Hunting

The fifth *Vimsati* of *Mānasōllāsa* has 292 verses to describe 21 varieties of hunting games that the royal people enjoyed as a sport, in winter season. Royal families hunted in a reserve forest, not far from the city and which was free from fierce animals but contained sober ones like deer, *sāṁbhar*, rabbits, peacock and varieties of birds.

Royal women, dressed in green short costumes called 'Dvipadis', enjoyed the hunting expeditions in the reserve forests. The text *Mānasōllāsa* gives the details of a hunting game called 'Dīpa Mṛgaya' that was in vogue during those days. A young healthy and trained female deer was made into bait – called 'Dīpa Mṛga'. *Dīpa* in Sanskrit means to shine, to rouse and that which excites and stimulates. Such a deer was trained to respond to signal calls, and taken to the forest with a rein like that of a horse. It was first made to mix with the wild ones. On the signal call, the trained deer would run to the master that was followed by the wild pack of deer, which were then hunted.

The lady is seen in B.F. 6, shooting the arrows. The *Dīpa Mṛga* or the trained young deer is seen with the reins, which the co-hunter is holding in the left hand (ref. B.F. 6a) and she holds a bundle of arrows in the right hand. The co-hunter is also dressed in a short, green-coloured *dvipadi*, with leafy decoration. The queen is seen with a *Brahma sūtra*, the sacred thread, that is indicative of a higher social status, which the co-hunter is not wearing.

Another hunting game the *Mānasōllāsa* describes is the 'Paniyaja'. On moonlit nights the queen with her associates would wait near water places concealed in the hollow of trees. Soaked chickpeas and greens were spread to attract the deers. The animals which came for a drink or for the grains were hunted.

In the sculpture, B.F. 23, the lady is seen waiting with the bow and arrow. Hunting was a strenuous game and ladies often hurt their foot in the process. First, aid was given by a hunting partner. On the right side we can see the partner massaging or dressing the hurt foot. Transportation of the game was also strenuous. The legs of the animals were tied and hung on either side of the pole that they carried on their shoulders. The attendant on the left is carrying the game, that were hunted.

3. Vanakride

Vanakride is described as a pastime pleasure in a garden. Someśwara describes how the royal women enjoyed in a garden that was at a suitable distance from their palace. Different kinds of fruit-bearing trees, like mango, jack fruit, banana, pomegranate, and scented flower plants like jasmine, *champaka, bakula,* were planted and maintained in the 'Vana', the garden, for the king to sport there for pleasure with select members of the harem. Royal women relished fruits which they could choose and pluck.

Apsara sculpture in Fig. 16 indicates a lady plucking a fruit. Women often hurt their foot as they strolled or played hide and seek in the garden for they were bare foot. First-aid was given by her assistants. BF. 35 indicates a lady holding a pebble, and whose foot is being examined for the hurt. She is resting taking support from a creeper. *Latāgṛha* was a bower surrounded with creepers, where varieties of aromatic flower plants and creepers were grown. In spring season, royal women plucked the flowers and buds. Flowers were woven into garlands or bouquets. They decorated themselves and the king with variegated floral ornaments on ears, hairs, wrists and neck.

A lady is seen in B.F. 31 adorning herself with a flower, and she is trying to figure out how it suits her as an ear-ring. She is wearing a flower in the centre of her forehead also. The assistant to her right is showing the mirror. Another lady to her left is seen giving freshly woven flower garland for the queen for her decoration.

4. Aquatic Sports – Jalakride

Summer time was spent in the *Dhārāgṛha,* a place with water jets or an artificial lake that was constructed to conduct sports, to beat the heat of summer. Mechanical showers, artificial water falls, streams of water gushing from sprouts of various animal models, were arranged for the enjoyment of royal families. Step-well was used to store water required for the *Dhārāgṛha.* Someśwara gives a detailed description of curtains that were dropped to cover the area where *jalakride* was arranged. One such summer time game was *sechanakride* where both men and women sprinkled water on each other. The king invited the distinguished personalities from all walks of life to participate in it. Cold and perfumed water was stored in big containers, made of gold and silver. Suitable syringe, made of gold, silver or cow's horn, were used to spurt water. The game was inaugurated by the young and beautiful women, dressed in white clothes, sprinkling red, yellow, sandal, and *chandana* water on the king, in the beginning and later the crowd participated in the game.

In B.F. 3, a lady is enjoying spurting water from a syringe. To her left, a man is filling the syringe with water from a big container. Another man is throwing a pot of water on the lady. It is interesting to note that the men and women played together without inhibitions, sprinkling water on one another. The other classics like *Yasas tilaka* and *Akhynaka-manikosha* also describe how the hot summer was beaten by the king, playing with royal women in Dhārāgṛha.

In B.F. 7, the queen is squeezing water from her hair, after enjoying the water game. The attendants are holding the mirror and a 'Veniguccha' for her decoration. Besides the organized sports and games, there were a number of amusements which the royalty and commoners enjoyed together – they were animal races and fights like buffalo, ram, and cock-fights. These amusements gave them a down-to-earth joy for happy living, to have a balanced view, and an association with the commoners.

Several indoor games are also mentioned in *Mānasōllāsa* – like *Chaturanga, Varatikakride,* a game of cowries, the *Phanida* or *Pashakakrida* (a dice game), *Prahelika* – the game of riddles which the women enjoyed in leisure time. The game of sticks (*Kolata*) was another indoor game of the female folk. Ladies played with a pair of painted sticks, in rhythm with the music of a folk song or Kolata songs. They moved in circular directions beating the sticks, and creating formations. On festive occasions men also joined the group for open-air performances, accompanied by expert players who delighted the crowd by performing acrobatics like touching the head with the toes and so on. Many temples have the Kolata scenes carved on pillars or on outer walls. Swing play was another amusement in the park.

5. Domestic Pets

Rearing pets was another hobby greatly enjoyed by the royal women. Pigeons, parrots, talking myna and monkeys were reared as pets. The sculpture of Belur clearly depicts the berries and grains that were used to feed the pets.

Pigeons were trained to carry letters and messages during Chalukyan period. The male bird was trained to carry letters, tied round its neck, which would fly to the required destination where the mate was kept.

In B.F. 4, the messenger bird is sitting on the right hand of the lady. In her left hand is the letter which was tied to the neck of the pigeon. A young girl, in short tight costumes, is assisting in untying the thread.

Parrot was another favourite pet bird. In B.F. 2, a lady is seen talking to her pet parrot. Her assistants are holding fruits, berries and grains for the bird.

In Figure 39, the lady is seen with another bird, which is playing with her necklace, sitting on her left arm.

Monkeys were also reared as pets of the royal woman. In B.F. 1, the lady is decorating herself and her pet monkey is being carried by a short and stout attendant who is standing on the right side.

In Figure 5, the pet monkey is teasing the lady by pulling away her robe and the woman is scaring away the monkey.

6. Fine Arts

The chapters from 10-34, of the fifth part of *Mānasōllāsa,* deals with *Gīta vinoda,* the field of music, the four types of musical instruments, the techniques of rendering *raga,* and rhythm patterns. Music, dance, drama, discussions and debates formed an integral part of intellectual pre-occupation. The queens of Chalukyan and Hoysala dynasties were great lovers of art and were well trained in instrumental music, percussion instruments, singing and dancing. Around 450 *ślokas,* from 950-1400, carry discussion on the intricacies involved with dance. B.F. 10, 14, 37, and 21 are some sculptures which indicate that the queens were musicians and dancers.

They entertained the king with their skills in the divine art. The dancers were trained to play and dance carrying the stringed and percussion instruments.

Mānasōllāsa says that the king and the members of the harem were well-versed in *Nāṭyaśāstra*. They were good at enacting dramatic situations. The king enjoyed the recitation of mythological and Purāṇic episodes through *Kathā vinoda*. It was 'Dvivaktra' where two people rendered it as a dialogue, or called *Chaturmukha*, when it was a group rendering.

A lady is seen here in Fig. 22, decorated like a 'Bhairavī' and enacting a related episode. All the accompanying musicians were male members, who were called *Kuśīlavanu,* the experts in instrumental music. Another sculpture, B.F. 28, depicts a queen going through a discussion, or narrating an episode from the scriptures. *Mānasōllāsa* mentions that Chalukyan queens were good debaters and took part in discussion sessions.

The activities of royal women and their enthusiasm for sports are described beautifully in the fourth and fifth parts of *Mānasōllāsa*. An artistic representation of such happy moments is carved in stone in the Chalukyan and Hoysala temples. The refinement in taste, love for adventure, animals, nature, and fine arts are all beautifully projected in the *Apsara* sculptures of Belur Cennakēśava temple. It can also be interpreted that the harem consisted of many wives, each one being good in some field, e.g., if the first wife was a musician or dancer, the second one was good at archery and the third was capable of amusing the king in water or garden sports. *Mānasōllāsa* can be considered as a primary text, before analysing the sculptures of Chalukyan or Hoysala temples.

IV

The Attendants of Apsaras

Each bracket figure at Belur temple has attendants, either male or female, helping to support the action of the main sculpture indirectly. The actions or the role played by the attendant images, their status and their decorations vary from theme to theme; when, *Apsara* is dressing, the attendants help her with more jewellery; when she is with a parrot, they offer fruits; when she is dancing or singing, they play accompanying instruments; when she is engrossed in a bow game, they supply more arrows. They perfectly match the *Dūtī Lakṣaṇa* or the various types of attendants a heroine can enjoy according to *Daśarūpaka. Daśarūpaka* (Part 2; 46) states eight types of *Dūtīs:*

Dūtyō Dāsī Sakhī Kārūr Dhātrēyī Prātivēśika,
Liṅginī, Śilpinī, Svayaṃ Ca Nētramitrō guṇānvita.

Dūtīs should be *Nētramitra* or pleasant to look; *guṇānvita* or shrewd and intelligent. In allocation of work, an attendant or *Dūtī* may be:

1. *Dāsī* - attendant or female servant
2. *Sakhī* - companion or female friend
3. *Kārū* or servant who does menial jobs
4. *Dhātrēyī* or daughter of a nurse or step-mother
5. *Prātivēśika* or neighbour
6. *Liṅginī* or an attendant who is literate and well-versed in *śāstras*
7. *Śilpinī* or attendant who is skilled in different arts
8. *Svayaṃ* or the heroine herself

Nāṭyaśāstra also informs that *Dūtī* has to be supportive to her mistress. She must accompany her in festivals, in gardens and other places and create an opportunity for the heroine and hero to meet. She has to be good-looking and be able to maintain secrecy of her mistress.

Nāṭyaśāstra explains in Ch. 34, Sl. 50-54, about the qualities of a *Nartakī* or the actress. A *Nartakī* should have physical beauty, feminine charm, good qualities, patience, and good manners. She should possess a soft and sweet voice, capable of singing in varying notes. She should be an expert in the representation of passion and feelings (*helā*, and *bhāva*), knowing the representations of *sattva*, and skilled in the art of acting or *abhinaya*. She should be skilled in playing musical instruments, have a knowledge of notes, rhythm and its patterns. She should be clever, capable of using the reasoning power and, above all, youthful in age with beauty. A dancer with these qualities and knowing the 64 types of arts is known as a *Nartakī*. The *Apsara* figures are carved with the qualities of a *Nartakī*.

Nāṭyaśāstra (N.S., Ch. 34, Sl. 48-49) also refers to a group of young ladies called *Naṭīs,* who are well-versed in music, aware of the intricacies of rhythm patterns, good at *abhinaya* and well-trained in dance. All the *Apsara* images depicting musical or dance activities, are accompanied by *Naṭīs.* The male artists who were good at playing instruments were called *Kuśīlavanu.* They are seen as dwarf figures along with the *Apsaras,* playing percussion instruments for rhythm or playing flute for melody.

Naṭīs and *Kuśīlavanu* are present as dwarf attendants playing music in all the *Apsara* sculptures that are engaged in activities of dance or music, as narrated in *Vēṇīsaṃhāra* (a drama by Bhasa) as:

Tatkimiti Nārambhayasi Kuśīlavaiḥ Saha Saṅgītakam, meaning the lady presented music along with the *Kuśīlavaiḥ.*

THE IDENTIFICATION OF THE TYPE OF *DĀSĪ* PRESENT IN THE *APSARA* SCULPTURES OF BELUR CENNAKĒŚAVA TEMPLE

Kārū is shortest in the group of attendants (may be two *tālas*) - half the knee height of the main figure (as seen in B.F. 1 and B.F. 2). They wear minimum jewellery and are stout and fat, doing menial jobs.

Dāsīs or attendants who help *Apsara* in all her activities other than ones where she is engrossed in music or dance. Carved up to knee length-probably three *tālas,* they appear better in status than a *Kārū,* by wearing more jewellery as seen on the left side of the main figure in B.F. 1.

Naṭīs appear in height as *Dāsīs* in three *tālas* but are slim and elegant with more jewellery and head decorations. They are present mostly with the brass cymbals when the *Apsara* is either playing an instrument or dancing as seen in B.F. 12, B.F. 29.

The male attendants seen as playing percussion instruments or flute (*Kuśīlavanu)* are carved up to knee level, probably three *tālas,* sometimes in sitting posture also as depicted in B.F. 20, 12 and 38.

Liṅginī is an attendant seen in B.F. 28, are slightly above knee level of the main figures and appear modest and serious by nature as they are literate and well-versed in *śāstras.* They are well-dressed like *Naṭīs* and are carved probably up to at three *tāla.*

Śilpinī is as tall as *Liṅginī* but helps *Apsara* in sporting activities as seen in B.F. 6 and 17.

Dhātrēyī (step-mother's daughter) appears equally well-dressed as a *Apsara.* She is carved up to hip level, up to three *tālas* as seen in B.F. 1 and B.F. 15 where the *Apsara* is admiring herself in a mirror. Only the *Dhātrēyī* wears a *yagñōpavīta,* like the *Apsara.*

Sakhī is carved above the hip level of *Apsara.* She is the tallest among all the attendants as seen in B.F. 4 and 27 carved up to four *tālas,* indicating more intimacy. They appear slim and young but with less jewellery and without *yajñōpavīta* and are present where the *Apsara* is with a parrot.

The inscriptional evidences of Chalukyan and Hoysala period address these attendants with a slightly different term:

1. The *Nartakī* was the *pātra.*

The lady who was the most skilled in pure dance, the art of histrionics and music was the prime dancer, who had the capacity to effectively enact the lead roles (*pātra*) of mythological or Purāṇic episodes and was called a *pātra.* She enjoyed a higher remuneration and a respectable social status as she danced for god in the temple everyday.

2. *Nati,* the co-artist, another dancer was a *Lachhani* or *Sāvagāni.*

Lachhani danced along with the *pātra.* She also appears to be equally well-dressed in bracket figures like the *Apsara.* Even *Lachhani* was a skilled and well-trained dancer who was well-versed in rhythmic patterns of dance and majored in singing and dancing. While *Lachhani* was a co-dancer, *Sāvagāni* was a co-singer.

3. *Dāsī,* a *Sūḷe.*

Sūḷe or *dāsī*'s allocated work was maintaining the temple and to keep it clean. She also assisted the *pātra* in her toilette, or in other activities like hunting. *Sūḷe* was a general term for the attendants like *Linginī, Śilpinī, Dāsī* or *Sakhī. Sūḷes* were of two types – one who stood with a *Cāmara* or fan was a *Cāmarasūḷe.*

One who stood by the side of a *Khambhā* (pillar) and assisted in other work was a *Khambhādasūḷe.*

They had further specification of right and left side ones with different work to do.

4. *Anuvalladasūḷe* – An innocent, young girl probably a daughter of a neighbour or a caretaker *Dhātrēyī* or *Prātivēśika* – can be compared to a *Sakhī.* She is the tallest in the group of attendants, depicting more intimacy that *Apsara* had with her. She is referred to as 'Kumari' in *Nāṭyaśāstra* (B.F. 4).

In the *Kuśīlava* group: (B.F. 12).

Harekāra or Instrumentalist.

Vaṃśiga – A flute player who majored in wind instruments. He enjoyed the highest status in the group of musicians with greater remuneration.

Maddalēkāra – A percussionist. *Maddalēkāras* were two in number – the first and the second one. Every *Apsara* figure depicting her music or dance recitals is seen with two *Maddalēkāras.*

Gāyaka – A singer.

In every recital of *Apsara,* all the above-mentioned artists participated.

V

A Brief Note on the Standing Postures Commonly Observed in Apsara Sculptures

Each sculpture, whether a deity, or *Apsara* as a deity, had to be sculptured in a definite posture, according to the *Śilpaśāstra*. For this, the concept of the deity and the dancing postures had to be studied thoroughly. Therefore, the knowledge of *Nāṭyaśāstra* became (compulsorily) infused into *Śilpaśāstra*. The *Āgamaśāstra* gives the characteristic of each sculpture as *dhyānaśloka* and the sculptor had to visualize the form in stone. Indian sculptors who carved dancing figures were guided by the principle of dance in movement and *dhyānaślokas* must have been definition of *Sthānas* (leg posture), *cārīs* (leg movement in progress) or *karaṇas* (combined movement of hands and legs) as given in *Nāṭyaśāstra.* Hence these dance sculptures are the authentic codification of art in stone, practised during that period of history. The sculptures which were created according to *Śāstramāna* (proportions of symmetry) are truly lovely. Sculptors were so much influenced and inspired by dance that even the act of combing hair or pulling a thorn from the sole, or holding a branch of tree were all portrayed as dancing figures observing the rules of dance.

A fact that intrigues the devotees in a temple is, why there are so many dancing sculptures in a temple. Sage Bharata answers that dance is occasioned by no specific need. It has come to use simply because it creates beauty, grace and attraction when performed. Dance is naturally loved almost by all people. It is eulogized as being auspicious and a source of amusement on occasions of general festivity, attainment of prosperity, marriage, childbirth and so on. Dance adds grace, attraction, and enthusiasm to an occasion. From a philosophical view, dance is an expression of joy. It is the sway of the body, in response to the nature of vibrations. It sets both the performer and the onlooker, into a movement of spirituality. Hence, dance is a sacred art for which reason, Hindu gods are represented in dancing postures–all having a certain meaning and philosophy.

Dance is represented in two forms. The pure dance movements or the non-interpretative dance and the interpretative dance where *abhinaya* (the art of communicating the meaning of a song in dance) is involved. Both forms call for a mastery over the required physical gesticulation of leg movements, hand movement, facial expression, etc. The leg postures that are used in dance, when used in a sculpture, makes it look like a dancing sculpture.

The standing postures, otherwise called *Sthānaka,* denotes *sthiti* or the static aspect. The position of the entire leg is considered with special reference to the position of the feet, the bend at the knee and the shanks. Each *Sthāna* is maintained till the movement of the leg – the *cārī* begins, and they are prescribed with certain specific usage, in *Nāṭyaśāstra* and *Abhinaya Darpaṇa.* Here, the *Sthānas*, that are commonly seen in *Apsara* figures are referred and each *Apsara* sculpture is studied with special reference to *Sthānas*. *Nāṭyaśāstra* has defined three postures for women (Ch. 13, Sl. 159-171) and six for men but they can be used by the contrary sex also (Ch. 11, Sl. 51-72). *Apsara* looks graceful and relaxed when she is observing *Strīstānakas* like *Āyata*

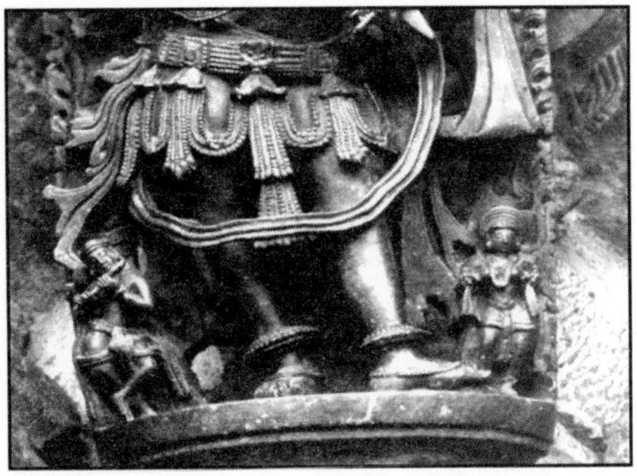

Fig. 1. *Āyatasthāna*

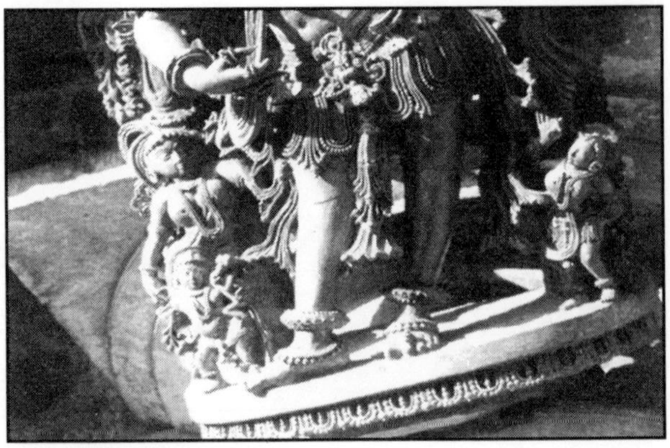

Fig. 2. *Avahitthasthāna*

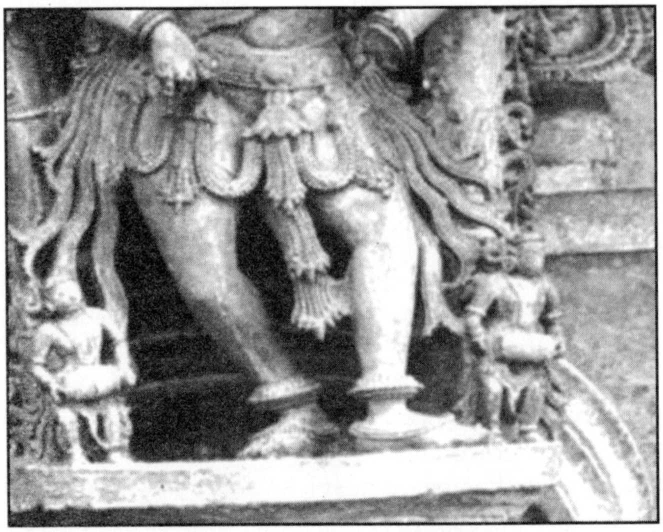

Fig. 3. *Maṇḍalasthana*

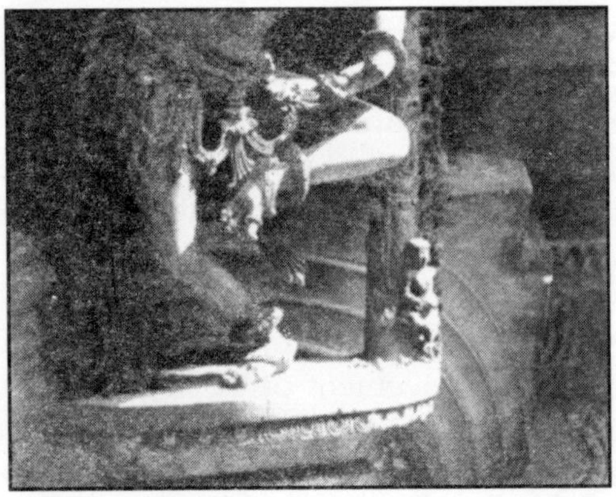

Fig. 4. *Aindrasthāna*

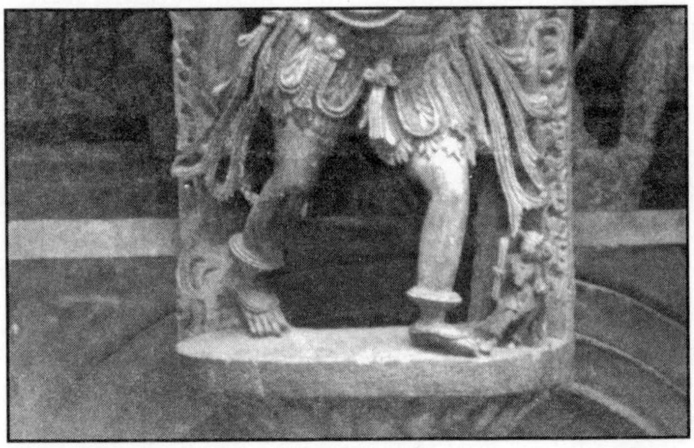

Fig. 5. *Ālīḍhasthana*

Pl. V. The standing postures (*Sthānakas*) of *Apsaras* at Belur Cennakēśava temple

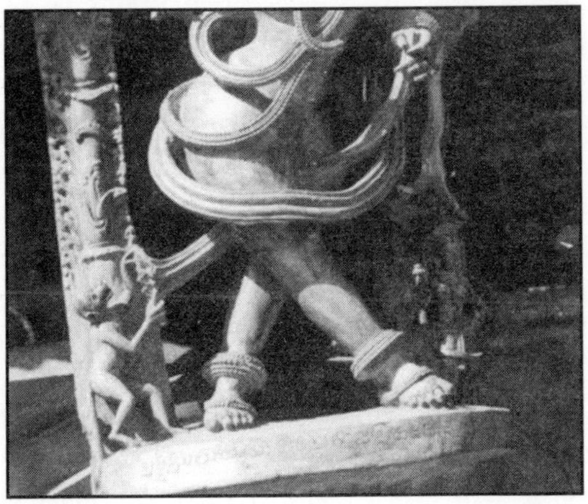

Fig. 1. *Svastikasthāna*

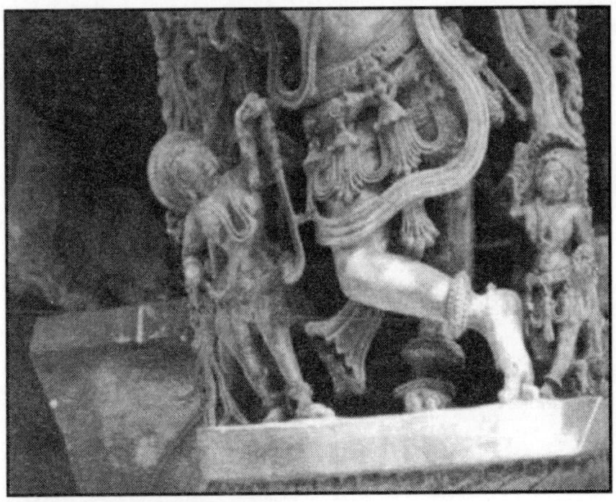

Fig. 2. *Svastikasthāna*

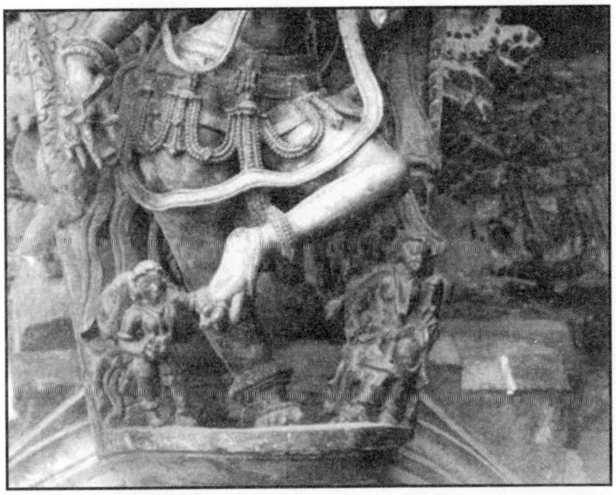

Fig. 3. *Ekapādasthāna*

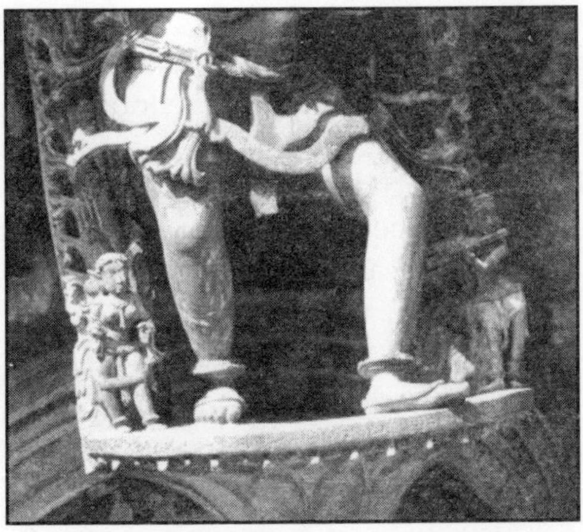

Fig. 4. *Vaiṣṇavasthāna*

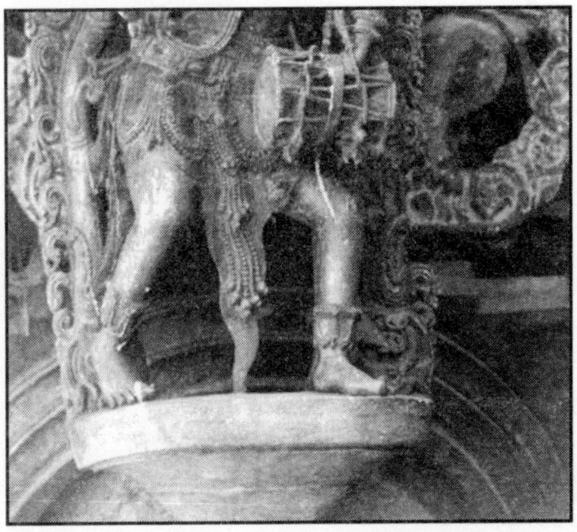

Fig. 5. *Vaiśākasthāna*

Pl. VI. The standing postures (*Sthānakas*) of *Apsaras* at Belur Cennakēśava temple and *Avahitta* (a resting posture of a lady) that are prescribed in *Nāṭyaśāstra*. *Maṇḍala* and *Aindrasthānas* are used when she is engaged in some art like playing an instrument or dancing. Her heroic posture is depicted in *Ālīḍhasthānas*. She depicts her hasty movements in *Svastikasthāna* and motionlessness in *Ekapādasthāna*. The *Vaiṣṇava* and *Vaiśākhasthānas* are used to depict the masculine posture (Ref. Plate V & VI).

a. *Āyata* - the right foot is in *Sama* (straight) and the other is placed obliquely at the side at one *tāla* (a measure of 10-12") apart. One hand is in *latā* (hanging freely) and the right hip is raised. This posture is used in first appearance of stage while conversing with dear ones, in expressing majesty, pride, profundity, agitations, observing carefully and indicating silence.

b. *Avahittha* - The left foot is in *sama* and right foot placed obliquely at its side, one *tāla* apart and hips are slightly raised to left. One hand is in *latā*. It is used to express satisfaction, graceful self-admiration, bashfulness, awaiting husband's arrival, anxiety, and erotic sentiment, etc.

c. *Maṇḍalasthāna* - Feet are obliquely placed 1-4" apart with toes facing sideways divergently. Knees are bent in half-sitting position. The body deflection may be either at two places, when it becomes *dvibhaṅgi* or at three places, when it becomes *tribhaṅgi*. This posture is used in the depiction of pure dance movements, holding an instrument, bow and such other things, large birds, etc.

d. *Aindra* - Standing in *maṇḍala* posture, one leg and the knee is raised up to the other knee level, and with the hand hanging freely in *latā hasta*. It is used to suggest graceful dancing posture, Indra, royal persons and a king.

e. *Ālīḍhasthāna* - The right foot of *maṇḍala* is extended by 3-4 *tālas*. This posture is employed in acts of heroic sentiments, self-confidence, release of weapons, duel of wrestlers and so on.

f. *Svastika* - When the right foot is kept across the left foot, the posture is *svastika*. When the shanks are crossed in *svastika*, it is used to show anger, negative mood, hurried movements, etc. (When crossed at ankle level, it indicates great joy, secrecy, etc. as seen in the posture of Lord Kṛṣṇa.)

g. *Ekapāda* – is standing on one leg, with the other foot and leg across the knee. It is used to indicate motionlessness, penance, etc.

h. *Vaiṣṇavasthāna* - Feet are 2.1/2 *tālas* apart in a knee bent posture. One foot is obliquely placed with toes pointing sideways. This is used to denote ordinary conversation in connection with various duties. It is to be used prominently in erotic, marvellous, heroic and odious sentiments.

i. *Vaiśākhasthāna* - Feet are 3.1/2 *tālas* apart, both obliquely placed and pointing sideways; the body weight is borne on the thighs, and legs are bent at the knee, with a raised waist position. This posture is used to bend the bow, for horse riding, and depiction of strenuous work.

The *Aindra, Svastika* and *Ekapāda* positions are descriptions according to *Abhiniya Darpaṇa* and the rest are according to *Nāṭyaśāstra*. All the dwarf figures of attendants are also carved according to the prescribed *Sthānas*.

VI

Rasa – Sentiments

Rasa means the essence, pith, the juicy and the best part of Indian dancing. *Rasas* or sentiments occupy an important place in the history of ancient Indian literature and fine arts. It is necessary to understand the basic structure of *rasas* (or sentiments) before relating them to the *Apsara* sculptures of Belur temple. It is easier to express emotions in literature or dance, but to bring it out in a sculpture is difficult. They are expressed through body movements as frozen *(Āṅgika abhinaya)* postures along with facial expressions and supported by other accessories. The main dancer had to be thorough with the mode of expressing *rasas* according to *Nāṭyaśāstra* as she had to enact the leading roles of the episodes of mythological or Purāṇic stories (the term *pātra* also means role in dramaturgy).

The aesthetic pleasure of *Apsara* sculptures is determined by how successful the sculptor is in expressing a particular emotion and evoking the *rasa*. The eight mental states or *rasas*, are commonly felt by human beings, and hence are natural.

The *rasas* are eight in number. According to *Nāṭyaśāstra,* Ch. 6, they are *Śṛṅgāra* (the erotic), *Hāsya* (the comic), *Karuṇa* (the pathetic), *Raudra* (the furious), *Vīra* (the heroic), *Bhayānaka* (the fearful), *Bībhatsa* (the disgustful), and *Adbhuta* (the marvellous).

Śānta, the supreme state of bliss, is sometimes considered as the ninth *rasa.*

Bharata gives the analogy of enjoyment of food in explaining the experience of aesthetic delight. Just like a person relishes the flavours of various spices while eating food, and in this relish gets satisfaction, so also a spectator relishes the permanent states of moods, aroused by presentation of various emotions, with the help of verbal, physical or mental gesticulation and gets joy in this experience. *Nāṭyaśāstra*, Ch. 7, explains that *rasas* are created by a certain cause for that particular mood (*Vibhāva*), the mode of expressing it (*Anubhāva*), and the durable effect it leaves on spectators' mind (*Sthāyibhāva*). (There may be some transitory states in *rasas* called *Vyabhicāribhāva*, which appear as wave patterns before stabilizing.)

A combination of *Vibhāva*, *Anubhāva* and *Vyabhicāribhāva* creates a *rasa* which is equivalent to various spices and the procedure followed in creating a food dish, which is enjoyed in total.

Vibhāva - The condition by which the actor experiences and feels about a particular state of mind or emotion, and that what is felt is *Vibhāva. Vi* stands for one's *jñāna* – a clear knowledge – the reason by which a sentiment is created. The physical gesticulations are determined by *Vibhāva*. Hence, *Vibhāvas* produce a sentiment. *Vibhāva* (the state of condition) has two categories.

Ālambana – the reason or root cause by which the sentiment arises.

Uddīpana – The accessories which excite or feed a *rasa*. They act as catalysts in enhancing the effect of *Ālambana*.

Anubhāva – it is the mode of outward gesticulations of mental states or *rasa*, which is transferred to the spectator. It is the external manifestation or indication of a feeling by appropriate symptoms. The physical action through which the audience are made to understand or experience a *Sthāyibhāva* is called *Anubhāva*. *Anu* means 'later'. *Bhāvyate* is to 'experience'. The way an emotion is expressed through gestures and facial expressions after it is felt is *Anubhāva*. The facial decoration and the different usages (*viniyoga* as they are called) of the eyes, eyebrows, chin, and mouth, demonstrate life in an artistic way, making movements beautiful and showing the psychological temperaments of characters. The facial expressions show the image of one's inner feelings. These sculptures depict a high degree of synthesis, that has been formed through a long historical period, the root of which can be traced to be as prescribed in *Nāṭyaśāstra*.

Vibhāva produces a sentiment and *Anubhāva* projects a sentiment.

Sthāyibhāva is the durable effect on human personality – The lasting or permanent feeling that is felt after experiencing a particular *rasa*.

Thus, the characters in a particular surrounding (*Vibhāva*) with fitting gestures (*Anubhāva*) cause to produce in the spectator a *Sthāyibhāva*, which is otherwise a sentiment successfully depicted. *Vibhāva* and *Anubhāva* which create a particular situation, have their roots in reality. Even in the illusion of reality created by the sculptors in *Apsara* sculptures, the spectator feels that it is actual reality for a time.

According to the relation or the effect of a *rasa* on *citta* or mind, *rasas* are categorized as *Vikāsa, Vistāra, Vikṣobha* and *Vikṣepa*.

Vikāsa (blooming) – It is the mood which blossoms or opens out the mind. *Śṛṅgāra* and *Hāsya Rasa*s are classified as a form of *Vikāsa* of mind.

Vistāra – expands or swells the mind. *Rasas* like *Vīra* and *Adbhuta* are known to act as *Citta Vistāra*.

Vikṣobha is the one which makes the mind turbid or disturbs the tranquility of mind. *Bībhatsa* and *Bhayānaka* are categorized under *Citta Vikṣōbha*.

Vikṣepa is the one which bursts out suddenly like a bullet firing out of a gun. *Raudra* and *Karuṇa* are grouped under *Vikṣepa*.

Śṛṅgāra, Hāsya, Vīra, Adbhuta and *Śānta* are pleasurable due to desirable *Vibhāvas*. *Raudra, Bhayānaka, Bībhatsa* and *Karuṇa* are non-pleasurable due to undesirable *Vibhāvas*. Feminine grace in youth is the support of sentiments in sculptures too, and they show changes in respect of face and other limbs. The variation in *rasas* offer a unique mode and testimony to the enduring beauties carved in this temple. It is truly beauty frozen in time.

---

* The depiction of *rasa* in *Apsara* sculptures bear no relation to any Purāṇic or mythological episodes, as there is no proof in support of this. Hence, it is viewed for a demonstration of how a particular *rasa* is to be conveyed through *Aṅgika, Āhārya* and *Sāttvika* modes. It is a demonstration of how a lady has to enact for a particular situation.

** In the author's observation, *Bībhatsa* (disgust) and *Karuṇa* (pathos) are not represented in *Apsara* sculptures as it contracts the *citta* – the mind.

VII

Apsara in Śṛṅgāra Rasa

Most of the *Apsara* sculptures are based on different aspects of *śṛṅgāra rasa*. *Śṛṅgāra* is called the 'King of Rasas' as it elevates the state of mind to *Śṛṅgā,* meaning a peak. The mind expands experiencing joy. The permanent mood – *Sthāyibhāva* of *Śṛṅgāra* – is Rati, meaning attraction and pleasure. Anything that is beautiful, pure and clean is compared to *śṛṅgāra rasa*. *Śṛṅgāra* in colloquial terms means beautification, leading to attractive appearance and is related to the youthful and mutual loving state of a hero and heroine in love. *Daśarūpaka* states that *Śṛṅgāra* has three stages – *Āyōgo Viprayōgaśca Śambhogaścēti Sa Tridhā-* (D.R., Part IV, Ch. 58) in relation to the state of mind of the hero and the heroine. *Āyōga* stands for acceptance of each other. But due to some reason the hero and the heroine have not yet met. Most of the *Apsara* sculptures depict *Āyōga Śṛṅgāra* as she is interested in the hero and is preparing herself for the meet. But the hero is not physically depicted in this group of 42 sculptures. Lord Cennakēśava is the hero of the *Apsaras*. *Viprayōga* is where the hero and heroine are separated. *Sambhōga* is where they are united.

The aspect of love in the sentiment *Śṛṅgāra* is made clear by the context such as pleasure of season, use of garlands, ornaments, objects of senses such as music and the like, going to garden and enjoying oneself there, hearing words about the hero or playing with him. The context in sculptures determine the nature of behaviour of the character of heroin – the *Apsara*. *Śṛṅgāra* is expressed through soft and delicate movements of limbs, smiling face and clever look in the eyes, pleasant state of mind, relaxed postures and gait. In her expression of love the *Apsara*'s efforts are based on longing (*abhilāṣā* in Sanskrit) to meet her beloved. She tries to decorate herself and exhibits anxiety before the meet. She is also depicted as waiting in a garden for her beloved.

Ramya dēśa, kalā, kāla, Vēśabhōgādi Sēvanaiḥ
Pramodātma ratihi saiva yunōranyonyaraktayoho (D.R., Part IV, Ch. 56)

Daśarūpaka quotes that *Śṛṅgāra* is evoked and depicted when the hero or heroin is rejoicing in a:

1. *Ramya dēśa* – Beautiful place like a palace or garden.
2. *Kalā* – Enjoying fine arts and immersed in music where the state of mind is pleasant and clear.
3. *Kāla* – enjoying a private time (like speaking or listening about the hero or enjoying *utsava kāla,* a festive time).
4. *Vēśabhogadi Sēvanaiḥ* – Enjoying or deriving pleasure from dress, ornaments, food, etc., which elevates the mind to a pleasant state. *Bhoga,* the experience of enjoyment is possible through the help of *manas,* the mind and not otherwise.

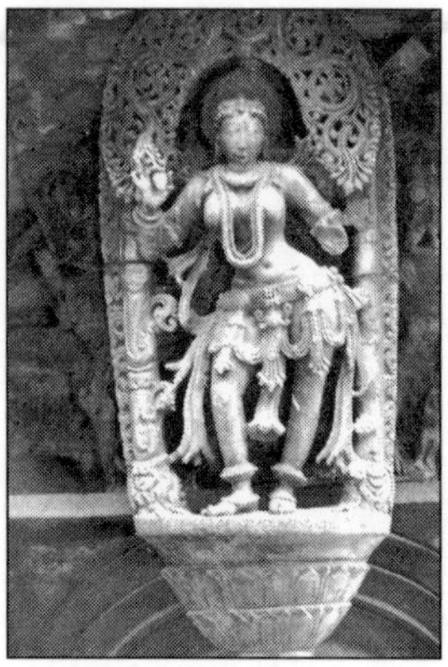

B.F. 16. *Apsara* in a garden

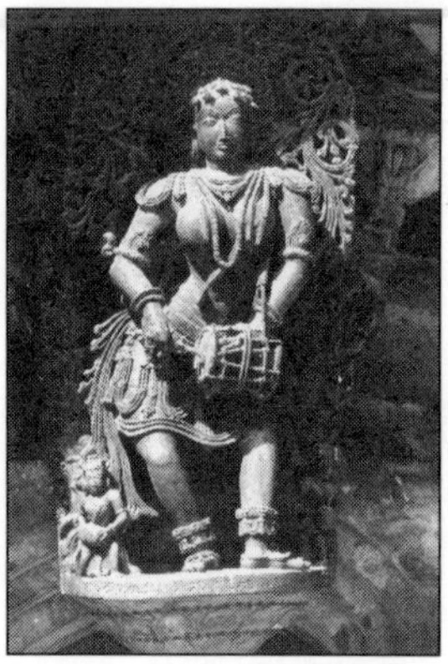

B.F. 10 *Apsara* playing a percussion instrument

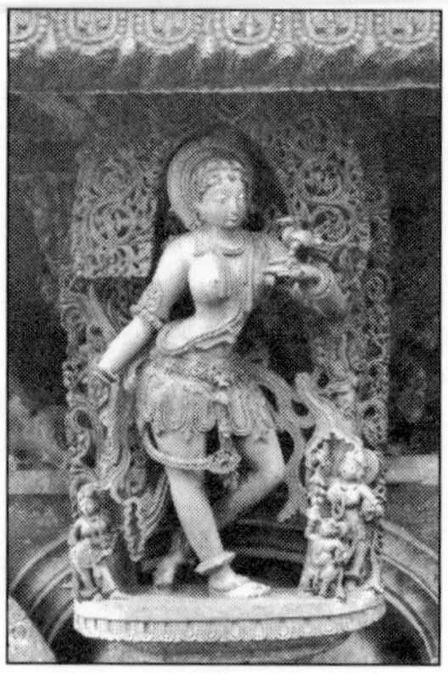

B.F. 2. *Apsara* with a parrot

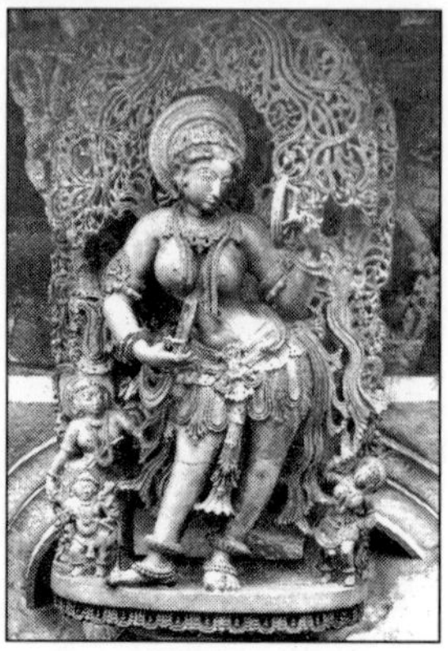

B.F. 1. *Apsara* admiring her charm in a mirror

In the *Apsara* images of Belur Chennekēśava temple, *śṛṅgāra rasa* is expressed in these four models.

1. *Śṛṅgāra* in a garden (enjoying a flower, fruit or plant)
2. *Śṛṅgāra* by actions depicting enjoyment in art forms
3. *Śṛṅgāra* in a pleasant time
4. *Śṛṅgāra* through dress (wearing jewellery and costume)

The analysis of sculptures in *śṛṅgāra rasa* is also supported by the actions of the dwarf figures depicted on either side of the main figure.

In category 2, dealing with *Kalā*, where *Apsara* is involved in music or dance, the attendants belong to the *Kuśīlava* group, who are well-versed in music and dance, and appear with instruments. The *Taṇdava vidhi kriya* as described in *Nāṭyaśāstra* is depicted here.

The other groups of *Śṛṅgāra* and the other rasa depictions are based on the type of attendants, as described in 'Dūtī lakṣaṇa' of *Nāṭyaśāstra*, and their actions. The sequence is viewed as a portrayal of a dramatic situation in sculpture. It may also be a frozen posture of *vachikabhinaya*, and the dwarf figures depict the thoughts of the main figure. The absence of accompanying instrumentalists, in a dramatic situation, support and confirm this analysis.

1. *ŚṚṄGĀRA* EVOKED IN A BEAUTIFUL PLACE (RAMYA DĒŚA)

Bracket Figures No. 16, 35

Apsara is enjoying in a garden and she is precisely like a *Śālabhañjikā*. In these images, she is bending or holding the branch of a tree, thus being in close touch with a tree indicating her association with nature, which is considered as a *Ramya dēśa* – a pleasant place.

Bracket Figure No. 16

Apsara is trying to pluck a fruit, standing in *Avahittha* posture. The *Avahittha* posture suggests the aspect of satisfaction (with the fruit). She is enjoying plucking a fruit, or enjoying the colour or feel of it.

---

* *Daśarūpaka* explains the characteristics of the types of *Nāyikās* (heroine) where a bashful young and innocent girl in the prime of her youthfulness is described as *Mugdha Nāyikā*. In B.F. 35, the *Apsara* may depict a *Mugdha Nāyikā*, who under the pretext of getting the thorn removed, or holding a branch, takes a second glance at her beloved. The fact that her concentration is not focussed on her foot or the skin deep prick but at something else, with a pebble in her hand, supports this analysis.

Bracket Figure No. 35

Apsara is in a garden either enjoying nature or waiting for her beloved, but has trouble caused by stones and thorns. She holds a stone in her right hand. *Apsara* has taken support from the branch of a tree to support herself to enable the attendant to examine her left foot, standing only on the right leg in *ekapāda,* where the left leg is placed across the right knee, suggesting motionlessness.

The *dāsī* to her right has removed the thorn from the *Apsara*'s foot, which she is holding in her hand. To the left is another *dāsī*, with a *chouri* in her hand.

Vibhāva - *Apsara* is happy, enjoying the beauty of nature in a garden (*Ramya dēśa*).

Ālambana - Love for nature and probably a meeting place with her beloved.

Uddīpana - The flowers and fruits, which intensify her interest in a garden. (It may be a *Apsara* waiting in the garden to meet her beloved.)

Anubhāva - Delicate and relaxed posture and a tension-free movement in a beautiful garden. She stands in *Avahittha* posture in B.F. 16 indicating her satisfaction.

Sthāyibhāva is Rati - pleasure.

2. *ŚṚṄGĀRA* – THROUGH ART (GANDHARVA KALĀ)

When the hero or heroine is involved in enjoying any art form like dance and music – the *Gandharva Kalā* – they are depicting *śṛṅgāra rasa* as it is categorized under blooming of the mind or *Citta Vikāsa. Nāṭyaśāstra* defines *Gandharva Kalā* as music and dance based on *Svara, tāla* and *pada* (words) executed with various musical instruments. This was the art loved by gods and *Gandharvas* who were proficient in music. *Apsaras* in *Gandharva Kalā* are carved according to the description of *Nartakī* in *Nāṭyaśāstra* who was referred to as *patra* in the inscriptions of Chalukyan and Hoysala period. The images are depicted involved in art like playing the *vīṇā* (a stringed instrument), the drum, the flute, singing with brass cymbals and dancing, thus exhibiting their knowledge in music and dance in-depth. They are shown as proficient in all four categories of musical instruments of an orchestra like *Tāta, Avanaddha, Suṣira* and *Ghana* (the stringed, percussion, wind and metallic instruments), other than being great dancers. The term *Saṅgīta* was always referred to in its triple aspect, viz., *Gīta* (song), *Vādya* (instrumental music) and *Nṛtta* (dance). It appears as if we can hear the sound of jingling bells, the rhythm of percussion instruments and the melody of flute around the temple walls.

In all the bracket figures depicting involvement in music or dance, the male attendants are accompanying on percussion instruments or wind instruments. They are called *Kuśīlava* according to *Nāṭyaśāstra* who are good at playing any instrument. As described in inscriptions of the Chalukyan period they are *Maddalēkāra, Vaṃśiga, Gāyaka,* etc. The female attendants are *Naṭīs*, the co-dancers who are slim, beautiful and well-dressed almost like *Apsaras* and provide the rhythm through cymbals, as they are good at the intricacies of rhythm patterns. They are called *Lachhani* or *Sāvagāni* in Chalukyan inscriptions.

According to Bharata, the term *Nāṭya* is very comprehensive, encompassing and synthesizing branches of vocal, instrumental music, dance literature, dramaturgy, histronics and other theatrical arts. The *Nāṭyaśāstra* dealt mainly with the intricacies of each division and the knowledge of which has been followed by Indian artists ever since it was formulated. The *Apsara* sculptures reflect how truly the Hoysala sculptors and artists followed the aspects of *Nāṭyaśāstra,* in their dance, music, dramaturgy and so on.

Some *Apsara* sculptures depict pure dance sequences, as there appears no theme that is supported by either the accessories held, or through the dwarf figures on either side. She appears in a dance posture with instruments and the accompanying artists are also playing music. This is discussed by Bharata in *Nāṭyaśāstra*, Ch. IV. Sl. 266-296, under the heading *Tāṇḍava Vidhi Kriyā* where the role of pure dance, in the preliminaries of a play, are explained. They are:

1. Arranging the auspecious musical instruments, seating of singers is observed in 'Kutapa', and all instruments are tuned.
2. Music without words is sung as 'Asarita',[1] and *Nartakī* plays *Nirgita* (a combination of sounds, or music without words) on a stringed instrument to satisfy the vanity of *Daityas* and *Danavas*. It is also called *Bahirgita*, as it is considered outside the play as a preliminary gesture.
3. The dancer makes an entry as the songs are sung with the accompaning instruments. Dancer performs a befitting *cārī*[2] (leg movement) and should perform 'Vaiśākha rechita Karaṇa' highlighting all the *rechaka* movements (see foot notes). Only rhythm instruments are played when she performs *Karaṇas*[3] and *aṅgaharas*.[4] All instruments are played when she performs for a song with words. She has to perform *cārī* (graceful leg movements) and *mahā cārī* (vigourous leg movement) to the song and then take an exit. This procedure is repeated by the co-dancer (*Naṭi*).

In my analysis and approach, the above-mentioned *Tāṇḍava vidhi kriyā* is easily traceable in *Apsara* sculptures when the accompanying instruments are studied carefully.

1. B.F. 13 - *Apsara* is indicating tuning of the stringed instrument.
2. B.F. 30 - She is playing *Nirgita* and *Bahirgita* on *vīṇā,* a stringed instrument
3. B.F. 14 - Music of the orchestra before the entry of the dancers.
4. B.F. 19, 21 - *Apsara* is performing *rechakas*[5] and *karaṇa* to rhythm instruments.
5. B.F. 8, 10, 24, 33 - May be representation of *cārīs* with varieties of percussion instruments.
6. B.F. 29 - She is probably indicating the use of stringed instrument to a song, which the co-dancer is singing and a melody instrument flute is played (this is without a percussion instrument).
7. B.F. 40, 41, 25, 38 - *Apsara* performing graceful[6] and vigours dance movements, (depicting *cārī* and *mahācārī*), to a *Gīta* that is sung by co-artist, and all instruments are played. This may be the representation of *Saṅgīta*, where dance, song, instruments are performed simultaneously.

The *Vibhāva* and *Anubhāva* remain the same for all sculptures expressing activities in art forms.

Vibhāva - Love for art.

Ālambana - *Apsara* is interested in enjoying and exhibiting her art and talent, by which she and her beloved share a happy mood.

Uddīpana - The right and left side attendants, either male or female, are participating in the orchestra by playing supportive instrumental music.

Anubhāva - Happiness or joy is expressed in a smiling face. Her flexibility and grace is expressed in the *tribhaṅga* posture, when she is dancing. Even while playing the instruments, *Apsara* is in a dancing posture as dancing was used to satisfy gods and *naṭ* (to dance) was the art of *Naṭa* or *Nartakī*. *Apsara* is engaged in *Gandharva Kalā* in two ways: *vādya* – instrumental music, and *Nāṭya* – the dance.

The *Apsara* sculptures in *vādya* group of holding or playing musical instruments can be further classified into five categories depending upon the instruments she is holding.

I. Engrossed in stringed instrument – B.F. 13, 14, 29 and 30
II. Depicting involvement in percussion instruments – B.F. 8, 10, 18, 33 and 36
III. Wind instrument – B.F. 11
IV. Singing and playing brass cymbals – B.F. 12 and 20
V. Graceful dancing postures and a representation of *Saṅgīta* – B.F. 11, 19, 21, 25, 29, 38, 40, 41.

Someśwara describes in *Mānasōllāsa* that *vādya* enhances the appeal of dance. There can be no dance without *vādya* and hence instruments are important for both music and dance recitals.

In all the figures of this category, *Apsara* displays a hairstyle that is suggested in *Nāṭyaśāstra*, for ladies in eastern part of India. Hair is tied into a *kośa*, and decorated profusely giving the effect of a halo. This is a suggestive indication that when a lady is well-versed in arts, she is above the normal human level. The veil which probably emerges from the back of the head is seen flying on either side of *Apsara* at the back.

A. Stringed Instruments ('Tata' Vādyas)

Apsara is playing four types of string instruments which are comparable to the present day (1) *Tambura* (*Tanpura*), (2) *Kinnari* or *Vicitra vīṇā*, (3) *Gottuvādya*, (4) Instrument resembling *swara maṇḍal*. These stringed instruments throw light on the types of instruments that were in use during the Chalukya or Hoysala period. *Nāṭyaśastra* (Ch. 33, Sl. 15) mentions that among the stringed instruments, *vipanchi* and *Vicitra vīṇā* are major limbs and *kacchapi* and *ghosaka* are smaller instruments, *kacchapi* is one stringed instrument, made of tortoise shell and *ghosaka* is a kind of *tanpura*, used merely as a drone. An interesting feature the author observes is that the stringed instruments, *vīṇā* or *tambura*, are not used as an accompanying instrument in the orchestra or *Saṅgīta* figures. Only the flute, percussion instruments are played and co-singers are present with the cymbals. The Chalukyan and Hoysala inscriptions mention about the financial payment that was given for *maddalakara, vamsiga, naṭī, savgani*, etc. and there is hardly any mention of *vīṇā* players.

B.F. 13

Apsara is plucking the string of a *tambura* which may be the *ghosaka* of ancient times. The instrument is now missing, but position of her hands indicate that in her left hand, she is supporting the base of the instrument, and with her right hand she is gently plucking the strings of the instrument. *Tambura* is a instrument, which is used as a drone to maintain the aspect of pitch in orchestra, to which other instruments and vocal music are tuned. Chapter V in *Nāṭyaśāstra* mentions about a stage called *Asrāvana* where musical instruments are adjusted for playing them in due manner. B.F. 13 may be a representation of the tuning of *tambura*, a preliminary stage that is observed before the performance.

On her right side is a co-singer, in a cross leg posture and playing the cymbals. To her left, is a *maddalakara*, with the percussion instrument. The *Apsara* stands in a beautiful *tribhaṅga*, with legs in *Aindrasthānaka*, where her left leg is raised to the right leg knee level. In the background, on the creeper,the sculptor has carved a lizard trying to catch a fly. (The purpose of this feature, is discussed in Part II of this book, ch. 3/3, dealing with the tuning of the mind.)

B.F. 14 (Tata Vādya)

The *Apsara* is playing an instrument resembling *Laghukinnarī*. She is holding the instrument in her left hand, the head of which is supported on her left thigh partially. In her right hand she holds a plectrum with which strings are plucked. A description of *Laghukinnarī* is given in *Mānasōllāsa*, in the chapter *Vādya Vinōda*, on musical instruments. It is a stringed instrument with two small gourds. The bigger version of this with three gourds is called *Bṛhatkinnarī*. *Laghukinnarī* was a popular instrument in those days. Now it is obsolete. The nearest comparison can be seen in *Vicitra vīṇā* (see Appendix).

She is supported for rhythm by two male attendants (*Kuśīlava*) on right side who are playing on *Edakka* and *Maddala* (see Appendix). On the right side are two female attendants; one of the *Naṭīs*, a *Savgani*, is playing on cymbals and the other one is standing. All are participating in the orchestral recital. The sweet smile on *Apsara*'s face indicates her happiness with the art. It looks as though she is beckoning the viewer to enter this beautiful temple, and enjoy the secrets of divine bliss. She is standing in *Maṇḍalasthāna.*

B.F. 29

Apsara is holding a stringed instrument which looks like the present day *swaramaṇḍala* or *santoor* in her right hand, and the decorative bamboo or wooden mallet in the left hand, to strike the string. It is a shallow wooden box with vertical row of strings (which can be identified as thin verticle lines in the instrument), held by posts for tuning. Beads are inserted in the string for fine tuning. The instrument is tuned to the scale of a particular melody. *Apsara* stands in *Āyata* posture, to reveal her appearance with the instrument. To her right is the *Vamsiga*, playing on flute, and to her left is a co-singer with cymbals. The absence of percussion instruments indicate that the *Apsara* is playing a melody-based *gīta* or song.

B.F. 30

Apsara is involved with a stringed instrument resembling *Gettuvādya* (see Appendix). The resonator in the front part of the instrument is broken. The body of the instrument is long, ending with a snake motif. The strings are struck with a decorative bamboo blade which she is holding in her right hand. In her left hand also she holds a smaller blade to move on the strings. It is also used as a rhythmic instrument. The front part of her left foot is slightly raised indicating that she is tapping her foot to maintain rhythm. Yājñavalkya says, music be it vocal or instrumental or dance, is not acceptable it if is out of rhythm – *Gītaṃ Vādyaṃ Ca, Nṛttaṃ Ca, Tālahīnaṃ Na Rājatē.*

Her recital looks like a solo performance even though she is supported by a *Kuśīlava* on the right side sitting and playing on a percussion instrument. The attendant to her left is indicating the rhythm. *Apsara* is in *Maṇḍalasthāna.* Her deep involvement in music is expressed on her face.

Nāṭyaśāstra in Ch. V explains the rules and parts of the preliminaries that are to be observed before the commencement of a play or *Nāṭya*. After the stage of 'Asravana' where musical instruments are tuned and adjusted, 'Nirgīta', the music of stringed instrument' is to be played initially to satisfy the vanity of *Daityas* and *Rakshasas*, so that they are not provoked to create any obstruction for the performance. This *Nirgīta* that is played on a *vīṇā*, does not convey any words, but involves the techniques of playing called *Karaṇas*. It is classified as a *Bahirgīta*, to satisfy the vanity of *Daityas*, which means it is outside the play. In B.F. 30, *Apsara* may be indicating the stage of *Nirgīta* or *Bahirgīta*. It is viewed so due to the absence of co-singers or flautist.

B. Percussion Instruments (Avanaddha Vādyas)

B.F. 8, 10, 24 and 33

Avanaddha is a class of covered musical instrument which are mostly used to indicate rhythm or tempo. It is a drum, the face of which is tightly covered with hide and the tightening and loosening of which changes the pitch of the instrument to high or low. The size and shape of the drum varies and even the surface of the face varies in diameter. Hence, there are hundreds of varieties of percussion instruments. They are called *puskara vādya*. The drum part of the instrument may be either made of wood or clay or metal.

Avanddha or percussion instruments are played on occasions like festivals, royal procession, musical or dance recitals, joyous celebration, and auspicious occasions like marriage, childbirth. To depict a battlefield, or an assemblage of fighters, large drums of loud noise are played. For household affairs, smaller drums are played.

Nāṭyaśāstra, Ch. 33, mentions various types of percussion instruments, the technique of playing them and the rules that are to be observed while playing them. The common percussion instruments as described in *Nāṭyaśāstra* are:

Mṛdaṅga, Paṇava, Dardura as major limbs. *Jhallari, Ankika, Pataha, Urdhvaka, Muruja, Alingya* as minor limbs. *Bheri, Bhambha, Dundubhi, Dindimas* are with slack, large and extensive surface, with a depth of sound.

1. *Mṛdaṅga* has the body made of clay, with two faces, which are covered with hide and is played by both hands. It is three and half *tāla* in length with a face of 12 fingers diameter.
2. *Paṇava* is a drum with two heads, thinner in the middle part and fastened with strings. It is sixteen fingers long and the face is eight and five fingers in diameter.
2. *Dardura* is shaped like a pitcher, which has one face that is sixteen fingers in diameter.
3. *Ankika* is three and a half *tāla* long, shaped like myrobalan, with two faces.
4. *Urdhvaka* is shaped like barley grain with two faces. It is four *tālas* long, with a face that is fourteen fingers in diameter.
5. *Alingya* is also with two faces in the shapre of cows tail.

The *Apsara* sculptures of Belur temple are with many varieties of perucssion instruments. Two percussionists are present in all sculptures involved in music, which indicates that two different instruments like *Mṛdaṅga* and *Paṇava* were played, to enhance the effect of music.

The percussionists employed different techniques or *Karaṇas*, as they are called, with strokes and rhythm patterns to enhance the pure dance sequences or the rhythm of instrumental music. The drum beats were played according to the age and status of the male or female roles, and the pattern of play also varied according to the sentiments that were projected in the ballet. The term *Maddalekara* for percussionist is mentioned in many Chalukyan or Hoysala inscriptions but it is not referred in *Nāṭyaśāstra*. Hence, it might have come into usage after the period of *Nāṭyaśāstra* compilations. The percussion instrument is played by *Apsara* with a stick called *koṇa*, which resembles the present day *edakka* or *chenda*.

B.F. 18 depicts three percusionists. *Nāṭyaśāstra* in Ch. 33 says that the three *puskara vādyas* – *Paṇava, Mṛdanga* and *Dardura* – should be placed facing east on the stage.

B.F. 10 also has three different percussion instruments. The percussionist to the left of *Apsara* is holding the drum vertical. The three instruments are *Mṛdaṅga, Paṇava* and *Dardura,* which are mentioned in the *Nāṭyaśāstra*.

The percussionists had to be well trained in applying proper plastering to drums. They had to be experts in the use of hands, with firm, swift and controlled strokes and with a complete knowledge of the intricacies involved with music and rhythm patterns. Their good health, energy and knowledge, added charm to all events as percussion instruments were indispensible in all recitals and functions.

B.F. 8

Apsara is dancing and playing a small instrument called *muruja* (or *pataha*, which has two heads and resembling the present day *ḍhakkī* (see Appendix). It is an hour glass shaped small drum, covered on either side by stretched parchment. Her left hand is inserted in the strap to support the instrument. With her right hand she is beating the drum with the help of a small stick. The beauty of this figure explains the *śloka* of *Nāṭyaśāstra* on *tāla*.

Takāraḥ Śaṅkaraḥ Prokto, Lakārō Lāsya Ucyatē.
Śivaśakti Samāyōgē Tālamityabhidhiyate.

She appears to be an embodiment of both rhythm and *lāsya* (grace) as she is in a brisk dancing movement, in *tribhaṅga*, with the rhythmic drum. The raised left leg suggests a vigorous rhythmic, jumping and turning step, which is indicated by the flying scarf on the left hand. Her small bud-like mouth is set in a beautiful and sweet smile and downward eyelids indicate her deep involvement in the art.

* *Mānasōllāsa* mentions that the *Nartakī* – the actress, was trained to dance, carrying and playing varieties of instruments effortlessly.

B.F. 10

Apsara is in a dancing pose in *Maṇḍalasthāna* beating a drum *Paṇava* that can be compared with *edakka* (see Appendix). This is one of the basic postures which the drum dancer has to observe as they carry the weight of the instrument while dancing. The drum is slung from the left shoulder. She holds a curved wooden stick in the right hand (called *koṇa*) and beats the drum with it. The left hand is inserted in the strap of the instrument to adjust the tension of the parchment. Rhythm or the discipline of *tāla* fixes the form and boundaries, offering scope to create varied patterns within. The variations of pitch, by the skilful fingering techniques, is indicated here, which adds thrill, making the rhythmic patterns more effective and interesting. She is beautifully decked with ornaments on arms and legs. She is frozen forever with her eternal, beautiful and blissful smile, with the eyes in *Mukula* expression (which is half-closed eyes with smiling expression indicating enjoyment). She is accompanied on either side by *Kuśīlava* male attendants playing percussion instrument. This is one of the most beautiful figures of Belur temple, which is preserved intact. To her left, stands a drum beater, who is holding the drum vertical. The three different percussion instruments are the representation of *Mṛdaṅga*, *Paṇava* and *Dardura*, which are mentioned in Ch. 33 of *Nāṭyaśāstra*, that are to be presented in the preliminaries of a ballet. *Apsara*'s involvement in rhythm instrument, presented in a dancing posture with the unique hip costume, ornaments, and the hairstyle constitute a unified beauty and form a unique style of Hoysala art.

B.F. 24

Apsara is a drum beater, half-sitting in *Maṇḍalasthāna*, in a graceful *tribhaṅgi* posture, but the drum is missing. Her hand position and the strap (broken) indicate the drum is like *eḍakka* even though the figure looks like in a dancing posture. She is supported on either side by male percussionists in sitting posture. Creative variations in rhythm patterns call for active participation of the intellect as it is based on the calculation of numbers and the grip over mathematics in concrete action. An important feature of *laya* is its capacity to infuse energy. It stimulates and enlivens music.

B.F. 33

Apsara is dancing in *Maṇḍalasthāna*, with a small drum that looks like *Jhallari*, which is now known as *Buḍubuḍikai* (see Appendix) in left hand. It is an hour glass shaped small wooden drum with both faces covered with skin. Two knotted chords are tied to it to strike the heads when shaken. In her right hand, she holds *chitaka tāla* (see Appendix) – a pair of wooden clappers. She is dancing beating both the instruments, expressing her skill and capacity. Male *Mṛdaṅgists* are sitting and beating *Mṛdaṅga* on either side.

This sculpture is a demonstration of the *Tālavadhana* – the art of exhibiting the attentiveness, skills and capacities of the artist in a music recital where different rhythm patterns are reckoned, at the same time. She is probably demonstrating a specific *tāla* pattern with the *chitika tāla* in her right hand and a speedier or a different *tāla* with the *Budubudukai* in the left hand. The attendants are with a different type of percussion instrument, to which she has to harmonise. Her dancing posture is indicative of another rhythm pattern, with her foot. Such a demonstration of academic interest requires intence practice, concentration and accuracy.

C. Wind Instrument (Suṣira Vādya)

B.F. 11

Flute was the most ancient and leading musical instrument. It is seen in almost all ancient Indian sculptures, depicting music and dance. The flutist was called *Vamsiga* in Chalukyan and Hoysala inscriptions who enjoyed the highest status among the instrument players. In B.F. 11, *Apsara* is in the dress of Kṛṣṇa, trying to imitate the flautist who is on her left side, and she is playing on flute. Her long hair is in the net of *Vyālakēśa* (the bottom of which looks like snake hood) and is tied and twisted. She is with a robe similar to the one worn by other male attendants, the central fold of the garment descending up to the knee level. But she is still wearing the anklets and *nūpura* on feet. She wears a feathery decoration (like the one in Kṛṣṇa idol) on her head. Her involvement in music is indicated by the eyelids in *ardha mukula* (half-closed). On her right side is a *dāsī* playing on the cymbals. *Apsara* is in *Vaiśnavasthāna* in *tribhaṅgī* posture. Her left leg is kept 2.1/2 *tālas* in front of the right one and toes pointing sideways.

* Generally in the temples and mansions of kings, the *Nartakīs* would enact the male roles also. They were strictly trained by their preceptors. Here *Apsara* is in the dress of a *Vamsiga*, playing the wind instrument.

D. Metallic Instrument – Cymbals (Ghana Vādya)

B.F. 12 and 20

B.F. 12

Here *Apsara* is depicted as a singer with *tāla* or *kaṃsāḷē* in hand (see Appendix) who guides the rhythm for devotional music or a dancer through brass cymbals. It is a pair of clappers with cup-shaped metal disc and deep central depression, made of bell metal. Cotton sling is tied to the disc. It is used for rhythmic accompaniment in devotional music and *saṅkīrtan*. They are classified under metal instrument – the *Ghana vādya*. *Kaṃsāḷē* dance is a group performance. The main singer beats the cup-shaped cymbals, sings and dances with enthusiasm and the co-dancers follow it. Her opened mouth suggests that she is singing. She has a beautiful smile on her face. To her right and left are *Kuśīlavas* playing percussion instruments and flute. On left side is a co-artist, the *Naṭī*, who is slim and well-dressed like the *Apsara* and playing the cymbals (*Kaṃsāḷē*). *Apsara* is standing in a beautiful *Āyata* posture with her.

B.F. 20

Apsara is singing and playing the brass cymbals in *Āyata* standing pose. She is singing the song and providing rhythm through cymbals *(Kaṃsāḷē)* to other singers or dancers. Even though the hands are damaged, the flying straps or woolen cords hanging from the instrument, indicate the instrument as cymbals. On the right side are two *Kuśīlavas* playing percussion instruments. On the right side is a young and beautiful male figure of another *Kuśīlava* playing the *Bāṅsurī* – the wind instrument which looks longer than the one used in B.F. 12.

B.F. 12 and 20 depict a musical orchestra called *Saṅgīta* as described in *Nāṭyaśāstra. Saṅgīta* means sung together in chorus, in Sanskrit. It is a song sung in many voices, a harmonious singing, accompanied by instrumental music and dancing, a triple simphony with a devotional theme, which is also called *saṅkīrtan.*

"Gītam, vādyam, Nartanam, ca trayam saṅgītamuchyate."

In B.F. 20, co-singer is not present; hence, it may be that *Apsara* is presenting a gīta or song as a vocalist. Though dance is described as the special field of *Apsaras,* they also had equal proficiency in singing and playing other instruments.

E. Graceful Dancing Postures

B.F. 19, 21, 25, 38, 40 and 41

Apsaras loved to dance and they performed for gods while serving as an inspiration to all dancers for generations. The graceful dancing postures of the *Apsara*s in this temple depict *Nṛtta* aspect of dancing. *Nṛtta* is based on rhythm, is related to visual pleasures and it belonged to the classical style as described in *Nāṭyaśāstra.*

Most of the *Apsara* figures engaged in *Nāṭya* are in *tribhaṅga* when body deflection *(bhaṅgī)* is considered. In her *sthānaka* (the standing posture) she is in a pose called *Aindra,* (standing with one leg bent and the other leg and knee folded and raised) or in *maṇḍala,* the hand hanging naturally in *Ḍōlahasta,* or *Latāhasta* in some figures. She is performing *rechakas* and *karaṇas,* the stages of which can be identified to a certain extent, depending on the accompaniments that are present. Most of these figures have all the accompanying artists like two percussionists, one flutist and a *Naṭī* or a singer – the *Savgani,* with cymbals. But, in B.F. 25, 38 and 40, a male artist is playing on cymbals which indicates that he is the dance teacher, the *Nattuva.*

B.F. 25

Apsara is dancing with a raised left leg in *Aindra* posture and the right leg is in a bent position (*Aramaṇḍi* – the half-sitting position). She has observed perfect geometry in placement of hands. She is probably performing a *karaṇa*. On either side, male attendants or *Kuśīlavas* are playing percussion instruments, cymbals (*tāla*) and flute. The man who is guiding the rhythm through cymbals may represent the dance teacher *Nattuva.*

* An interesting feature of this sculpture is that the *Apsara*'s left and right hands are placed in the physical positions of the *Mūlādhāra*, and the *Sahasrara chakras*. This indicates that she is demonstrating the awakening and the flow of the *kuṇḍalini śaktis* through oneness with music and dance. The philosophical details on *kuṇḍalini chakras* are discussed in part 2 of this book, in ch. 3/7.

B.F. 38

Apsara is standing in *tribhaṅga* in *Maṇḍalasthānaka*, and tapping her left foot. She is performing a *pada rechaka,* the turning movements of ankle and *kaṭi rechaka,* by moving her waist region.

Her right hand is in a beautiful *Ḍōlahasta* (dropping freely and as the left hand is damaged, it is difficult to trace the *hasta mudrā* or the hand gesture). She is supported by two *Kuśīlavanas* on right side, who are playing percussion instruments. On the left side are two more *Kuśīlavas* playing cymbals and flute. The male artist playing on cymbals may be indicative of *Nattuva,* the dance teacher. The figure is a beautiful sculpture with the entire group of co-artists participating. According to *Tāṇḍava vidhi kriya* of *Nāṭyaśāstra,* when dance, vocal music, and instruments are presented together, she is presenting the *Nāṭya,* or performing to a *gīta* in *lāsya* – a graceful mode of presentation.

B.F. 19 and 21

Apsara stands in *Maṇḍalasthāna* in a very graceful *tribhaṅga* posture. Her right hand is dropped in a free hanging *Ḍōlahasta* and the left hand raised up above the head, depicting *hasta rechaka.* On either side are *Kuśīlavas* playing on percussion instruments. Her rhythmic movement in dance is indicated by the tapping of her left foot. According to *Tāṇḍava vidhi kriyā,* she is performing the *rechaka* and a *karaṇa* to the rhythm of percussion instruments. Her left foot is slightly raised from the ground, indicating *pada rechaka.* B.F. 21 looks like a continuation of the *rechaka* movement from B.F. 19. The foot which is slightly raised in B.F. 19 is lifted in B.F. 21. The wrist and neck movements show a continuation of the movements of B.F. 19. She may be indicating the performance of a *karaṇa,* performing only to the rythym of percussion instruments.

B.F. 40 (on the Navaraṅga Pillar)

Apsara depicts a beautiful dancing pose in *Aindrasthānaka* and a *tribhaṅga* posture. She may also be depicting an *Akasakichari* (where the foot movement is off the ground). The male attendant on her right is playing a percussion instrument. On the left the *Nattuva* teacher is sitting and playing cymbals. Another male artist is playing a percussion instrument. She is probably performing the pure dance sequence (*karaṇa* in *tāṇḍava* style). She is seen at a moment where the right leg is forcefully bent, after stamping of foot, and the left leg is bent and raised, clearly indicating the classical style of dance. The force of her movement is indicated by her neck scarf fluttering on either side above the shoulder.

B.F. 41 (on the Navaraṅga Pillar)

Apsara is standing in *Maṇḍalasthāna* and is in *tribhaṅga,* with *Ḍōlahasta* where the right hand is hanging in a graceful posture. Here she is elevated to the status of a goddess by wearing a *mukuta* (crown) with a nimbus. She wears beautiful ornaments on her arms. To her right are two *Kuśīlavas* sitting and playing on *Maddala.* The attendants to her left are playing on cymbals and flutes. *Apsara* is demonstrating the delicate movements of waist and hands, which are *kaṭi* and *hasta rechakas.* The total orchestral presentation (where *gīta, vādya, nṛtya* are

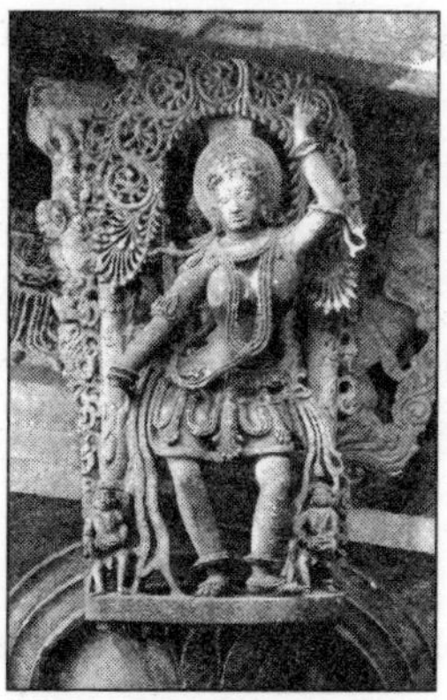

B.F. 19. *Apsara* in a graceful dance movement

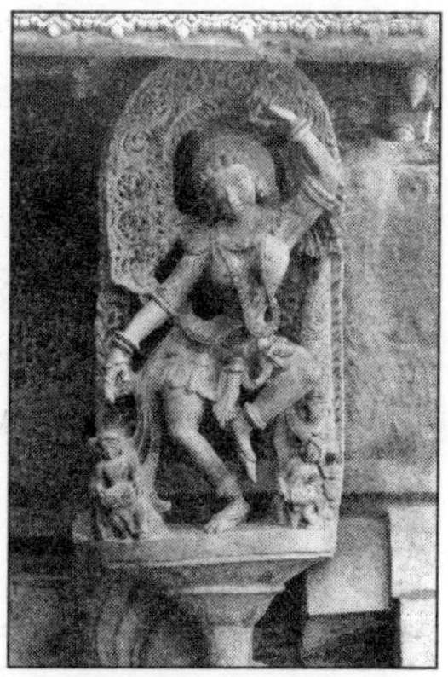

B.F. 21. *Apsara* in a graceful dance movement

involved) is called *Saṅgīta*. The two different percussion instruments who are always present with dance or music sculptures, indicate that they embellished the recitals with variation in tempo and techniques, that acted as an interesting and invigorating aspect in recitals.

Apsaras are traditionally classified as *laukika* (worldly here is as an artist) and *daivika* (divine). *Laukika* is depicted in the normal attire of a dancer and *daivika* is where she is present with a crown and a nimbus. It may also be a stage where a dancer is elevated to the status of a goddess, by excellence of her virtues and excellence in art, or that their personality is godly and creative, with the depth of knowledge they had gained.

* B.F. 41 may also be a representation of Queen Śāntalatādevi who was the wife of the Hoysala King Viśnuvardhana, who was known to be properly trained in dance and music.

3. *ŚṚṄGĀRA* IN A PLEASANT TIME (RAMYA KĀLA)

B.F. 2, 3, 4, 27 AND 39

Śṛṅgāra rasa is evoked when there is a talk either with the hero or somebody is talking about the hero with the maiden. In the bracket figures 2, 4, 27 and 39, *Apsara* is associated with a pet parrot. Parrot, in Indian art, is frequently associated with *Apsaras,* with three thoughts. It may denote a friend – a soulmate, with whom the heroin shares her personal thoughts in a casual relaxing time of gossip, or it may denote the soul or the 'paravāṇī' in philosophcal persuits. Thirdly, it is the vehicle of Kāmadeva, the god of love. Hence, the parrot is associated with love messages. In this temple *Apsara* is either listening to its words about the hero or she is trying to receive or send a message through it. Parrot is a symbolic gesture of love and a carrier of love messages. *Apsara* is soft-spoken as she can hold the bird in her hand. *Apsara* is depicted as a *Śṛṅgāra Nāyikā* standing in a graceful *Āyata* or *Avahittasthāna*. The absence of accompanying instrumentalists indicates that she is not in a dance recital. Probably she is depicting a sequence of a play, where a live bird is brought into picture. It also suggests a *Vāchika* mode of *abhinaya* where pleasant words are exchanged with the parrot. The attendants are different here than the ones present in the previous chapter.

Sakhī, a close friend of *Apsara,* is always present in this group of bracket figures, who looks taller than the other attendants.

* *Śṛṅgāra,* the erotic sentiment, has two bases – union and separation. B.F. 2, 4 and 27 indicate a state of temporary separation from her beloved, for which reason the *Apsara* is distressed. She is enthusiastic to hear a love message from her pet bird, as she is anxious for the delay caused by the hero in meeting her. She engages herself in hearing about her beloved through her pet parrot, or through the letters sent by him.

In B.F. 2, 4 and 27, the *Apsara* indicates *Viprayoga śṛṅgāra,* a temporary separation from her beloved. She longs to hear a message from or about her beloved. The parrot is symbolic of love notes or sweet notes.

B.F. 2

The maiden is seen standing in a relaxed posture, holding a pet parrot in her left hand. Her gaze is fixed on it with full attention. On the right side a *dāsī* is looking whether her lady's beloved is coming or she is trying to maintain privacy by avoiding intruders. To the left of *Apsara* are two attendants. The taller one, a *dāsī,* is holding a bunch of berries in her right hand for the bird and in the left hand she holds a corn. The shorter fat attendant is a *kārū* with a corn (or fruit) in her left hand and the right hand is pointing to the bird, probably encouraging it to speak.

Vibhāva: The parrot in *Apsara*'s hand, which is evoking *śṛṅgāra rasa*.

Ālambana: Lady is all attentive to hear the name or message of her beloved.

Uddīpana: The attendants are tempting the bird and encouraging it to speak up.

Anubhāva: A relaxed cross-legged posture without any tension. The love with which she is holding the bird, the sight of love and anticipation, with slight drooping eyelids, a smiling face and a side look gives the indication of joy and good temper evoking *Śṛṅgāra*. Glance is *Lalita* with eyes in a smiling expression. She stands in a *svastika* leg posture, the legs crossed at ankle region, which hint joy and secrecy.

Sthāyibhāva is *Rati* and mood of love.

B.F. 4

The maiden is standing with a pet messenger bird in her right hand. In her left hand she holds a bunch of messages and the left side young attendant *Sakhī* is helping her with the message by pulling the rope. At the same time she is watchful to maintain secrecy from others. (The increased height of the attendant, up to the waist of the *Apsara*, probably speaks of the intimacy the lady has with the attendant.) A *dāsī*, the right attendant, may be holding something for the bird in her left hand also looks disappointed. The lady's gaze and sight is fixed on the parrot with a bent head position. *Śṛṅgāra* is evoked as there is a message from the hero which is opened.

The left attendant who looks very young, girlish and innocent may be the representation of the child artist called *Anuvalladasūḷē*, as described in Chalukyan inscriptions which are dealt with Chapter III on *Apsaras*, of this book.

Vibhāva - The bird which has brought the message.

Ālambana - Her love for her beloved and a messenger bird.

Uddīpana - The message in which the lady is interested, for which she is entertaining a messenger bird.

Anubhāva - *Apsara* is standing in *Āyatasthāna*, and the right hand is in a *latāhasta* on which a bird is sitting. Her gaze at the parrot and the bent head turned sideways is *Anchita* head posture, indicative of worry that is caused with the letters held in her left hand. The glances are *karuṇa*, where the upper eyelid is fallen, and eyeballs lowered (N.S., Ch. 8). Head is in *adhogata*, bent downwards in disappointment in B.F. 4. *Āyata* posture is also indicative of a worried state of mind.

Sthāyibhāva - Love.

B.F. 27

Apsara is probably conversing with her pet parrot. (The hands are damaged, but the action of the attendant, who is showing fruits for the bird, confirms that the *Apsara* is holding the parrot in her left hand.) The right hand is in an encouraging gesture for the bird, which she is holding in her left hand. On the left is a *Sakhī*, the attendant (who is comparatively taller suggesting more intimacy with the lady) is also encouraging the bird to speak, with a fruit which she is holding (between the thumb and the forefinger) in the right hand. The left hand is broken. *Sakhī*'s hair is decorated with *Śikhājāla*, a net holding her long hair with pearly decoration at the bottom.

Vibhāva - The bird by which *śṛṅgāra rasa* is felt.

Ālambana - The desire in *Apsara*'s mind to communicate something to her beloved through the bird.

Uddīpana - The encouraging bribe that is being given by the attendant to promote the action.

Anubhāva - A posture in *Āyatasthāna* which indicates a state of anxiety. Glance is *śūnya*, indicating where the eyes are in *sama* or normal position but expressing blankness in a staring look (that is not focussed on the bird she is holding).

B.F. 39 (On the Navaraṅga Pillar)

Apsara is in a garden. A parrot, her pet bird, is perching on the maiden's left arm band. The bird has lifted her *hāra* or pearl necklace with its beak. *Apsara* is trying to divert the attention of the bird by showing a bunch of fruits to it. Attendants or *dāsīs* have accompanied the *Apsara* to the garden. *Apsara* shows an expression of embarrassment with shyness. She is *Lajjānvita,* as her upper eyelids have fallen in shyness and eye lowered, after hearing something from her pet parrot. She is standing in *Avahittasthāna* in a *tribhaṅga* posture. *Avahitthasthāna* is indicative of happiness here.

B.F. 3 (Utsava Kāla)

Apsara is participating in the festival, playing 'jalakride' or the water game. She is holding the syringe in the left hand and the right hand is in the position of pushing the piston. Part of the right hand is broken. However, the attendant's actions support that she is partaking in the game of 'jalakride'. According to *Daśarūpaka*, the lady who is in a joyful state of mind, and shows enthusiasm for a game, is classified either under *Swadhina bhartruka* (one who is enjoying the company of her beloved). *Apsara* in B.F. 3 exhibits the characters of a *Śṛṅgāra Nāyikā* who is in a happy state of mind.

To the right is an attendant who is supplying perfumed water in a pot. To the left is a male attendant who is filling the syringe with the coloured water. The mischievous smile on the *Apsara*'s face, her enthusiasm in the game of colour depict *śṛṅgāra rasa* in *Utsava Kāla*, and she depicts a *Śṛṅgāra Nāyikā*, as sprinkling of coloured water is an expression of love.

Apsara is indicating *Vaisnavasthāna* in her leg which is indicative of an enthusiastic activity of *śṛṅgāra rasa*.

4. *ŚṚṄGĀRA* THROUGH DRESS (VEŚA BHOGADI SEVANAI)

Nāṭyaśāstra (Ch. 24, Sl. 9 to 11) and *Daśarūpaka* (Part II, Ch. 47-48) speak about the inborn qualities that a lady is adorned with, in her youthfulness. Feminine grace in youthful period, supports the sentiments of *Śṛṅgāra*. The natural physical graces are called *Bhāva, Hāva* and *Helā* which arise from one another and are aspects of *Sattva* (natural character). *Hāva* (emotion) manifests itself in the change in position of eyes, eyebrows and the neck, indicative of erotic sentiment. *Helā* is the emotion arising out of *Hāva* and is expressed as graceful body movements. *Bhāva* is the feeling that arises from the other two. The various natural graces which a lady exhibits like amorous gesture, graceful hand movements, confusion, manifestations of affections and pretended anger are the outcome of *Helā, Hāva* and *Bhāva* (the inborn qualities).

Adorned with these natural graces, a lady exhibits involuntary (without effort) graces, some of which are seen in *Apsara* images as follows.

Śobhā (beauty) - it is the grace acquired by limbs due to beautiful form, youth and loveliness heightened after or before the enjoyment of love.

Kānti - the charm arising out of beauty.

Dīpti - the radiance in high degree of charm.

Mādhurya (delicacy) - the soft movement of limbs in moderate condition which are tender and beautiful *(Lalitā)* in nature.

The images of *Apsara* in the activity of decorating herself exhibit all these natural and involuntary graces. She portrays herself as a *Śṛṅgāra Nāyikā*. Her enthusiasm for self decoration is due to her youthfulness and love for her beloved. The process of dressing up by *Apsara* can be classified into three distinct stages. (1) *Kēśa Śṛṅgāra,* (2) *Ābharaṇa Śṛṅgāra,* and (3) *Śṛṅgāra Avalōkana* meaning the hair decoration, adorning with jewellery, and lastly, admiring her charm in the mirror.

The efforts of *Apsara* are based on longing (*abhilāṣa* in Sanskrit) to meet her beloved. She tries to decorate herself enthusiastically. She is seen in a relaxed posture, with a relaxed state of mind, her graceful posture enhancing the natural grace she is adorned with, and there is a total absence of negative thoughts. The erotic sentiment (*Śṛṅgāra*) is in accordance to *Ayoga Śṛṅgāra,* which is expressed through the enjoyment of garlands, unguents, ornaments, decorating oneself where the mood or the state of mind is generally happy, connected with the desired objects.

According to *Nāṭyaśāstra,* Ch. 25, Sl. 210-211, a description of eight types of heroines according to their state of mind in relation to the hero are described. Among them *Vasakasajja* is a heroine who decorates herself enthusiastically before meeting with the beloved. B.F. 7, 42, 31, 32, 1 and 15 depict various activities of a *Vasakasajja Nāyikā,* where she is engrossed in decorating herself.

A. *Apsara* in 'Kēśa Śṛṅgāra' (Hair Decoration)

B.F. 7

Apsara is proudly displaying her thick and long hair. She is examining her hairdress, after decorating it with *Śikhājāla*. It is a decorative net running through the length of hair, with beaded decoration at the bottom. She feels the neatness of her *Śikhājāla* before tying it into a knot, which was a popular hairstyle in the western part of India.

The right side attendant, a *dāsī,* is assisting her with a comb in the right hand and a *vēṇīguccha,* a garland of flowers or an ornament, in the left. The *dāsī* to her left is holding a mirror for her lady. *Apsara* is standing in *Āyata* leg posture, with the body weight shifted on right hip in a relaxed way. *Apsara* depicts a *Vasakasajja Nāyikā* who is decorating her hair.

B.F. 42 (on the Navaraṅga Pillar)

Apsara is standing in a cross-legged *svastika* posture in a relaxed mood, examining the neatness or thickness of her *Śikhājāla*. The *dāsī* to the left is ready with a *vēṇīguccha,* a garland of flowers for further decoration. The right side *dāsi*'s hands are damaged.

Vibhāva - Decorating her hair, examining the neatness of *Śikhājāla.*

Ālambana - Reason for decorating may be her natural desire to look good or well-groomed as she is a youthful maiden who is interested in her hero.

Uddīpana - Supported and encouraged by attendants with accessories like comb, mirror, flowers, etc. a perfect set-up of lady in *Śṛṅgāra.*

Anubhāva - A relaxed standing posture, with legs in *svastikasthāna.*

Sthāyibhāva - Pleasure of decoration *(Ratī).*

B. *Ābharaṇa Śṛṅgāra* (Decoration with Ornaments)

Decorating with profuse ornaments has been regarded as a symbol of traditional Indian dance. It is the reflection of aesthetical sense of Indian beauty concepts. Adorning oneself with a variety of ornaments is a means or device for characterisation and expression form, integrating interpretative performance in fine arts. Decoration with excessive jewellery can be regarded as an emblem of Hoysala art.

B.F. 31

Apsara is holding a small jewellery (or flowers) in her left hand and wondering how it suits her. The right attendant, a *dāsī* is holding a mirror for her lady. The *dāsī* to her left, is giving her a floral ornament, probably an attachment for the hip belt for further decoration or it may be a garland of flowers. *Apsara* is confident of her *Kānti* (charm) which is expressed in her *Hāva* and *Helā* (position of eyes, eyebrows and neck) and she stands in graceful *Āyatasthāna* to indicate that she is observing herself carefully. *Apsara* depicts a *Vasakasajja Nāyikā,* where the heroine adorns herself with jewellery and decorates enthusiastically before meeting her beloved.

B.F. 32

Apsara is trying to fix the stud of her ear-ring or *Karṇa kuṇḍala* but has dropped the screw of ear-ring in confusion. The *dāsī* to her left, has located the screw, which she is showing to the *Apsara.* To the right of *Apsara* is a monkey sitting, which probably suggests the restless state of mind. The beauty of the *Śikhāvyāla* tied into a knot is seen here *(kośa).*

Vibhāva - The desire to look more beautiful.

Ālambana - Decking herself up to perfection for her beloved. The presence of monkey has caused confusion for which reason she had dropped the ear stud.

Uddīpana - The *dāsīs* helping her out with ornaments.

Anubhāva - The look of examining how the jewel suits her confirms her desire to look more beautiful. The *Hāva* or her movements are full of *Mādhurya* and tenderness in B.F. 32. She is seen *Alidasthāna.* Her hasty movements indicate that she is in a hurry to welcome her beloved, but the monkey has confused her.

Sthāyibhāva - Śṛṅgāra - Ratī.

C. *Śṛṅgāra Avalōkana* (Admiring her Charm in a Mirror)

In B.F. 1 and 15, *Apsara* is projected as a *Śṛṅgāra Nāyikā* who has all the enthusiasm to look beautiful. We see the presence of a *Dhātrēyī,* a step-sister, as an attendant along with the *Apsara.* She is well dressed like her mistress, wears a *Brahma sūtra* like the *Yajñōpavīta,* and comes up to hip level of the main figure. She is not seen in the previous two stages of grooming, like hair decorations or jewel decorations. She looks like a *Nāṭī*, but since she is not holding any instrument, she is classified as a different attendant. *Apsara* depicts a stage of *Vasakasajja Nāyikā*, where she decorates herself enthusiastically before meeting her beloved. This is one of the aspects of *Sambhoga Śṛṅgāra*. In B.F. 1, she is a heroine dressed up for the union, and stands holding the mirror to make sure that she is presentable in her outward appearance.

B.F. 1

Apsara is in the final activity of dressing up. She is admiring her own beauty (*śobhā*) and radiance (*dīptī*) by looking into the mirror. She holds a comb in her right hand to give a final touch to her hair and a mirror in the left hand. She is almost done with her toilette with beautiful and elaborate head decorations, arm, hand, finger jewellery, various necklaces, hip belt and anklets but the attendants are encouraging her to wear a few more ornaments. Her leg posture, *Avahittasthāna*, indicates the feeling of satisfaction and self admiration. To her right, is the attendant *Dhātrēyī* offering a bangle. She is classified as a step-sister, who wears a *Brahma sūtra* (*yagñōpavīta*) like her mistress. To her left is a slightly shorter *dāsī* giving a small piece of jewellery (like a broach) in her right hand. A short and fat attendant, *Kārū* is with them, carrying a pet monkey and a bunch of berries for it.

Vibhāva (depiction) - *Apsara* is trying to give a final touch to her appearance. She is satisfied with her make-up and admiring herself in the mirror.

Ālambana (root cause) - Her youthfulness and the hero for whom she has dressed up.

Uddīpana (supporters) - Both attendants are encouraging the activity by offering more jewellery.

Anubhāva (mode of expression) - Her graceful standing posture is in *Avahittasthāna* with her body deflection in *tribhaṅga*. The look of satisfaction on her face admiring her *Śobhā* (beauty) has given an extra *dīptī* (radiance) to her face, thus depicting *śṛṅgāra rasa*. *Avahittasthāna* of leg is also used to indicate anxiety other than satisfaction. The *Apsara* may also interpret her anxious state of mind about her appearance.

Sthāyibhāva – is Ratī or love.

B.F. 15

Apsara is looking at her image and trying to enhance her appearance. She is holding a comb in the right hand and a mirror in the left trying to give a finishing touch to her elaborate hairstyle. She is in a relaxed mood in the process of decorating herself, standing in a *tribhaṅga* posture with the feet in a crossed position called *svastika*. To her right is a *Dhātrēyī*, a step-sister (up to hip level) offering a *vēṇīguccha*, a garland of flowers, for more decoration. The *dāsī* to her left is offering a necklace with a pendant.

Ālambana (root cause) - Her youthfulness and the hero for whom she has dressed up.

Uddīpana (supporters) - Both the attendants are encouraging the activity by offering more jewellery.

Anubhāva (mode of expression) - *Apsara*'s self-admiration of her charm, gives a perfect set-up of *Śṛṅgāra*. Her legs in *Svasthikasthāna* reveal a joyous state of mind, her youthful grace highlighting the aspects *Helā* and *Hāva* in depicting a *Sthāyibhāva* of *Ratī*.

All the sculptures depicting *śṛṅgāra rasa* are grouped under *Citta vikāsa* as a happy atmosphere blooms the mind.

NOTES AND REFERENCES

1. Music when it is sung without words (meaning) and with dry words, is called *Asarita* and should be sung before the commencement of the ballet.
2. Cārī is the movement of one leg (at a time) involving the coordination of the movement of foot, shank and thigh and is a sub-unit of a *karaṇa*.
3. *Karaṇa* is a movement of unit, where a *cārī*, hand movements and movements of other parts of the body are involved. (N.S., Ch. IV, Sl. 30-34).
4. *Aṅgahara* is a group of *karaṇas* in dance.
5. *Rechakas* are the graceful and embellishing movement of the neck, hand, waist and ankle region that add grace to dance movements. (N.S., Ch. IV, Sl. 246-254).
6. When *cārīs* and *karaṇas* are performed gracefully, it is called *Lasya* mode of presentation and it is performed vigorously (with heavy stamping of foot) or throwing the leg high up vigorously is called *Tāṇḍava* mode of presentation, or *mahācārī*).

VIII

Apsara in Vīra Rasa

B.F. 6, 17 and 23 – *Lakṣaṇa* of *vīra rasa* (D.R., Part IV, Ch. 79)

Vīraḥ pratāpa Vinayādhyava Sāyasattva mōhā Viṣāda Naya Vismaya Vikramādyaiḥi.

Heroism, prowess, politeness and firmness are the *Vibhāvas*, characterized by absence of love and sadness. Enthusiasm is its *Sthāyibhāva*.

Heroism befits men and women of high calibre. Enthusiasm is its *Sthāyibhāva*. *Vīra rasa* is displayed in acts of courage, valour, physical strength and praise with politeness. It is born out of heroic enthusiasm, firmness and there is no sign of love or depression. *Apsara* is depicted as a lady, skilled in heroic and courageous sport like hunting. The *āhārya* mode of *abhinaya* is expressed here, where there is an indication in the change of costume, weapons, with live and dead animal representation.

The text *Mānasōllāsa* gives the details of the royal hunting game called *Dīpa Mṛgaja* that was in vogue during the Hoysala period. (*Mānasōllāsa*, a text that was written in AD 1126, by the Chalukyan King Someśvara gives an account of the political, cultural and social aspects of that period. It has the details of the royal hunting game that women played.) A young, healthy and trained doe (female deer) was made into a *Dīpa Mṛga* with the reins like those of a horse. Two hunters would go to the forest with *Dīpa Mṛga* and the deer would be tied to a tree, or allowed to mix with the wild ones. Attracted by the young doe, a herd of wild deers would appear, which the hunters would hunt, hiding under the cover of bush.

Apsara depicts this activity in B.F. 6, 6a, 17, and 23. The leaf-bordered skirt which the *Apsara* and her attendants are wearing is a suggestive indication that they are involved in hunting activity, or hiding behind a bush. Her hairdress is a representation of the style that was popular in the southern part of India, where hair is tied into a jar-shaped bun, called *Kumbhi bandhaka*. *Nāṭyaśāstra* (Ch. 11, Sl. 93-95), gives a description of the four acts relating to the use of bow and arrow in dramaturgy. They are:

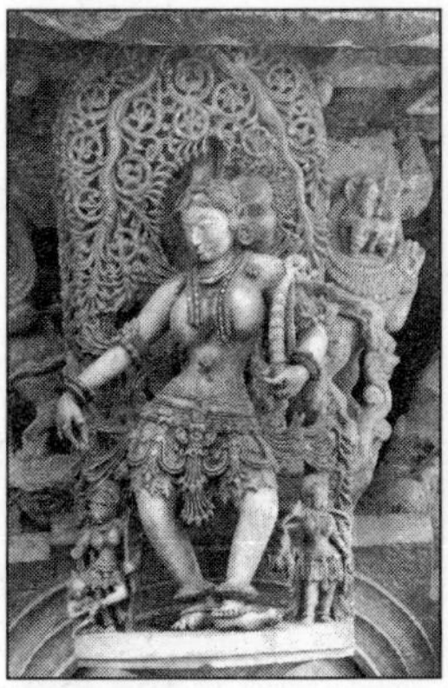

B.F. 23. *Apsara* as a huntress

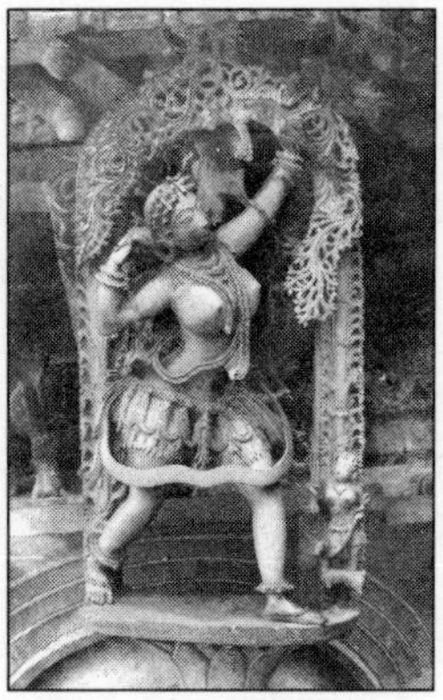

B.F. 6. *Apsara* as a huntress

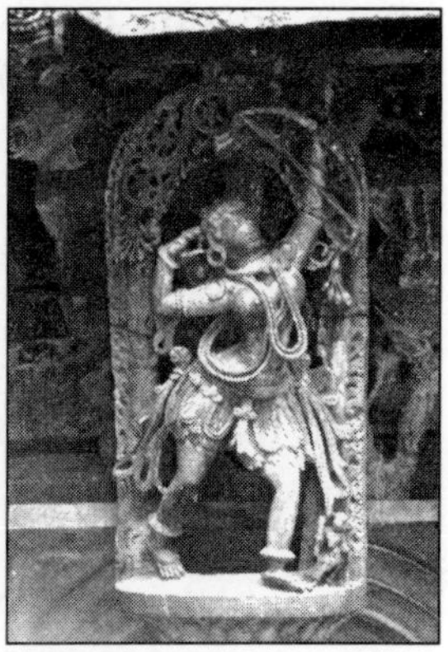

B.F. 17. *Apsara* as a huntress

Preparing - *Parimārjana*
Taking an arrow - *Ādana*
Taking an aim - *Sandhāna*
Shooting the arrow - *Mōkṣana*

The preparing stage, *Parimārjana,* is the holding or bending of the bow. *Ādana* or *grahaṇa* is taking the arrow. B.F. 23 depicts these two stages. Taking an aim, the *Sandhāna* is represented in B.F. 6 and shooting or release of arrow that is *Mōkṣana* is in B.F. 17.

B.F. 23

Apsara is holding a bow in the left hand (which is damaged) and an arrow in her right hand. She wears a leafy hip costume befitting the heroic game. She appears waiting for the game in *Maṇḍalasthāna.* The attendant *Śilpinī* to her right (or the mini figure of the *Apsara*) is also holding bow and standing in *Ekapādasthāna,* suggesting motionlessness, as she is getting her foot examined that is pricked by a thorn. They are silently waiting (suggested by *ekapāda*) for deer to come near them. The attendant to the left holds the dead animals, that are tied to a pole which they have hunted. It is a representation of *Parimārjana* and *Ādana,* where according to *Nāṭyaśāstra,* she is preparing for the hunting game with bow in the left hand and an arrow in the right.

Vibhāva - Enthusiasm in a shooting game

Ālambana - A desire to hunt as she is aiming at a game. They are actively participating in the game *Dīpa Mṛgaja.*

Uddīpana - The attendants are encouraging with more arrows, and an animal like deer which they want to capture.

Anubhāva - The stretched hands and legs in *Ālīḍhasthāna* (in B.F. 6 and 7) indicate her heroic gesture. The head is turned up slantingly in *udvahita,* with a tucked-in chin giving a majestic look, full of confidence.

Sthāyibhāva - Shows enthusiasm.

Vīra rasa is grouped under *Citta vistāra* as the mind expands or swells under the heroic emotions.

B.F. 6

Apsara is sporting a hunting activity in the costume of a huntress. Her hairstyle is comparatively simpler and the waist belt is lined with a leafy decoration, that is indicative of green coloured costume. She holds a bow in her left hand and shooting an arrow after pulling the string. The position of the hands is indicative of this action. It is a stage called 'Sandhāna', where she is taking an aim. Her head is turned up looking focussed at her aim seriously. She is standing in *Ālīḍhasthāna* (Ch. VI), where the feet are kept three *tālas* apart, which is a *sthāna* indicated in the *Nāṭyaśāstra* for heroic activities. On her left, she is assisted by an attendant, *Śilpinī* (an attendant who is skilled in certain arts, B.F. 6a), standing with the *Dīpa Mṛga,* with the reins like that of a horse in her left hand and a bundle of arrows in her right.

B.F. 17

Apsara has shot an arrow at the game. The attendant is assisting her mistress by offering more arrows. The position of the right hand and her facial expression indicates the completion of the activity. She stands in a beautiful *Ālīḍhasthāna.* Her right leg and left hand trace a graceful curve, which is enhancing the beauty of the heroic posture. Her position of head suggests *udvahita,* with a tucked-in chin. According to *Nāṭyaśāstra,* this is the last stage in the action related to bow and arrow, called *Mōkṣana,* where the arrow is shot at the target.

IX

Apsara in Bhayānaka Rasa

Fear is the basic mood of this *bhayānaka rasa*. The reasons for fear being loud noise, unpleasant things, emptiness, forest, etc. It is expressed in jerky movements of legs and hands, faltering and quick steps, fearful or stunned look, covering the body parts with hands, shivering, etc.

Lakṣaṇas of *bhayānaka rasa* (D.R., Part IV, Ch. 86):

Vikṛta Svara Sattvādēr Bhaya Bhāvō Bhayānakaḥ.
Sarvāṅga Vēpatu Svēda Śōṣa Vaicitrya Lakṣaṇam.

Screaming, trembling of hands and feet, paralysis, perspiration, seeking safety, running away and the like are the characteristics of *bhayānaka rasa*.

Apsaras were proficient not only in pure dance but in *abhinaya* and the histrionic art. They are decribed as good actresses in *Nāṭyaśāstra*.

B.F. 5, 26 and 34 indicate *bhayānaka rasa*.

In B.F. 5 and 34, the *Apsara* is dressed in a hairstyle called *Kumbhi bandhaka* which according to *Nāṭyaśāstra* is the style prescribed for the ladies in the southern part of India.

B.F. 5

The wild monkey has pulled the robe of the *Apsara* when she is dressing up (as she is without the waist belt and skirt). The maiden, out of fear has been trying to run away; at the same time she is holding a cut branch of the plant, and is trying to scare away the monkey. She is trying to pull the other end of her robe in her left hand. The lady looks absolutely frightened with a serious face. The attendant to her left is unaware of the incident as she is just standing like a guard with an object, like a stick in her hand. To the *Apsara*'s right is the naughty monkey, which is pulling the robe. The sentiment of fear is merged with anger resulting in agitation. Her gait is a hurried action of fast steps, with escaping movement – a result of the pursuit of a ferocious animal.

Vibhāva – The lady is frightened because of the monkey which is disrobing her.

Ālambana – Fear of the wild monkey and the fear of nudity.

Uddīpana – Her loneliness as the attendant is unaware of this happening.

Anubhāva – Her wide open fearful gaze fixed on the monkey, trying to chase the monkey and trying to run away from it. Both eyelids are expanded and the central part of eyes project great fear. She shows glances of *Bhayānvita* or fear is struck (N.S., Ch. 8, Sl. 58). She is depicting *Baddha Svastikasthāna* in legs, a suggestive posture of showing anger.

Sthāyibhāva is fear and it is categorized as *Cittavikṣōbha*, as it has disturbed her tranquility of mind.

B.F. 34

The *Apsara* is again troubled by a monkey as it is pulling her robe. She is trying to run, at the same time attempting to chase the monkey with a stick. Her left hand clasps to her stomach in fear and right hand is in action of throwing a stick at the monkey. The attendant on left side is unaware of the monkey's sudden appearance as she is just guarding her lady. To *Apsara*'s right is the monkey (which is damaged); only the legs and the deformed body reveal the monkey's presence. The *Apsara* depicts the actions that are to be used, while demonstrating or expressing the sentiment of fear in B.F. 5 and 34.

Vibhāva – Monkey's action of pulling the robe by which the lady is frightened and she is attacking the monkey too.

Ālambana – The unpredicted action of the monkey as it is in a wild mood.

Uddīpana – The attendant's silence, which is making the *Apsara* more scared.

Anubhāva – Action of running away; left hand holding on to the stomach out of fear and trying to run away from the wild monkey; the eyes express a fearful look on beholding the monkey. Both eyelids are expanded fully, pupils centred and in protrusion, she is *Bhayānvita* (N.S., Ch. 8, Sl. 58). Head movement is *vidhuta*, a fast jerky side movement, which results in flying of her hair. She is indicating a gentle *Vaiśākasthāna* – a posture that suggests an exit movement.

* The *anubhāva* or the action of running away with big steps of B.F. 34, and B.F. 5 can be considered as the action in movement of the *anubhāva* of *bhayānaka rasa*.

Sthāyibhāva is fear. It is grouped under *Cittavikṣōbha*, where the mind is disturbed or the tranquility of mind is lost.

B.F. 5

The wild monkey has pulled the robe of *Apsara* when she is dressing up (as she is without the waist belt and skirt). The maiden, out of fear has been trying to run away, at the same time she is holding a cut branch of the plant, and is trying to scare away the monkey. She is trying to pull the other end of her robe in her left hand. The lady looks absolutely frightened with a serious face. The attendant on left side is unaware of the incident as she is just standing like a guard with an object, like a stick in her hand. To *Apsara*'s right is the naughty monkey, which is pulling the robe. The sentiment of fear is merged with anger resulting in agitation. Her gait is a hurried action of fast steps, with escaping movement – a result of the pursuit of a ferocious animal.

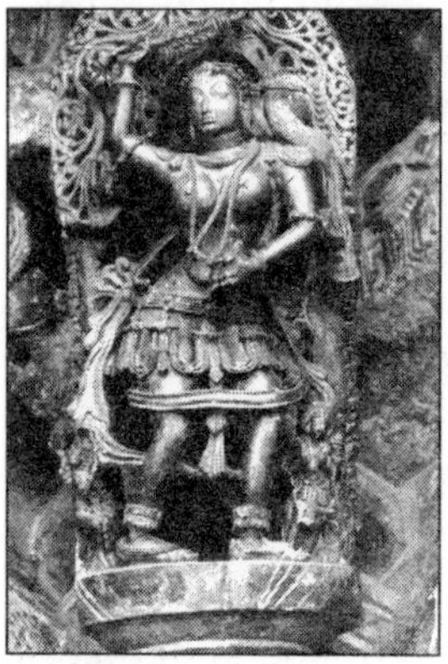

B.F. 34. *Apsara*'s encounter with a monkey

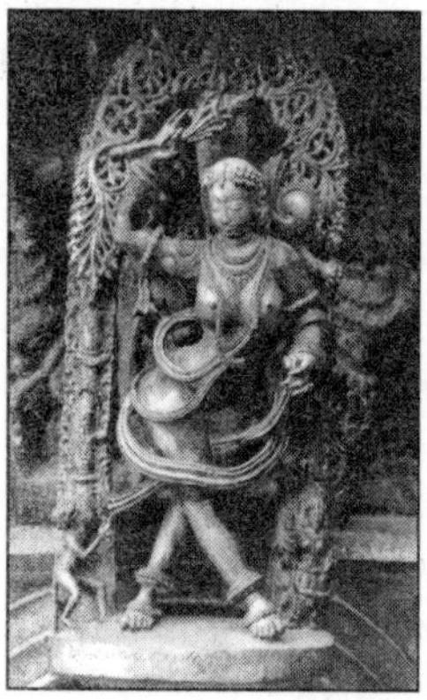

B.F. 5. *Apsara*'s encounter with the monkey

Vibhāva – The Lady is frightened because of the monkey which is disrobing her.

Ālambana – Fear of the wild monkey and the fear of nudity.

Uddīpana – Her loneliness as the attendant is unaware of this happening.

Anubhāva – Her wide open fearful gaze fixed on the monkey - trying to chase the monkey and trying to run away from it. Both eyelids are expanded and the central part of eyes project great fear. Glances of *Bhayṇvita*, fear struck (N.S. Ch 8, Sl 58). She is depicting *Baddha Svastikasthṇa* in legs, a suggestive posture of showing anger.

Sthāyibhāva is fear and it is categorized as *Cittavikṣōbha*, as it has disturbed her tranquility of mind.

B.F. 26

Apsara has seen a scorpion on her robe, which she is wearing. Out of fear, she is shaking the pleated part of the *saree* with her right hand. The other part of her dress is still intact on her left leg, which she is holding with her left hand. The scorpion has fallen down. The left side attendant (a *dāsī)* is too scared as she is clutching her stomach with her left hand and the right hand is near the head in desperate fear. The other attendant, to her right, is not aware of the scorpion's presence as she is just standing, guarding her lady when she is changing her clothes. The *Apsara* is scared of two things: one, the scorpion, and the other, her unplanned exposure. A scene of fear is created as the lady is too scared. Fear has taken the upper hand in forcing the *Apsara* to forget her modesty.

Vibhāva – Scorpion's presence, which has caused fear and confusion.

Ālambana – Seeing the scorpion as it is an unholy, poisonous thing that stings.

Uddīpana – The confusion, which the left *dāsī* is experiencing and her inability to help in the fearful situation. The *dāsī* to her right is unaware of the scorpion.

Anubhāva – Jerky movements, shaking of the cloth which she is wearing, with fear in her eyes. The *dāsī* to her left is looking down at the scorpion with fear-filled expression and confusion in movements. Glances of the *Apsara* are *Bhayānvita* (N.S., Ch. 8, Sl. 45 & 58); her eyelids are expanded fully with pupils centred and protruding. She looks vacant (*Śūnya*) in anxiety (N.S. Ch. 8, Sl. 62). Her vigorous shaking of the *saree* is depicted in her *Yajñōpavīta* drawn to one side. She is standing in *avahitta* posture.

* According to the *Nāṭyaśāstra*, the gesticulation of body movements to portray a *rasa* is of three varieties, depending on the status and calibre of the role.

The *uttama* or the heroin of high calibre has suggestive and subdued actions.

Madhyama or a *dāsī* has a slightly inferior mode of communicating a feeling. The attendant to the left of the *Apsara* in B.F. 26 might suggest the *madhyama* mode of gesticulation for *bhayānaka rasa*.

Kaniṣṭa is the inferior and exaggerated mode, befitting persons of low calibre.

X

Apsara in Raudra Rasa

Lakṣaṇa of *raudra rasa* (D.R., Part IV, Ch. 81)

Krōdhō Matsara Vairi Vaikṛtamayaiḥ Pōṣō'sya Raudrōnujaha,
Kṣōbha Svādhara Daṃśakampa Bhrukuṭī Svēdāsya Rāgairyutaḥ.

Anger is born out of a jealous or challenging enemy, defamation, etc. *Raudra* is expressed by biting one's own lips or teeth, knitted eyebrows, eyes and face turning red in colour, etc.

Anger is the *Sthāyibhāva* of *raudra rasa*. It is caused by inviting an opponent for a war, argument, etc. Here the *Apsara* indicates *raudra rasa* by her decision to win over her enemy. It is expressed in staring harsh looks, her firm-footed step, etc.

In the B.F. 9 and 22 the *Apsara* is dressed like Kālī or Bhairavī as she appears with the aspects of Lord Śiva as Bhairava holding *Khatwanga*. The mouth of the skull is shown wide open, which is an iconographic indication of the symbol of devouring. She wears a head crown which is studded with mini skulls. She holds a mace which has the top of a skull. In Figure 9, she holds something like a piece of flesh, or a small knife, in her right hand. The attendants are male, both announcing the movement of Bhairavī with the sound of drum. It looks like the *Apsara* is enacting the role of Bhairavī, in a Purāṇic episode. The accessories used here is classified under *Nepathya Raudra* according to *Nāṭyaśāstra*. N.S., Ch. 34, Sl. 48-54 speaks of the representation of the terrible sentiment in three ways.

1. Terrible make up – Representation of blood or having a piece of flesh in hand.
2. Terrible in limbs – Tall, hefty with prodigious physical frame and holding weapons of various kinds.
3. Terrible in nature – A person with red or cruel eyes, tawny hair, rough voice, arrogant looks like scolding others (*krodhon matta*) and whose gait is wide, three *tālas* apart and raising the feet high.

Vibhāva – Display of skull in crown and in mace creates a feeling of anger which she is depicting.

Ālambana – Her desire to destroy the enemy by the use of the mace.

Uddīpana – Using mini skulls in the crown (indicating her previous victories) and using the skull as her mace, and the sound of drums to enhance the ferocious gait.

Anubhāva – She looks furious; her face is devoid of a smile or delicate looks and head is in a *sama* position. She is in *Maṇḍalasthāna*, in B.F. 22, dancing a *cārī* (leg movement) to the loud drum beat after her victory over the enemy.

The glance is *Raudri* (N.S., Ch. 8, Sl. 49), a pitiless glance, eyelids still, expressing energy and prowess, eyebrows knitted in furious sentiment. The jaws are tightly pressed and side cheeks are drawn in, showing anger.

In B.F. 9, *Apsara* as Bhairavī is in *abhaṅga* posture where her left leg is positioned one *tāla* in front of the other leg and the weight of the body is borne on the right leg. It suggests a heroic posture. In B.F. 22, she is in *Maṇḍalasthāna*, depicting movement from the previous one.

Sthāyibhāva is *krodha* or anger.

It is classified under *Chitta vikṣepa*, where there is an outburst of emotions.

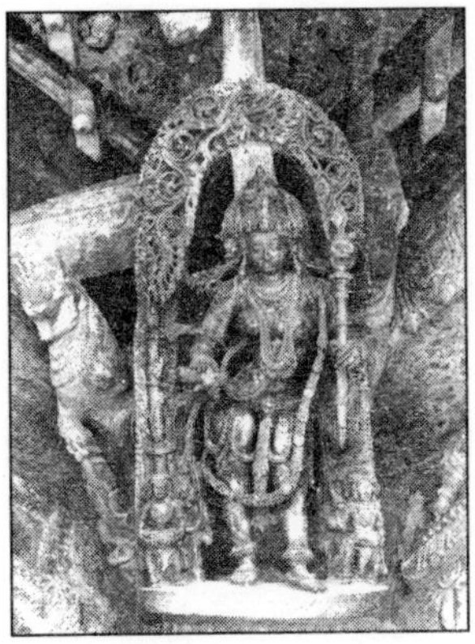

B.F. 9. *Apsara* appearing as Bhairavī

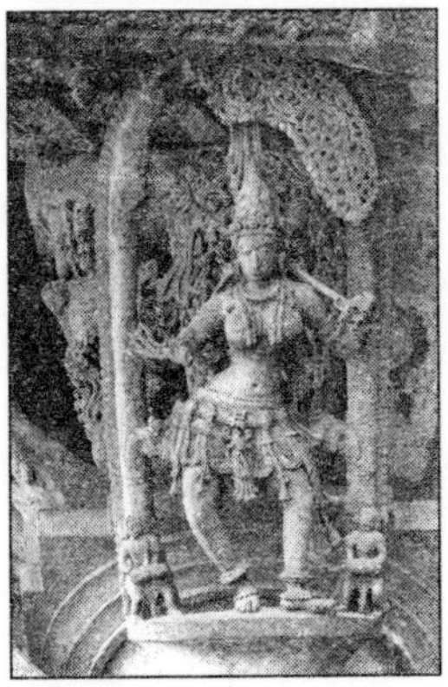

B.F. 22. *Apsara* appearing as a Bhairavī

XI
Apsara in Adbhuta Rasa

Lakṣaṇas of adbhuta rasa (D.R., Part IV, Ch. 85)
Atilōkaiḥ Padārthaiḥ Syād Vismayātmā Rasōdbhutaḥ

Adbhuta (astonishment or wonder), is the *Sthāyibhāva*. It is expressed on seeing heavenly beings, extraordinary feats of men, like magic show, excellence in artistic achievements, huge mansions, temples, etc. It is expressed with wide open eyes, spontaneous expression of appreciation by words and happiness either by words or by giving gifts, etc.

B.F. 12 and 20: The *Apsara* is standing in *Āyatasthāna*, and playing on *Kaṃsāḷē* (cymbals); even though her left hand is damaged in B.F. 12, the right hand reveals the lower part of cymbals. As a singer, she is in full appreciation of God. Her lovely smile shows her involvement in singing – an overflow of joy on seeing the figure of God; this gesture is indicative of the evoking of *Adbhuta rasa*. In B.F. 20, she is accompanied on the right by two male attendants (*Kuśīlava*) playing *edakka* and *maddala*. The male attendant to the left is giving supporting music on the flute. On the left is a *Naṭī*, a co-dancer or co-singer-dressed almost like *Apsara* and playing on cymbals.

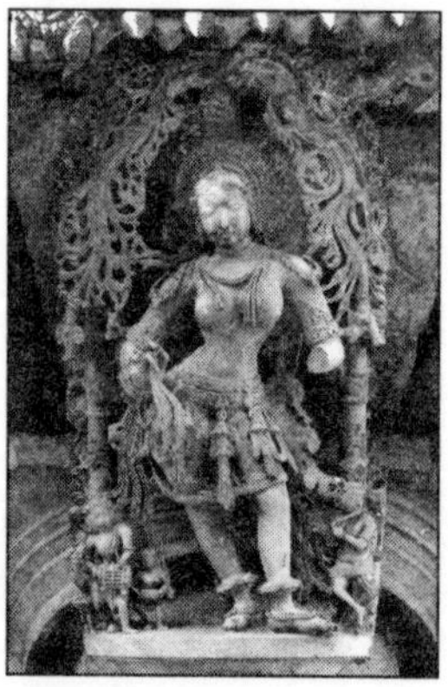

B.F. 20. *Apsara* singing and playing cymbals

Vibhāva – Singing a song in *saṅkīrtan* (in praise of God).

Ālambana – Her total concentration, probably in admiring the figure of God, expressed in the performance of singing.

Uddīpana – Supported by other instruments.

Anubhāva – Slightly opened lips, exposing her beautiful teeth, a lit-up face with a smile and a slightly bent head – a frozen posture of nodding head in appreciation called *Parivahita* (N.S., Ch. 8, Sl. 25) where the head is turned alternatively to the two sides of the shoulder. The glance is level, fully widened indicating *Vismita* (N.S., Ch. 8, Sl. 60).

Sthāyibhāva – Astonishment, created by the sight of God.

It is classified as *Cittavistāra* as it swells the beautiful mood.

XII

Apsara in Hāsya Rasa

B.F. 11, 18 AND 36

Vikṛtakṛti Vāg Vēśai rātmanō'tha Parasya Vā.
Hāsaya Syāt Paritōṣō'sya Hāsyas Triprakṛti ḥ Smṛtaḥ (D.R., Part IV, Ch. 82)

When there is something contrary to propriety, talk or dress, reproduction of behaviour of others, by imitation in parody, *hāsya rasa* is evoked (*Hāsya* meaning laugher). Laughter may be felt by the performer or audience. In the *Apsara* images 11, 18 and 36, the *Apsara* has sported a male appearance, which is classified under *Vikruta veśa* – a mimicry or dramatic representation through dress and costume. *Nāṭyaśāstra* says that (Ch. 35, Sl. 31-32) in temples and mansions of kings, the performance would be enacted by women with male roles also. The preceptors should teach it with effort to ladies. *Nāṭyaśāstra* (Ch. 24, Sl. 14-15) also describes in the category of natural grace, an aspect called *līlā* and *vilāsa*, where the lady imitates the behaviour of her beloved male persons through speech, gestures and ornaments which are delightful, and inspired by affection. It is a sportive mimicry called *Rūpānurūpa*.

One of the late Chalukyan temples at Bagali, which is situated in the Bellary district of Karnataka, has many interesting sculptures which are related to descriptions of *Kāmasūtra*, in the *śikhara* part of the temple. One such sculpture depicts a dancer, possibly a *Dēvadāsī*, exposing the veil of a eunuch which indicates that eunuchs were sometimes employed in *Sūḷēgēri* with *Dēvditis* as care-takers. *Daśarūpaka* mentions the term *varśavara* for eunuchs who are employed as attendants in a palace. Even some of the old literary works like *Mahābhārata* give an account of services provided by eunuchs in the harem. Arjuna as *Bṛhannaḷe*, an eunuch, was teaching dance to a princess Uttarā. It is probable that the three male bracket figures which look very much womanish but for the absence of breasts may be figures of eunuchs. However, considering the *Rūpānurūpa* theory that is described in *Nāṭyaśāstra*, these three bracket figures, Nos. 11, 18 and 36 are dealt in this book as female figures in male dress.

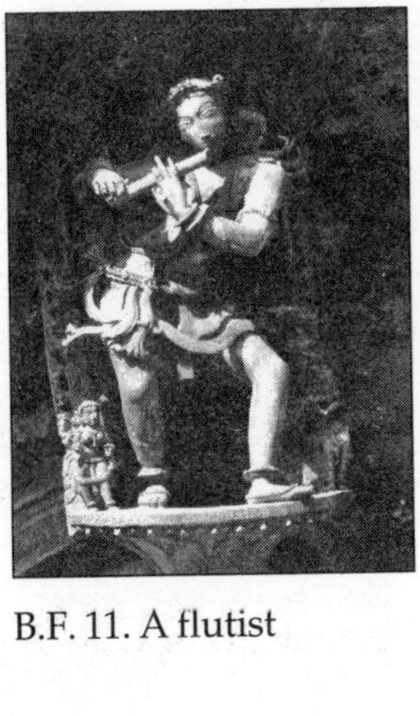

B.F. 11. A flutist

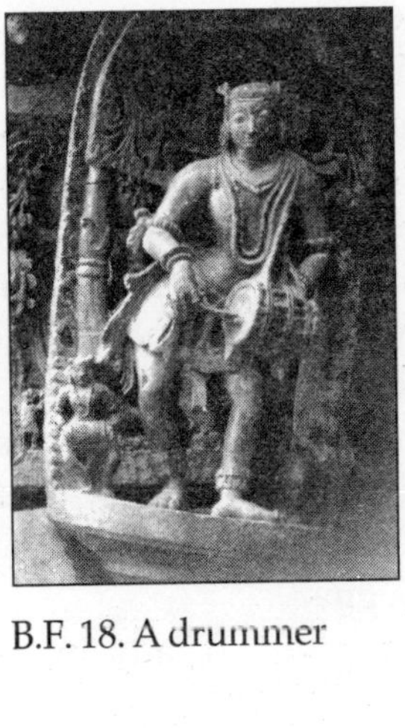

B.F. 18. A drummer

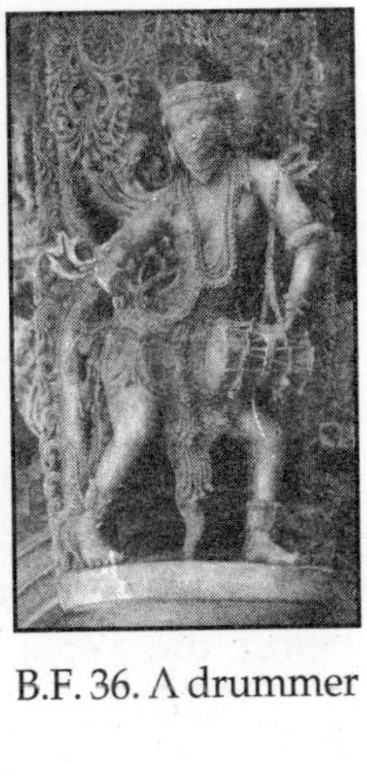

B.F. 36. A drummer

Apsara in B.F. 11, 18, 36 is in sportive mimicry with the dress of Kṛṣṇa, a young tribal man and a drummer. These relevant changes are of special kind, relating to standing or sitting postures, as well as gait and movement of hands, eyes, eyebrows, etc. They are called *Rūpānurūpa* where roles are imitated befitting the form, like a woman in a male role or a male in woman's role, skilfully done for fun. The leg ornaments worn by the B.F. 11 are decorative, which is not seen in a male instrumentalist, which supports that it is *Apsara* mimicking a flutist.

This dramatic representation was in vogue even in heaven by Rambhā, Urvaśī and other *Apsaras*.

B.F. 11

Apsara has amused herself by wearing the masculine dress of Kṛṣṇa. She wears a turban around the head, the end part of which is flying at the back. She is without the usual decorative half skirt but wears a robe around her waist. She appears with less jewellery and has tried to imitate a masculine face. On her head, she wears a furry crown. On her left is the flautist whom she has tried to imitate. On her right is a *Naṭī* playing on metallic cymbals.

Vibhāva – Sportive mimicry of Kṛṣṇa or the Vamsiga.

Ālambana – A person in whom she is interested.

Uddīpana – The image of Kṛṣṇa or the flautist, which she has tried to imitate to amuse herself and others too.

Anubhāva – Her eyelids are contracted initiating and winking and a smile to produce laughter in others. She is standing in *Vaiṣṇavasthāna*, which is a graceful masculine posture according to *Nāṭyaśāstra*.

B.F. 18 AND 36

The *Apsara* has dressed herself like a young tribal drum player. She sports an upturned moustache and artificial beard and on her head a small turban is wound, which is tied at the left. She has stuck some feather-like accessory on the right. The costume is just a robe worn around the waist along with her hip belt. The narrow waist and curve of hips indicate feminine form. She is playing the drum which she is beating with a stick. She looks comical with a mischievous smile.

Apsara is in a male dress. In B.F. 18, she appears in *Maṇḍalasthāna*, like a young tribal drum beater with a turban on head and a feather stuck in it. B.F. 36 also depicts her in a male dress and beating the drum like *Paṇava*. The central fold of the garment descends in a short conical form up to the anklet, the lower part ending in a point, which is protruding forward. In both figures she is standing in *Vaiṣṇavasthāna*, a masculine posture, where legs are kept 3.1/2 *tāla*s apart and knees bent in half-sitting posture. B.F. 18 and 36 indicate the three basic leg postions that are held by drum dancers. B.F. 18 depicts the first basic posture which the drum dancer, has to observe. The second, a slightly deeper posture is indicated by the percussionist on either side. B.F. 36 depicts the third basic posture, which a drum dancer has to practise as they carry the weight of the instrument while dancing. All figures with percussion instrument whether in the main sculpture or the attendant players, are carved observing these postures strictly.

*The 'Pungchol' drum dancers of Manipur style, start their performance observing these postures even to this day.

**Apsara* with a percussion instrument is always supported by two *Maddalekaras*. When the main artist relaxed, the other two would continue with the recital. *Nāṭyaśāstra* in Ch. 33 explains that the "Pushkaravādyas" (percussion instruments) are to be placed facing east on the stage, before the *Nāṭya* begins.

Vibhāva – *Vikṛtaveśa* – A lady in a different dress with funny movements.

Ālambana – Her desire to imitate a drummer (probably a *Kuśīlava*).

Uddīpana – Her hairband, upturned moustache and an artificial beard.

Anubhāva – Her funny leg posture, a mischievous smile to create laughter in others. In B.F. 18, she stands in *Maṇḍalasthāna* and in B.F. 36, she is in *Vaiśākasthāna* suggesting a strenuous movement that she is depicting.

Sthāyibhāva – Amusement.

Hāsya rasa is catogorised under *Chitta vikāsa,* as it blooms the state of mind. *Apsara* with the characteristics of *hāsya rasa* indicate fun-making, teasing and humor.

XIII
Apsara in Śānta Rasa

B.F. 28

shama Prakarṣō 'nirvācyō Muditād ēsta Dātmatā (D.R., Part IV, Ch. 53)

Na yatra dukham na sukham na chinta na dweśa rāgou na cha kachid iccha

The *Lakṣaṇas* of *śānta rasa* are: where there is no sadness, happiness, worry, desire, lust, envy or passion; this state depicts the sentiment *Śānta* or bliss.

The *Apsara* appears like a lady well-versed in *Śāstras*. She holds the *tālapatra,* the palm leaf bundle, in her left hand and explains it to others. In her right hand, she holds the *chin mudrā* or *haṃsāsya mudrā* (as seen in the figure of Buddha) or the hand used in giving *Upadēśa* (advice) where the tip of forefinger touches the tip of thumb. In her act of teaching some scriptures, she is standing in *maṇḍala* with a peaceful look. Her head, eyes, eyebrows, all are in *sama* position, depicting a peaceful state of mind. It also supports a *Nartakī*'s capacity, an insight into literature other than being proficient in fine arts and heroic sports. She stands in *Āyata* posture, to indicate her appearance on stage.

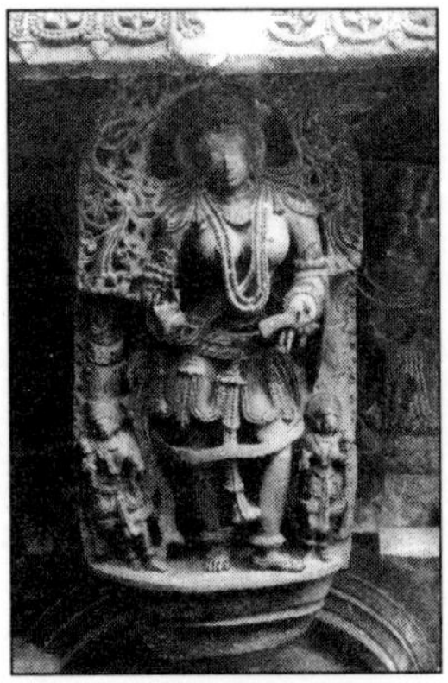

B.F. 28. *Apsara* holding the scriptures

On her right and left, are attendants called *Liṅginī. Liṅginī* is also well-versed in literature and enjoys a better status than *dāsī*. She is up to thigh level of the main figure, well-dressed like *Apsara*. She holds a fruit in one hand and a *Caurī* (a fan) in the other hand and appears calm like the main figure. They may also represent the role of *Cāmarasūḷē*, an attendant with a fan or *Cāmara*, as described in the inscriptions of the Chalukyan era which are described in the third chapter on *Apsaras* of this book. The right and left attendants are standing in *Āyata* and *Avahita* posture. A peaceful atmosphere is depicting *śānta rasa*.

* The attendants are calm, holding a fruit and a *Cāmara* which philosophically indicates that the *Apsara* is beyond the botherations of *Annamaya* and *Pranamaya kośas* – the sheaths of the botherations of body and mind. She is in the field of knowledge and hence peaceful.

Epilogue – Part I

The transformation of prayer halls from rock-cut shrines to huge structural monuments developed through time, as in most traditions of human art. Hoysala monuments involved lavish labour and skilled workmanship. Hoysala rulers and architects believed more in the sculptural richness than architectural massiveness, to attract commoners to visit a temple. In the Medieval period, temples that were built between 9th and 13th century AD across India, the noticeable feature was the inclusion of dancing sculptures in the form of *Apsaras* on the outer walls or in the *Navaraṅga*, irrespective of religion. The Hindu temples and the Jain Basadis, whether built in *Nāgara* or *Vesara* style, had dancing beauties in stone, as seen in the Konark temple, Khajuraho temple group, Delwara temple at Mount Abu, and the Hoysala temples. High literary activity and adoption of music and dance as forms of worship in temples, were probably the reasons why dancing sculptures became an integral part of temple architecture. Various commentaries on the art of dance and dramaturgy were written between the 9th and 13th centuries by poets and scholars. To mention a few, *Daśarūpaka* by Dhananjaya and *Nāṭaka Lakṣaṇa Ratnakośa* by Sāgaranandi were written between AD 920-1100. *Naṭya Darpaṇa* was written by two Jain poets, Gunachandra and Ramachandra between AD 1100-1175 and in 12th century AD. The great poet Sāradatanaya wrote a text, *Bhāva Prakāśika* and *Saṅgītarathakara* was compiled by Sarangadeva. All these texts dealt in detail about the chapter *Rasa* and *Bhāva*, the expressive part of dance and drama. The rulers who were patrons of art were inspired by these texts and adopted them in their art and culture. Thus, the art of dance gained popularity and got channelised according to these texts.

People had to be attracted to temples even before they entered them. This was achieved when *Raṅgabhoga* services were introduced. Thereafter, dance and music became an integral part of daily worship, with dancers living up to the expectations by drawing a huge crowd. A good-looking young dancer with all her attributes and talent was always been sought after by the audience.

Analysing the dance of *Apsara*, according to the classifications of *Nāṭyaśāstra,* dance is handled in two ways. *Uddhata* or *Tāṇḍava* (vigorous and forceful) and the *Sukumāra* or *Lāsya* (graceful and soft). *Apsaras* depict the *Lāsya* type of presentation, which is very graceful and befitting women. Her presentation of dance can be ascribed to *Nāṭya,* which is a complete form consisting of music, dance and communication through expression. Her pure dance movements or *Nṛtta* part is rhythm-based classic dance, which is clearly evident in the usage of percussion instrument and cymbals which help to guide the rhythm. She has depicted her art of communication – the *abhinaya* – through *Bhāva,* the feelings contained in a situation. The dancer had to undergo intensive training to gain command over the *Nṛtta* part like a thorough understanding of exercise, and usage of the major and subsidiary limbs, the *cārīs*, *karaṇas*, *aṅgaharas*, *rechakas* and *hasta mudrās*, all required for *Nṛtta* part of dance presentation effectively. *Abhinaya* is communicated in both *Lōkadharmi* classification which is simple, realistic with natural behaviour like in B.F. 15, 31, 32 and in the *Nāṭyadharmi* classification, where it is conventional, artistic and stylistic like in *vīra rasa* or *bhayānaka rasa* depiction. *Abhinaya* is further made easily understood by the onlookers through the liberal usage of accessories of *Āhārya abhinaya* like weapons (bow and arrow, mace), objects (like mirror or ornaments) or live animals like monkey, deer, bird, scorpion and so on (which are called *sanjiva*) according to *Nāṭyaśāstra*. Hence, the codified *hasta mudrās* are seen in a lesser degree, and in many figures the fingers are damaged, which makes it further difficult to trace the codified hand gestures. On the contrary, the *Padasthānas,* the position of legs, are observed strictly according to the *Nāṭyaśāstra* and *Abhinaya darpaṇa*. Traditional Indian dance ballet with the characteristic of playing a story or a puranic episode involved singing, acting, dialogue, recitation and pure dance movements. It demanded proffeciency over various artistic catagories such as literature, music dance and fine arts. Dance postures are used as a medium in the *Apsara*s of Belur temple, to show the hypothesis of a dramatic situation with artistic standardisation. The dance postures along with the ornaments and the accessories complement each other in depicting her performance-perfect.

Apsara figures depict all four types of *abhinaya* like *āṅgika* (physical expression), *vāchika* (through words), *āharya* (accessories and make-up), and *sāttvika* (related to mind). In the *āṅgika* mode she has meaningfully utilized the major, minor and subsidiary limbs (*āṅga, pratyāṅga, upaṅga*) for communication like the prescribed use of leg and waist movements, the delicate positioning of arms, hands and fingers and the position of neck, head and so on, all indicating the *āṅgika* mode of *abhinaya*. In *vāchika* mode, where singing and words are involved, two figures indicate that she is singing by herself with the cymbals. In her association with the pet parrot for message, the actions of the attendants suggest that she is exchanging pleasant words with the bird; thereby the usage of prose and poetry is depicted through *Vāchika abhinaya*. In the *āharya* mode, the varieties of hairstyles depicting regional identification, the various accessories, jewels, costume (*vīra rasa* costume is different from that of *bhayānaka* or *hāsya rasa*), all advocate the knowledge the sculptors had, with *āharya* aspect and the use of *sanjiva* (animals). In the *sāttvika* mode of *abhinaya*, the *Apsara* presents a beautiful picture of the characterization she is depicting. Her inner feelings and state of mind is effectively reflected in her facial expressions. The dancer, who modelled for these sculptures, had to present the various types of emotions according to the theme of ballet, whenever called upon to do so, without losing herself in the emotion she was depicting. She also had to be proficient of expressing the *rasas* through *āṅgika*, *vāchika*, *āharya* and *sāttvika* modes of presentation as *Nāṭya* was a mimicry of the ways of the world in classical style, endowed with various emotions and situations.

In total, of the four types of *vṛttis* (a style in composition) that are described in *Nāṭyaśāstra*, *Apsara* exhibits *kaiśiki vṛtti*, which is full of delicate emotions, expressed by a beautiful woman like *Apsara*, supported by costumes, music and cultivated dance – all melting together to pleasantness. N.S., Ch. 1, Sl. 46-50 mentions that Lord Brahmā created the nymphs with specific names (like *Mañjukeśi*, *Sukeśi*, *Sulochanā*, *Manoramā*, etc. which are more than 32) who were the personification of different aspects of skill and embellishment of a drama, and gave them over to Sage Bharata for his production. The *Apsaras* at Belur temple are embodiment of these qualities with a form.

Majority of the *Apsara* sculptures depict *śṛṅgāra rasa* as it takes the performer and spectator to *Śṛṅgā* – a peak level. The dancing sculptures through their involvement in the act of playing an instrument or depicting geometrical dance postures, project *śṛṅgāra rasa*. According to

Daśarūpaka, when the heroine is enjoying an art form she is in the mood of *Śṛṅgāra*. In most of the figures under this category, *Apsara* is frozen forever with her eternal smile exhibiting great warmth and serenity. Her smile in figures like B.F. 8, 10, 12, 14, 20 is so inviting as if she knows the secret of eternal happiness. The sculptures which depict her personal grooming in various stages of toilette, express the state of anxiety which a bride experiences, either by dropping the screw of the ear pendant or trying out how she looks with a different ear-ring. She expresses a look of satisfaction over her appearance when she is admiring herself in a mirror. She is depicted as a *Vasakasajja Śṛṅgāra Nāyikā* in the act of decoration (*nāyikā* is a term used when her state of mind is in relation with a hero). She is again a *virahot kantita Śṛṅgāra nāyikā* when she associated with a parrot (suggestive of a love message). She receives the bird in B.F. 2, but looks disappointed with the message in B.F. 4 and sends her worries through the bird in B.F. 27. Every sculpture has some accessory to hold in hand; hence, the actual *hasta mudrā* or hand gestures, which is a distinguishing feature of Indian dancing, is hard to trace.

I have observed that in *Apsara*'s depiction of *vīra rasa*, the sculptures which precisely depict the *Dīpa Mṛga* hunting game as described in *Mānasōllāsa*, the figures are not sequentially placed. But the game is traced in beautiful dancing figures. Her actions are sculptured according to the 'Nyayas' of using bow and arrow, according to the conventional *Nāṭyadharmi* mode, which is discussed in Ch. VIII on *vīra rasa* of this book.

In trying to bring out the expression of *bhayānaka rasa*, there appears to be a healthy competition between the sculptors, as two figures are carved with the same theme, but with slight variation. In B.F. 26, where the *Apsara* is associated with the scorpion, the depiction of *rasa* is purely *Bhayānaka*, whereas in B.F. 5 and 34, where she has an encounter with a monkey the emotion of fear is overlapped with the mood of anger to a certain extent, and hence the *Apsara* appears in an agitated mood. However, her fear and the resulting jerky movements are beautifully captured in stone. In her depiction of *raudra rasa*, her *cārī* movements, the use of mini skulls, and the mace, have enhanced the effect of anger and determination, even though her enemy is not seen. The absence of extra arms suggests that it is a dancer's costume and not to be confused for an image of goddess. In the depiction of *adbhuta rasa*, the captivating smile and a slight bend of the head, with a look of appreciation in eyes hints that *pātras* were also good singers. Even here two sculptors have adopted the same theme but the face looks different, which suggests that the dancers who modelled for these sculptors were different.

In the figures B.F. 11, 18, 36, which are categorized under *hāsya rasa*, it was difficult to conclude whether it was a man looking feminine or a lady mimicking a man. The curvaceous waist and hips with the absence of breasts along with a mischievous smile looks a bit comical. The leg ornaments of B.F. 11, 18 are feminine, which made me conclude they are *Apsaras* in a man's dress. The flutist and the percussionists in other sculptures (B.F. 12, B.F. 20, B.F. 10, etc.) are without leg ornaments. *Apsara*'s depiction of *śānta rasa*, in the act of reading out something from the palm leaves suggests *pātras* also gave a bit of religious discourse in their daily performances or perhaps she is studying or explaining the theoretical part of dance. Her attendants on either side holding a fruit, and a *Chāmara*, suggest that, the *Apsara* has surpassed the veils of *Annamaya* and *Pranamaya kośas*. (The details on *kośas* are discussed in Ch. 2-3, part II, of this book.) The depiction of *Apsara* playing all four categories of instruments in dancing postures probably suggests that the *pātra*s or the *Nartki*s sequenced their recitals with different instruments alternated by pure dance, expressive dance and literary recitals to break the monotony and ensure variety to retain public curiosity. The representation of dance in sculptures give a clear picture of the style in which the contemporary dancers performed. The refined dance postures indicate about the refinement that had come about in the art of Hoysala artists, sculptors, promoters, general public, etc. In Indian temple dancing sculptures, both feminine and masculine forms were frequently idealized. The slim waist, heavy breasts, lithe limbs, youthful sensuous poise was the outcome of idealized feminine grace moulded in the frame of *Śāstramana*. The belief that the measurements of human body as prescribed in *Āgamas*, ought not to be disregarded under any circumstance, came into vogue during this period also. The artist was thus handicapped and imagination had no freedom of action. The genius of the artist, regarding his imaginary skills, took a second place while making an image. He was hard struck with the rules of *Āgamas* and he could fashion the images as best as he could within the framework of *Āgamas*. The departure from the rules laid down authoritatively in *Śāstras* was not easily tolerated. Hence they look different from Greek or Roman sculptures, which are close to human anatomy. However, Hoysala *Apsaras* kept the proportion more close to realism than the Chalukyan dance figures, where the limbs are over-emphasized with long proportions. Even though the jewellery is in no way very different from the jewellery used by the current Odessey or Bharatanatyam performing dancers, The *Apsaras* look over-decked because of their short stature and the medium of stone. However, the excessive decorative patterns and costumes make the images more symbolic, attractive and endow Hoysala art with unique beauty.

Sculptures with musical instruments have played a very prominent part in the development of the cultural heritage of India. Sculptures are like visual documentation of various aspects like love for art, musicians, musical instruments, the method of playing the instrument and the social status of the artists, at that particular period. Hoysala artists have made an attempt to keep a record of at least a few of the various instruments, that were in use during Hoysala era. It mirrors the in-depth knowledge in the use of musical instruments the intensity of love for dance and music that the patrons, the sculptors and the models had, and the interest with which the public supported the field of music. Through the *Apsara* sculptures, the sculptors have depicted the four main category of instruments like *tata*, *suṣira*, *avanaddha* and *ghana* which were used in a solo or orchestral performance.

Besides the instruments, *Apsara* figures also enlighten us on the jewellery, objects used, dress code for both men and women, hairstyles they observed and many other such interesting facts. The *Apsara* in bare bust should not be interpreted for eroticism, as probably that was the dress code observed during that period. This view gets stabilised when *Apsara* sculptures in the temples of other parts of India (like Mount Abu or Gujarat step-wells) that belong approximately to the same period are studied. Probably, cutting and stitching a cloth was not in practise and cloth was used only for wrapping around the organs.

It is only when we visualise ourselves as sculptors and try to carve a figure in stone, a deep philosophical theme, through young charming and dancing *Apsaras*, who do not look like yoginis, that we can appreciate the divine merit the Hoysala sculptures were endowed with.

Apsaras are more than successful in bringing out the glory of the past. These figures of artists hint that dance and music were deep-rooted among Indians much before they were expressed as dancing sculptures. The diplomatic ways in which the Hoysala rulers maintained harmony and tolerance in religious sects, and managed to get continued patronage and support from public through dancers, speak volumes on the capacity of the dynastic rulers. Equally well the *pātras* or *nartakīs* as *Apsaras* have glorified the rich heritage and tradition of our culture, which differentiated Indian temples from those in other countries.

Appendix

MUSICAL INSTRUMENTS USED BY *APSARA* IN BELUR CENNAKĒŚAVA TEMPLE

(Number Reference is According to Vādya Darśan,
Sangeet Natak Akademi, New Delhi)

No. 12	BĀNSURĪ Aerophone (BIHAR)	A bamboo tube with a beak-shaped blowing hole, six finger holes and a fipple. Used in folk music and dances. Used by shepherd and cowherd communities of Bihar.
No. 26	BUḌUBUḌUKAI Membranophone (TAMIL NADU)	A small, skin-covered hour glass shaped instrument made of brass. Two knotted strings strike the skin heads when shaken vigorously. Used by Kudu Kuduppandi, a wandering tribe of South India.
No. 27	BURRAKATHA DAKKI Membranophone (ANDHRA PRADESH)	A pitcher-shaped brass vessel having short neck and round belly. The wider end covered with skin with the help of cotton cord through hoops and an iron ring. Suspended from neck, played by hands. Used by Burrakatha balladeers.
No. 41	CHENDE Membranophone (KARNATAKA)	A wooden cylindrical drum with both the faces covered with skin. Tied with the help of iron hoops. Suspended from the neck and played with sticks. Used in *Yakshagana.*
No. 47	CHITTIKA TĀLA Idiophone (KARNATAKA)	A pair of wooden clappers with clashing surface. Jingle bells attached on outer ends. Clapped by one hand rhythmically. Used by devotional singers. Occasionally used in folk music.
No. 51	DAKKI Membranophone (KARNATAKA)	Hour glass shaped drum, skin heads on both sides with the help of bamboo hoops. Held by its middle part, one face struck by stick. Used by mendicants and folk singers. Also used during traditional and ceremonial occasions.
No.58	ḌAMARU Membranophone (TAMIL NADU)	An hour glass shaped body made of brass. Faces covered with hide fastened by cotton cords. A knotted cotton cord attached on opposite ends on the bracing cord. Held by one hand, the player makes the knots to strike drum heads. Used by Kudukuduppi Andi of Tamil Nadu.

No. 64	DAVANDI Membranophone (TAMIL NADU)	Hour glass shaped small drum of brass. Hooped parchment is stretched over both the faces. Held in left hand and is struck by a thin wooden stick by right hand. Used in religious, auspicious occasions and temple services.
No. 82	DHOLU Membranophone (KARNATAKA)	Bi-facial wooden cylindrical body. Faces covered with skin suspended from the neck. Played with two sticks. Used in community group dancing and folk ensembles.
No. 87	EḌAKKA Membranophone (KERALA)	An hour glass shaped two-headed drum, slung from left shoulder. The right face is struck with a stick, while the left hand is used for varying the tension of the parchment by pulling and releasing the cotton cord worn round the waist of the drum. Used as a part of instrumental ensemble, in the rituals conducted in the temples of Kerala. Also as an accompaniment of Kathakali and Mohiniattam classical dances.
No. 94	GETTU VĀDYAM Chordophone (TAMIL NADU)	An instrument with round wooden resonator, long neck and bent peg box ending with a lion motif. Also contains an extra resonator. Strings four in number, made of steel, are struck with a bamboo blade and stopped by another blade, used as a drone cum rhythmic accompaniment. A rare instrument.
No. 123	KAMSALE Idiophone (KARNATAKA)	A pair of clappers with a cup-shaped metal disc and a deep central depression. Made of bell metal. Thick cotton sling is tied to the disc. Used as rhythmic accompaniment in devotional music and dance of Karnataka.
No. 125	KARADI VĀDYA Membranophone (KARNATAKA)	A barrel-shaped bi-facial wooden drum. Faces are covered with skin and tied with the help of iron rings and cotton cord. Decorated cloth is covered over the instrument. Played by either hands or sticks. Used in folk and traditional music and dance.
No. 147	MADAL Membranophone (ORISSA)	A bi-facial barrel-shaped drum made of baked clay. Both the faces covered with parchment and tied with dense leather facing through hoops. Black paste loading on both faces. Suspended from the neck and played by hands. Used in tribal community dances.
No. 164	MRIDANGAM Membranophone (SOUTH INDIA)	A popular bi-facial drum of Carnatic music, made of jackwood. A cylindrical body tapered at both the ends. Layered parchments, fastened to leather hoops and kept intact and tight by leather braces, at times small pieces of wood are also put in-between these braces to facilitate the tuning. Black paste loaded on right face in layers. Very fine flour dough applied on the left face before the performance and taken out immediately afterwards. Used as an accompaniment in South Indian classical music.

No. 214	RUDRA VEENA Chordophone (NORTH INDIA)	A long tubular body made of wood. Two large-sized round, resonators, made of fine quality gourds placed under the tube, at an equal distance from centre. Four playing strings one of steel and three of copper tied to the hook on lower end, stretched parallel to the tube and go to the ornate tuning pegs. Two drone strings mounted on the bridges on either side of the tube, stretched and tied to their respective pegs. Twenty-four brass-fitted raised wooden frets, fixed on the tube, with the help of wax. The resonators are richly decorated with wooden floral carvings. Carvings on the peg box as well. The lower end of tube is chiselled out like a bird and serves as a base for the wide flat ivory bridge. While playing, one gourd rests on left shoulder and the other on right thigh. Played with wire plectrums worn on right hand fingers. An instrument used in North Indian classical music.
No. 220	SANTOOR Chordophone (JAMMU AND KASHMIR)	A trapezoid wooden box, 120 steel strings, stretched on 30 wooden bridges in sets of four on each bridge. Bridges are arranged in a set of fifteen on each side. Struck by bamboo mallets. It is placed on a triangular wooden stand while playing. Used in traditional music of Kashmir called Sufiana Qalam. Has now acquired an important place as a classical music instrument.
No. 246	SWARMANDAL (NORTH INDIA)	A shallow wooden box with twenty-five strings tied to string-Chordophone holding posts and tuning pins. Beads are inserted into the strings for fine tuning. Strings are strummed by right hand fingers. Used for accompaniment in North Indian vocal music concerts. An open string harp category.
No. 268	TAVIL Membranophone (KERALA)	A large barrel-shaped bi-facial drum made of jack wood, both openings covered by layered skin and tied over the rim with the help of bamboo hoops and braces. Played by hand and stick. The left face of the drum is loaded with paste from inside. Used in folk and traditional music particularly in the instrumental ensemble called *Periya Melam*, in the accompaniment to Nagaswaram, a double reed wind instruments.
No. 295	VICITRAVĪṆĀ Chordophone (NORTH INDIA)	A long wooden shaft rests on two huge resonators, which are made of gourd, of equal diameter and height. Five main, three drone and eleven sympathetic strings. Three bridges, one main, one secondary and a small bridge for sympathetic strings. Played with plectrums worn on the right hand fingers and stopped by glass or stone piece, held in left hand. Used in North Indian classical style of music. Also called *Batta Been*.

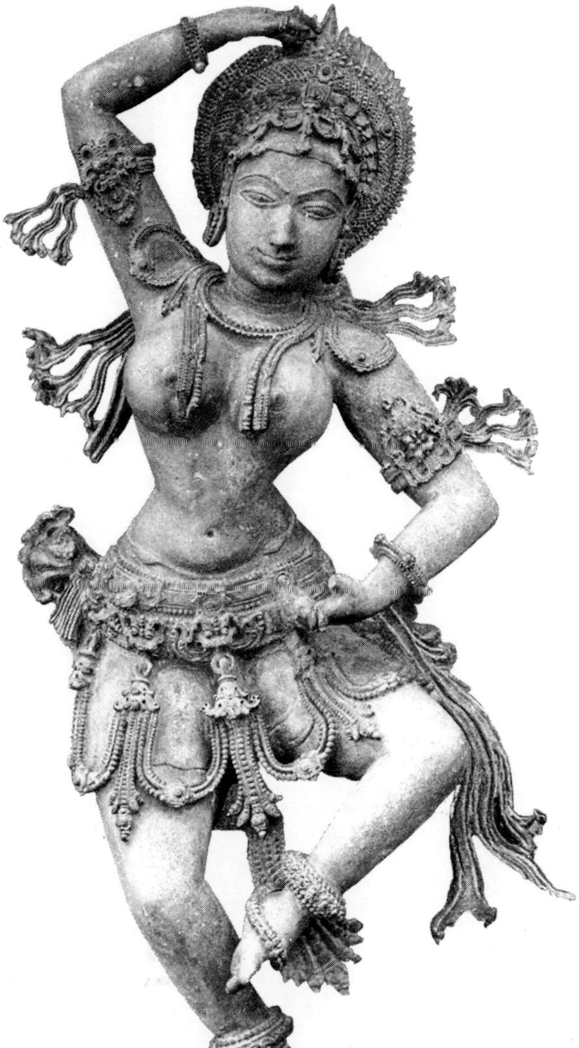

PART - II

APSARA – The Philosopher

I

Introduction

God is bliss. Human mind is forever searching for an enduring state of happiness, without realising that the mind itself is constantly on the move. The *Apsara* sculptures are carved with a basic theme of search for happiness and search for bliss. There is an inner urge in every human being to be blissful. As it cannot be bought either by material wealth or created, the search for the source of eternal happiness is constantly groped for in the outside world. The two fields of this search are the outer world and the world within. Some *Apsara* sculptures depict their search for happiness in the outer world with materialistic objects or sensual pleasures. With that she looks happy momentarily, as long as the objects are existing. Her unhappiness even after enjoying momentary pleasures, are due to her unstable and restless state of mind, as the mind and sense organs can enjoy pleasures only to a certain extent, and then pleasure itself becomes a source of pain. The mind swings from pleasure to impulsive actions of anger, fear or vanity, etc. Some *Apsara* sculptures depict her to be in a stable and blissful state of mind, where she is involved in activities relating to music (*Jñāna* in general, but here, the *Jñāna* is through *Nādayoga*). This knowledge, which she acquires by her self effort by imparting training in a field to the wandering mind, enables her to activate the divine core within, from which flows the perennial stream of peace and tranquility and thus locate the source of blissfulness. She looks satisfied with her involvement in the art of music and dance, as satisfaction is the character of eternity manifest. The dissatisfaction during the relationship with the temporal world and the satisfaction and peace she acquires with the world of meditation on sound (where the focus on her physical body or ego is absent) is depicted through the *Apsara* sculptures. In other words, momentary happiness and bliss are manifestations of the mind, which are studied through the activities and which is an outcome of *rājasik* (unstable) or *sāttvik* (goodness and purity) quality of thoughts. The knowledge or *Jñāna*, which she developes by her effort, gives her the bliss which she fails to acquire from the materialistic objects. Her unhappiness is defined by her unstable and fluctuating state of mind, which swings from pleasure to displeasure.

The forty-two *Apsara* sculptures in the Cennakēśava temple at Belur are carved to project the personality dominated by *Rajoguṇa* and *Sattvaguṇa*. *Apsara* sculptures project two phases of activity. Firstly, *Rajoguṇa*, where even though she is physically and mentally active, she is not enjoying a state of harmony or peace from within. Second phase is *Sattvaguṇa*, where she gets into a process of learning and self-introspection. She gets to know the fundamental knowledge of a right, *sāttvik*, peaceful living and the process of elevating oneself from the mundane to the knowledge of supreme self, within. This theme of the logic of spirituality is depicted in *Apsara* sculptures, through the path of *Nādayoga*. Twelve sculptures are categorised to depict how she is under the influence of *Rajoguṇa* and is involved in various schemes, to satisfy her desires with the awareness that she is just her physical body. Three sculptures are grouped to depict a transitory state of mind where she is realising that her non-blissful state is due to her ignorance, and she is destroying the veils of ignorance with the arrows. Twenty-one sculptures (where her mind is not focussed on her body) depict how she is transformed into a *sāttvik* person where she is involved in various stages of *Nādayoga*, a path of music, which she has chosen for her enlightenment. These sculptures indicate that, yoga with *nāda* is not an instantaneous process, the immediate pleasures of enjoying a song; *preyas* as it is called, is different from meditating on *nāda*) and does not happen overnight. It calls for a transformation of thought process in the begining. Further, the body and mind have to be tuned, for a steady focus on *nāda*, effort should be given to meditate on *nāda* and finally harmonise both physically and mentally, to become one with it.

The temporary and non-permanence of external beauty, the permanence and eternality of inner beauty that is gained by way of activating the inner self, seems to be the basic theme of these 42 *Apsara* sculptures. Hence, it is essential for the reader to understand the *guṇas*, the quality of actions, the four states of the soul – the *avasthās*, the *kośas*, the sheaths, that cover the soul, and the seven *chakras*, which explain the level of awareness. The author has attempted to build up a link between these philosophical aspects, the psychological states and the actions of these *Apsaras*, as the quality of actions are based on the texture of thoughts which is in line with the level of self-awareness.

In all the 42 sculpture, the *Apsara*s appear equally well-dressed and adorned with a lot of jewellery, irrespective of whether the theme they are projecting is related to *Rajoguṇa* or *Sattvaguṇa*. The classification is based on her thoughts and actions, through which she is projecting her priorities in life. The *sāttvik* qualities are gained here through the path of *Nādayoga*, the science and therapy, which has the capacity to transform a person from gross or basic level of mere existence, to a creative personality with higher intellectual capacities.

The sculptures are adorned profusely with jewellery as they are basically *Apsara*s who are always embellished with precious stone jewellery in the sculptural art. Probably the Hoysala rulers have chosen this medium to express the high level of wealth, prosperity and material success they enjoyed. The intricate carvings in the temple with a special attention to *Nādayoga* in *Apsara* sculptures depict their love for art, architecture, philosophy and devotion to God. The analysis here is based on the thoughts behind the actions and not on the ornamentation.

This part of the book explains the psyche of un-evolved state of mind, withdrawal from the same and a process of evolution of mind in the first two chapters. Chapter III explains the intricacies, power and effects of the sound on human mind, the *Anāhata* and the *Āhata Nādayoga* and finally oneness with it depicting Godly characters. Hence, before going into the details of the topic of *Nādayoga*, it is essential to know what the *avasthās* and the *guṇas* mean.

1. THE FOUR STATES OF THE SOUL – THE 'AVASTHĀS'

Jīva in Sanskrit is defined as the soul, the individual spirit, the feeling of being. Human beings are endowed with the greatest manifestation of awareness that is analyzed as the grades of consciousness, through which every human lives. Every human is aware of something, but the sphere, area and depth of awareness differ. The soul while identifying life, experiences four planes of consciousness called *Jāgrut*, *Svapna*, *Suṣupti* and *Turīya* states, an exhaustive study of which is given in the *Mandukya Upaniṣad*. The *Mandukya Upaniṣad* is probably the very first scriptural literature in the world, where life has been considered in its totality.The ancient sages had come to their conclusion on life after an exhaustive observation.

When the mind identifies itself with the physical body, or the spirit is in reference with the gross body of food and vital sheaths, it is called *Jāgrut avasthā*. It may be in relation to the functioning or appearance of gross body. *Jāgrut* is called the wakeful state also as it enjoys the experiences of the wakeful world. The third mantra of the *Āgama prakaraṇa* of *Mandukya Upaniṣad* explains:

"Jāgarita sthāno bahis-prajñāḥ", meaning, in the field of waking state, one is conscious of the external world (of objects).

When the soul detaches from the physical body and roams in the realm of mind, it is *Svapna avasthā* or the dream state. The soul in dream state attaches to the subtle body or the inner world of mind and emotions. The fourth mantra explains:

"Svapna-sthāno antaḥ prajñāḥ", meaning, in the field of dream state, one is conscious of the internal world.

When the spirit identifies with the intellect and gets one with it, detaching from the physical body and mind (emotions), it is called *Suṣupti avasthā* or the deep sleep state. It is called deep sleep as the soul is withdrawn from the agitations or activities of the body and enjoys a peaceful state of being, that is really relaxing. It is a state of consciousness, where a man gets close communion with God, though he remains in a forgetful state (forgetful to the physical body or passion). The fifth mantra explains,

"Yatra supto na kascana kamam kamyate na kascana svapanam paśyati, tat suṣuptam", meaning, in the state of deep sleep, one does not desire any objects, nor does he see any dream. The consciousness is full of bliss and one is an enjoyer of bliss.

Beyond the *Jāgrut* (wakeful), *Svapna* (dream state) and *Suṣupti* (blissful state) *avasthās*, the soul exists in a fourth phase of silence, the zone of divine bliss, the domain of truth, which is called *Turīya avasthā*, where the self or soul is totally withdrawn from the body, mind, intellect and the spirit unites with the supreme soul in a state of oneness with God. Union with God can be explained as the soul getting into a pure state, reflecting the godly characters of perpetual bliss, where even the flashes of *māyā* fail to make an impact. The Upaniṣads call this state as *Turīya*, meaning 'the fourth'. The discovery of this state of God consciousness enables one to discover the 'self'. The seventh mantra explains,

Nāntah prajñam na bahis prajñām- na ubhayataha prajñām,

Prapañca upasanam- śāntam, śivam, advitam, caturtham manyate sa ātmā sa vijñeyaḥ, meaning, that which is not conscious of the internal subjective nor the external objective world, and free from the world of all phenomena. The soul is peaceful, auspicious and non-dual – which is considered as the fourth state of awareness.

2. 'GUṆAS' – THE TEXTURE OF THOUGHTS AND ACTIONS

Action is the insignia of life. Man cannot live without actions. The activities of a person reflect his thought process. These two together can be called *guṇas*. *Guṇa* means the attitude with which the mind functions. The nature of *guṇas* have no separate existence and attributes inherent in a substance. It is compared to the properties of a material. Under the influence of different climatic conditions of the heart, mind and thoughts, *guṇas* are classified as:

1. *Tamas* - *Tamoguṇa* - a phase of inactivity. The mind is steeped in inertia and indifference.
2. *Rajas* - *Rajoguṇa* - a phase of passionate activity and vacillating emotions.
3. *Sattva* - *Sāttvikguṇa* - a phase of bliss, the highest quality of mind: poised, serene, equanimous and above worldly passion or excitement.

These three in different proportions attribute different flavour, influencing the mental and intellectual calibre of an individual. The three *guṇas* are always present in every human's heart, but each will be competing to gain their upper hand. It may so happen that *Rajoguṇa* may win over *Tamo* and *Sāttvikguṇa*, or *Tamoguṇa* gaining an upper hand when the power of intellect is weakened. The *Sāttvikguṇa* wins when the mind listens to the intellect. The role of a human in his lifetime is to gradually rise from *tamas* to *rajas* to *sattva* and reach the trans-*sattva* wherein lies the supreme self – the spiritual enlightenment.

The behaviour of the mind when it comes under the influence of each *guṇa*, is to be analysed and understood according to the actions and thoughts of *Apsaras*, which are classified according to, *Rajo* or *Sāttvikguṇa*.

Tamoguṇa which is expressed in action of misjudgement, indiscrimination, wrong comprehension, idleness and inertia, is not seen in *Apsara* sculptures. *Tamas* means mental darkness, meaning the light of intellect fails to support the thoughts and actions. When *Tamoguṇa* is powerful, it results in ignorance, inertia (of body and mind), hallucinations and an imbalanced state of mind, which is not depicted in the 42 *Apsara* sculptures. *Rājasik* intellect gives wrong understanding of righteousness and unrighteousness. It wrongly interprets the ethical and non-ethical values of life, resulting in erroneous performance of actions. Under the cover of *māyā* – the illusion, infinite desires make the physical body over active with a wandering mind lacking contentment and that makes a person *rājasik*.

An attempt has been made by the author to correlate the *guṇa* – the thought textures – to the *avasthās*, the state of the soul, with the *Apsara* sculptures. According to Nimbaraka school of Vedānta, who flourished in the 11th century AD after the time of Ramanuja, and who was one of the five principal commentators on *Brahma sūtras*, has discussed about the various and interesting features of the soul like its nature, size, number of souls, states of the individual soul, kinds of souls, its destination and so on. Describing the kinds of soul, Nimbaraka explains that there are only two kinds of souls, viz., souls in bondage and the freed souls. The souls in bondage associated with the mental relationship towards objects, comforts of material bodies and mundane existence. The freed souls are detached from material objects and mundane existence. Regarding the four states of individual soul, he explains that soul in the wakeful state is the knower, doer, and enjoyer, but the enjoyment manifests into various forms. In the deep sleep or the *suṣupti* state, the soul is just the knower and enjoyer, but the enjoyment does not manifest into forms. It is an eternal bliss.

This logic was most convincing to relate the *avasthās* to the psychological states and actions of the *Apsara* sculptures. The soul in bondage with material body is correlated with the *Rājasikguṇa* as they appeared to be interlinked, and the soul with no reference to material objects or body, is correlated with the *Suṣupti avasthā* as the quality of thoughts are *sāttvik* by nature.

The transformation from *rājasik* to *sāttvik* personality is not sudden. It has a transitory state of changing process like realising the merits and demerits of material pleasures, and preparing for a *sāttvik* style of life which is grouped under the *Svapna avasthā*.

3. MANIFESTATION OF *RAJOGUṆA* IN *JĀGRUT AVASTHĀ*

Rajoguṇa puts a person into action. The personality under this *guṇa* is naturally passionate, goaded by innumerable desires and deep attachments to self and to worldly pleasures. Ch. 14/12 of the *Bhagavadgītā* gives a clear picture of the behaviour patterns, under the influence of *Rajoguṇa*.

The mind in this phase relates to the gross body, the *kośas* made of food and vital air. The mind obeys implicitly the impulses of flesh, becoming a slave to the physical body, feeding and looking after it. This attitude develops like urges and attachments which will not allow a human mind to understand things as they should be understood. The waking state or the *Jāgrut avasthā* is the first of the four states of consciousness, symbolising the visible sphere. Its relation to the gross body promotes the ego which has a hunger that can never be appeased, and sense objects are the base for cognition. The quality of values or motives is expressed through the quality of thoughts, entertained, which further determines the texture of actions. Actions are thus a faithful expression of the inherent thought pattern. The actions of a *Rājasik* person seek gratification of one's own personal ambitions or selfish desires, as the *Rājasik* quality is characterised by activity passion and agitation.

An attempt is made by the author to study the inter-relations between the wakeful state of awareness (*Jāgrut avasthā*) and the *Rājasik* thought textures (*Rajoguṇa*) that characterise the human personality, which are depicted through some of the *Apsara* sculptures. The behaviour pattern, as explained by Swami Chinmayananda, can be summarised as the following, which are compared with the bracket figures, the explanations of which are discussed in the analysis of individual sculptures.

1. The actions are done with the expectations of a result (B.F. 1 & 15) as the mind believes itself to be his body.
2. *Rājasik* mind has fluctuating moods, as the thoughts in gross body enjoy pleasure (B.F. 16) and sense organs brood over pain (B.F. 35). The thoughts and deeds remain tied to the limitations of the body.
3. Mind often gets confused as actions are not focussed (B.F. 32). The mind gets easily agitated and worried.
4. *Rājasik* mind entertains *rājasik* joy which has a taste for the joy of gross body. It senses thrill and excitement from objects and indulgence. Comfort is the source of joy (B.F. 3).
5. The joy experienced is momentary and leaves craving for more of the same or hunts for new desires (B.F. 26).
6. Lifestyle becomes superficial. The time and energy is spent in pleasure and comfort seeking activities, satisfying the greed. The person here feels that the world is meant for enjoyment and the definition of happiness is an ever-changing phenomenon (B.F. 31, 1 & 15). The love for self is predominant here.
7. Pride over their possessions, and vanity – the thought of pride over their capacities – gives pleasure which becomes habituated (B.F. 7 & 42).
8. Fear and anger, the disturbing emotions, sometimes gain an upperhand under the influence of *Rajoguṇa* as sudden or constant fear manifest into agitations resulting in anger, deluding the rational capacity or choking the discrimination. In extreme cases *Rajoguṇa* may slip into *Tamoguṇa* where uncontrolled anger expresses itself in cruelty, physically assaulting the opponent to satisfy the personal ego (B.F. 5 & 34).

The mind acting according to these *Rājasikguṇas* can be classified in *Jāgrut avasthā* where the physical body is the only reference the mind has. It is not aware of the existence or capacity of the inner soul. The mind is compared in 4-5 sculptures with a monkey that is present with the *Apsara*, because of the restless state of mind, fluctuating thoughts, teasing nature and finding temporary comfort when basal requirements are met. Here *Apsara* indicates how a person believes himself to be the body, and the mind in this strata gets used to expecting rewards for their actions. *Rājasikguṇas* are expressed in sculptures where *Apsara* is amusing herself with physical decorations, executing superiority over lesser beings or entertaining oneself through pleasure games. The yearning of the soul for blissful state is ignored by her mind, as she believes herself to be her body, the pseudo self. There is, thus, a lack of harmony between the soul and the mind, which is the cause of her restless state.

Around 12 *Apsara* sculptures indicate the influence of *Rajoguṇa* in them.

4. ANALYSIS OF *APSARA* SCULPTURES IN *JĀGRUT AVASTHĀ* – A RESTLESS STATE OF MIND

Apsara sculptures are classified on the basis of their thoughts and actions depicted to (1) *Jāgrut* (wakeful state), (2) *Svapna* (dream state), (3) *Suṣupti* (deep sleep state), and (4) *Turīya* (blissful state) *avasthās*. The *Jāgrut avasthā* corresponds to *rājasik* qualities and *suṣupti avasthā* corresponds to *sāttvik* qualities. *Svapna avasthā* is an intermediate state while *Turīya avasthā* is the supreme state of bliss. Each sculpture has dwarf attendants on either side of the main figure, whose actions reinforce the thoughts of the main figure.

In the category of *Jāgrut avasthā*, *Apsara*s depict a state of mind which is under the influence of *rajas*. They appear passionate with lot of schemes for happiness, desires and emotions. Their mind always identifies with their body. The aspect of *tamas* which is a phase of physical inactivity and improper judgement of mind, darkness and delusion are not seen here. When *Rajoguṇa* predominates, the personality is active, enterprising, restless, greedy and longing for appreciation. Activity and enterprising here mean that the actions are motivated by extreme egoism and intentions are to fulfil and satisfy ego-centric and selfish desires, which are in pursuit of a search for happiness. Restlessness is an experience that is lived through by *rājasik* personality. Because of restlessness, an individual fails to enjoy quietude. *Jāgrut avasthā* means a wakeful state of awareness, where the mind tries to satisfy the demands of the physical body, i.e., the five sense organs and the five organs of actions are satisfied. The mind relates the soul to be the body, or the gross body, the outermost shell and life is a conscious existence with the body. The person is hardly aware of the mental or intellectual selves.

In the wakeful state, the *indriyās* (senses), the *prāṇa* (breath), the *manas* (mind), *buddhi* (intellect) and the ego are operative and functional. This is experienced as life at biological functions. The self enjoys, the gross matter and the consciousness is projected outwards.

The *Apsara* sculptures are analysed according to the characteristics of *Rajoguṇa*. Activity and dynamism are the main characteristics and the other *guṇas* are ambition, restlessness, passion, pride and vanity, haste or anxiety, superficial lifestyle, fluctuating moods, and schemes for pleasure which are correlated with the actions depicted in *Apsara* sculptures.

A. Ambition to Look Good

B.F. 1

Apsara is deeply attached to her body, which is a quality under *rajas*. Her efforts are focussed on two things – looking more beautiful and in impressing others. She is still dissatisfied with her appearance which is evident in her trying to shape her curly hair with a comb. The assistants are giving her more ornaments, as the lady is still not satisfied with her appearance. Her interest in life has not gone beyond her body. Hence she is classified under *jāgrut* or wakeful state with her mind focussed on the gross body. She is interested in self and ego satisfaction. Happiness (*sukha*) is in gross pursuits, exciting and momentary joy.

The *Apsara*'s mind is compared to the qualities of a monkey, which the attendant is carrying. She is restless as her mind is craving for more. Her mind is pampered which is indicated in the dwarf carrying a monkey in her lap and offering more fruits to it. Life is meant here for base level momentary pleasures, which are like the short-lived reflections in a mirror that stay as long as the person is there. The dwarf figures in total indicate qualities like a pampered and unsteady mind, aspiring for more, which are the qualities of *Rajoguṇa*. The monkey is indicative of the qualities of a pampered and unsteady mind, aspiring for more – which are the typical qualities of *Rajoguṇa*.

She depicts a stage of *jāgrut* or wakeful state of awareness, with her mind identifying with her gross body.

B.F. 15

The theme is same as B.F. 1. The *Apsara* is deeply attached to her physical body and spends her time and energy in decorating herself. Her awareness has not gone beyond her physical body which means she is either not aware or does not care for the inner and true personality that is within her. Her mind is longing for more of the pleasure sources or seeking varieties in it which is conveyed through the dwarfs offering her more jewellery. Looking more beautiful, a reference to her body and decorating it for an appreciation from others or for social acceptance, is her purpose. Her mind is under the sway of endless longings for things not yet accomplished, for objects not yet acquired and for profits not yet gained.

Her mind is identifying herself as her body, a typical *rājasik* quality with reference to the gross body. Self-identification is a movement of energy, and her thoughts identify with the sensation, which narrows down the vast energy potential that is within. She is representing the qualities of *Jāgrut avasthā* – a wakeful state of awareness. In B.F. 1 and 15, the *Apsara* stands with a mirror to make sure that she is presentable in her outwardly appearance, and thus indicates her trust in the mirror implicitly. She is not concerned with her inner soul or the potential. Looking beautiful is her sense of strength.

B. Passion

B.F. 26

It is a sculpture projecting a theme on what passion is and its consequences which will result as pain indicated by a scorpion. According to *Bhagavadgītā* (XIV.7), *rajas* is of the nature of passion. Psychologically, passion is the main symptom which is expressed in life as a million different urges, desires, emotions and feelings. Such a passionate person is being goaded by desires for things not yet acquired. Life is spent in endless activities, fulfilling the desires of passion. The joy experienced is not enduring and leaves craving for more of the same or hunts for new desires of habituated pleasure seeking. Passion makes a silent entry into the human mind, much like the silent movement of the scorpion which had sheltered in her *saree*. The sculpture suggests that it should be shaken off at the early stage or else the pain of it may have to be endured.

The aspect of confusion that the *Apsara* is experiencing is conveyed through the dwarf figure, which is to her left. Her confused intellect fluctuates between moods and thoughts and is therefore indecisive. Scorpion is indicative of the pain associated with passion. The figure is a clear picture of *Jāgrut avasthā* in awareness, where the mind is trying to fulfil the agonising desires of the *Annamaya* and *Prāṇamaya kośas* the gross body – obeying the impulses of the body.

* For a betterment in lifestyle, one has to concentrate on *Bhogavairāgya* (ref. Ch. 3.6, Part II) which guides a man to relieve himself from short-lived pleasures and seek a perpetual and lasting source of happiness.

C. Pride and Vanity

B.F. 42 and 7

Apsara is displaying her neatly groomed thick and long hair with a feeling of pride. She is so possessive of her capacity and is deeply attached to it which she wants to further decorate with the garland of flowers as her concept of beauty is at the physical level. To her, life means glamour and competition. Happiness (*sukha*) is in gross pursuits and momentary pleasures. More indulgence in physical aspects arise out of deep attachment to the physical body, which is a manifestation of mind under *Rajoguṇa*. Life and energy are spent in superficial decorations of the body, being unaware of the better capacity of the soul that is within. Through her sense organ of *sparśa* or touch, she is exhibiting the *rūpa* (form) of her long tresses which hints a feeling of 'I like'. When the mind and senses identify with the necessity, attachment dwells. The vast self-energy gets channelised into it, which later on becomes like a constant pressure, and investigation stops when pressure becomes more. The qualities of pride and vanity (pride over one's capacity) makes her attached to her gross body and she is in *Jāgrut avasthā* in her consciousness.

D. Haste and Anxiety

B.F. 32

Apsara is trying to adorn herself with an ear-ring in haste and she has dropped the back stud, which is picked up by the attendant sitting to her left. The activities of hurried actions are beautifully depicted in this sculpture, in her posture. When a person is under the influence of *Rajoguṇa*, the actions or duties that one performs are under tension. *Apsara* is restless in her mind, for which reason her action of fixing an ear-ring is defective, and it is not focussed. The mind is confused in the state of anxiety and actions become incomplete due to oppressive restlessness. A monkey that is sitting to her right, symbolizes her restless state of mind. It is also indicative of her mind not being involved in her action, in which case however small a work is executed, it becomes chaotic due to confusion. Her mind is 'Chanchala' or impatient and restless, which is usually compared to the mind of a monkey. The awareness is at gross body level, state of consciousness is at *Jāgrut avasthā* as she clearly indicates her association of mind to her physical body and its decoration.

E. Superficial Lifestyle

B.F. 31

Apsara is standing with an ear-ring (or a small flower) in her left hand and observing in the mirror (as shown by the attendant who is to her right side) to check how it suits her. Another attendant to her left is giving another piece of jewel or a garland of flowers.

Apsara is in an artificial life, with a superficial thinking, as she is not aware of her real self, the intrinsic wealth within her and its capacities. She is engaged in making her external appearance better, displaying a competitive feeling, and more for the social approval, which is a typical thought process under *Rajoguṇa*. Her mind finds joy when basic requirements are met and comfort is through objects and indulgence. She implicitly trusts the mirror, which reflects only the outward appearance. She is not aware of the truth of the non-permanence of the external beauty and the permanence of inner beauty.

She is in the influence of *Rajoguṇa* with her mind focussing on the gross body which is attributed to *Jāgrut avasthā*, where her state of consciousness is in a wakeful stage.

F. Fluctuating Moods (Pleasure)

B.F. 16

Apsara is enjoying plucking a fruit in a garden. Her mind in the *jāgrut* state of self-awareness and wanders in the pleasure garden of sensual objects. The sensual demands of the five sense organs are always taken care of at this state. *Apsara* plucking a fruit is a symbolic gesticulation of satisfying the senses, which is a character of *Rajoguṇa*. It also means the pleasures in life are different from happiness.

The mental and the intellectual equipment in a human body has the capacity to keep in record the impressions of the pleasures or pains experienced, which are called *vāsanās*. The *vāsanās* are like the un-manifest records. Desires and thoughts spring from *vāsanās* just as the grooves cut in a music record and actions are outcome of the *vāsanās*. *Apsara*'s interest in the fruit can be classified as the pleasure that she has experienced (not necessarily enjoying a fruit). The mind in *Rajoguṇa* fluctuates from pleasure to pain and hence results in a restless state.

G. Fluctuating Moods (Pain)

B.F. 35

Apsara is depicting the hurt that she has experienced on her left foot, caused by a pebble or thorn which the attendant is attending to. She holds a stone in her right hand.

Apsara's hurt on the foot can be explained for the pains that she has experienced in the past (not necessarily a pebble hurting her foot). When a person is under the influence of *Rajoguṇa*, the moods go fluctuating from pleasure to pains of *vāsanās* and make the mind toss higher and tether with agitation. This is the cause which takes away a stable and tranquil state of mind. The mental activities brood over the past or excited for no reason, which does not serve any purpose. Control over the mind can be achieved only through *jñāna* – knowledge or spiritual practices.

Apsara is referring to a state of physical reference – an awareness of *Jāgrut avasthā*.

H. Scheme for Pleasure

B.F. 3

Apsara is enjoying a fun time in playing game of water – *jalakride*. Even though the sculpture's hands are badly damaged, the dwarf figures who are supplying water and the other one, who is filling water in a piston syringe, indicate the game is in progress.

Psychologically, *Apsara* is trying a new event in search of happiness. The thrill that one enjoys in the game of coloured water is a momentary happiness that lives as long as the game is there. Later, the mind again goes searching for another sport or another scheme for better thrills, which is a quality under the influence of *Rajoguṇa*. *Rājasik* pursuits seem very attractive and easy to get joys, resulting in habituated pleasure seeking. Lifestyle becomes superficial and life is spent in comfort or pleasure seeking activities, that promisses some joy, but true joy still remains a mirage.

Apsara indicates the *Jāgrut avasthā*, where the awareness is at the gross body level. She is either still not aware of the better person who is within or she is not bothered to care for it.

I. Anger

B.F. 5

Lord Kṛṣṇa says in *Bhagavadgītā*, Ch. 3. 37, that,

Kāma esha krodha esha, rajoguṇa samudbhava.

This means passion and anger are born out of *Rajoguṇa*.

Apsara is angry with the monkey that is teasing her and she is trying to chase the animal away, by throwing the branch of a plant on it.

Human mind has many powers. 'Vikṣepa' is the state of mind which bursts out suddenly like a bullet firing out of a gun. This power of mind is also classified as projection, which is a quality of *Rajoguṇa*. The person under its influence interacts, creates, acts, and changes from his normal self very quickly. When the person slips down further in his behaviour pattern, he is slipping into *Tamoguṇa* where he is unable to perceive things as they are. The overlapping of *Tamoguṇa* in B.F. 5 & 34, in hiding the truth, makes the illusion or unreal problem seem very real. She has no patience to deal with the situation with a calm mind and expresses as being impulsive and unpredictable. Her enraged reaction is because of the ego, which has created an illusory compartment in which she dwells. Since ego demands respect, and demands destroy love, she is unable to cope up with the situation.

Apsara is indicating that her mind is disturbed and has turned violent due to a teasing situation, depicted through the monkey, which is pulling her veil. Her anger has enraged the monkey also, which is depicted in the monkey showing its teeth or screaming at her. It accounts for the quality of argumentation in the mental world. The body tries to detoxify the impaired glandular secretions of a disturbed mind through heavy breathing, which manifests as harsh voice and actions. Her awareness is compared to that of a monkey (animalise) called 'Vikruta puruṣa' where life is at a primitive state of mind. Anger, lust and passion are some of the powerful obstacles between human soul and supreme soul; unless these obstacles are cleared by *śama-dama* (ref. Ch. 3/6, Part II), it is impossible to experience a blissful state. Her awareness is at the gross level, in *Jāgrut avasthā* or at wakeful state where she is responding to a situation in an impulsive way.

J. Fear and Anger

B.F. 34

Apsara is scared of the monkey that is teasing her and she is getting angry with it. She is trying to chase away the monkey with a branch, which is in a dilapidated state to her right side.

Apsara clearly depicts the emotion of fear. Her eyes are wide opened and fear struck. In her left hand she is holding on to her tummy and seeking safety. She is trying to run away from the animal in a nervous hurry. Fear is a negative emotion which poses as an obstacle in the path of yoga. Negative thoughts, when harboured, ferment the mind. Physiologically, they impair the glandular secretions, which build up toxicity in the body and nerves behave in a disturbed state, leading a person to a confused state with a blurred vision. It is called a state of *'Citta Vikṣobha'* which makes the mind turbid and diffused, shattering her peace of mind. The position of her left hand indicates the *Svādhistāna chakra* of her body, where her awareness is still in the emotive phase and they seek comfort in running away from the situation temporarily, or try to gain an upperhand to satisfy the ego through power. The restless state of mind is like that of a monkey, with awareness which is called *Vikruta puruṣa*. Her uncontrolled anger is slipping down as *Tamoguṇa,* as her actions appear to be animalistic and cruel to the opponent. To satisfy her ego she is overpowering. Her mind places herself to her emotional levels and she does not care for the soul that is within her, which is the striking quality under *Rajoguṇa.*

- *Taittiriopanisath* explains that the feeling of duality and egoism are the root cause of fear which is called *avidyā*. The human fails to understand the omnipresence of Brahman and treats himself as a separate entity, feeling egoistic, which gives rise to fear or anger. A person who identifies himself with the Brahman has no fear, and freedom from fear is the way for better spiritual life.
- Fear, love and hatred are the three flavours of the same emotion. They can be interchanged. When love predominates, fear and hatred disappear.

II

Svapna Avasthā – The Process of Transformation

The transformation from *rājasik* to *sāttvik* is not a sudden procedure in life. *Rājasik* mind gets saturated with mundane pleasures in a short while, and the mind hunts for a higher level of bliss. It becomes aware of the presence of an inner soul and its capacities. It starts judging for a better source of intellectual and spiritual life. The basic demand at this transitory stage is discrimination and self-judgement, to get relief from *avidyā* (ignorance) and *māyā* (illusion; believing in non-real source of happiness). The veils of *māyā* like greed, passion, lust, etc., which are considered as enemies of *sāttvik* mind, are destroyed with the arrows of discrimination.

The most essential requirement for the transformation of the mind from *rājasik* to *sāttvik* is trapping and bringing under control the ever moving mind, which is compared with a deer/ gazelle, for its speed. In other words, it is silencing of the mind.

Svapna avasthā is a sacred stage as it is the first step of self-realisation. The realisation that dawns about how every pleasure left her where she was, and failed to elevate her to a state of bliss, instigates her to come out of the mesh of *māyā* and locate the right path for bliss.

In sculptures (B.F. 23, 6, 17), *Apsara* is shown involved in a hunting game. She is shooting the arrows (of discrimination) to destroy the obstacles of *māyā* and *avidyā* and one sculpture shows the action that she has shot the arrow (B.F. 17).

Once the mind is set on spiritual thoughts, *Apsara* shows how one has to get into *svādhyaya*. *Svādhyaya* is the study of scriptures, focussing and expanding one's knowledge by effort as depicted in B.F. 28, where *Apsara* is showing *jñāna mudrā* in the right hand suggestive of her concentration and in the left hand she holds scriptures, which she is going through. The study of any subject should be understood and put into everyday life for betterment of spiritual life. Constant study and its practice, will lead one to have communion with God.

From the stage where *Apsara* decides to destroy the obstacles of *māyā*, begins her *svādhyaya* – the practice of her study phase – and nowhere is there reference to the physical body or emotions of the physical world. It is just a happy state of mind. *Apsara* indicates the path of *Nādayoga* for betterment of life style.

1. ANALYSIS OF *APSARA* SCULPTURES IN *SVAPNA AVASTHĀ*

B.F. 23, 6, 17

The subtle body has two components, viz., the mind and the intellect. The mind is nothing but flow of thoughts. When the thoughts are withdrawn from the physical world or when they are released after satisfying the needs of the physical body, the mind enters into a different world of subtle body, which is identified as *Manonmāyā kośa*. Here again the mind acts at two levels – the subconscious and the unconscious level.

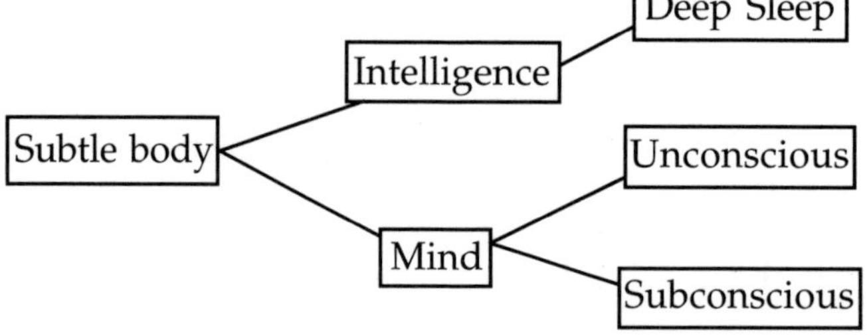

When the conscious mind is quiet, the subconscious mind floats up, which is called a dream state. It is the first stage of withdrawal from the outer world. This stage is compared to the nature of a relief valve, through which tensions and pressures of conscious level are released. Dream is a sacred stage of mind, between the waking and the sleeping (bliss) state, as the mind emerges from a putrefying stage and marches its first step to a refined state of realisation. This subconscious stage is like a platform upon which the unassimilated thoughts assimilate. The personality is temporarily released from the constriction of wakeful state. It is a stage of parade of thoughts, where the mind unfolds its *vāsanās* (a record of pleasure and pain). The intellect or the *buddhi* stands detached watching the parade of thoughts and later decides on the course of action to command.

Under the influence of *Rajoguṇa* in *Jagrut avasthā*, the mind fails to see things as they are. In *Svapna avasthā*, the mind is inquisitive to clarify its judgement, and in *Suṣupti avasthā*, it gains clarity to see things as they are.

There are three sculptures which are classified by the author under the dream state or *Svapna avasthā*. In all three, *Apsara* is holding bow and arrows and outwardly looks as though she is involved in a game of hunting. When analysed philosophically according to her state of mind and activities, it indicates that she has no desire for her body now. Her mind is no longer engaged in decorating herself or in a scheme which are ways for temporary happiness. The *Apsara*, through these sculptures, indicates that the mind looks for a source of happiness that stays forever and it is no longer agitated by negative thoughts of passion, greed or restlessness. The first step in the subtle thinking is the stage of controlling the wandering mind; only then it can locate the source in which the mind can be channelised. The capture of the wandering mind, and setting a goal to channelise the mind are depicted beautifully and very meaningfully through the picture of deer, bow and arrows, etc. The sculptures are not placed in a series, the reasons for which are yet to be known. Even though hunting is a game befitting *rājasik* personalities, the symbolic significance of a captured deer, bow and arrow are considered here. Bow symbolizes stored energy, will power, divine or terrestrial power, a long range weapon and an obvious emblem of war. Arrow represents penetration by perception. They are symbols of sun and sometimes shown as piercingly sweet darts of love, according to the symbolism of weapons of ancient world.

A. A Parade of Thoughts

B.F. 23

Apsara is standing with a bow in her left hand and the arrow in the right hand is damaged. It appears she is in a dilemma regarding her action to execute. The figures on either side represent the parade of thoughts – the impressions of pain and the reward. To her right is her own miniature figure, where she is getting her foot examined for the hurt. To her left is a figure carrying the game, that is hung to the corners of a pole (a reward of hunting game), indicating that the path of higher bliss may be painful initially on one hand followed by a reward on the other. This is depicted symbolically through *Apsara*, carrying the bow and arrow which are the equipment to destroy the obstacles of the *māyā*. This is the subconscious level of withdrawal of mind from wakeful state. She is in a stage of introspection, channelising her thoughts towards a blissful state. The subtle body, or the mind, in the first stage oscillates between doubts and realities. If supported by the intellect, she elevates into the second stage which is a spiritual state of mind failing which, she slips into a lower state of mind seeking basic pleasures.

*According to *Bhagavadgītā*, Ch. 6/7, pain and pleasures are the pair of opposites experienced by the mental zone. While heat and cold are the stimuli that are felt and experienced by the body, pleasure and pain are experienced by the mind. Honour and dishonour are the evaluation and reaction of the intellect. These are the pairs of opposites experienced from the world of body, mind and intellect. The dwarf figures on either side of B.F. 23, represent the pleasure and pain of the mental zone.

*A self-controlled and peaceful man remains balanced under the influence of the opposites, experienced by the three zones.

B. *Manōnigraha* (Capturing the Mind)

B.F. 6

Apsara is shooting arrows. The attendant is standing with a deer that is captured, holding some more arrows in her right hand.

This phase is symbolic of the mind's withdrawal. The mind which is always wandering in the garden of sensual thoughts with high speed is captured and brought under control. The deer which the attendant is holding in a snare indicates the mind that is brought under control.

Apsara is indicating that the intellect of the subtle body has judged to uncover or destroy the cover of *māyā* (illusion) and *avidyā* (ignorance). She is aiming the arrows for a higher level, which indicates that her vision, her aim and goal is at a higher level of awareness. She appears in a hip dress with leafy decoration, which suggest she is prepared to relieve herself from *avidyā*.

This suggests a phase of her intellect commanding the mind to become quiet, so that it can be channelised for a better purpose of refined thinking. *Apsara* indicates a phase of elevation into a calmer state of unconscious mind, from the agitation of wakeful state and hence she is in a dream state which is called *Svapna avasthā*.

C. Destruction of *Avidyā* (Ignorance) and *Māyā* (Illusion)

B.F. 17

Apsara has shot an arrow to an object at a higher level, which is indicative that her vision and goals are for a higher state. This is the third sculpture in the dream state, where the mind is totally withdrawn from the wakeful state of the world. Her vision and goals being higher, has elevated her from gross to a subtle level. The arrows she has shot, are suggestive of the intellect (*buddhi*), that has been guiding the mind, which is now under control, to clear the obstacles that are there as ignorance and *māyā*, and make way to have a clear view of what God/the supreme bliss is. This also hints through *Apsara*, that the source of bliss is seen only after the intellect makes a right judgement, regarding *Nityānitya viveka* (ref. ch. 3.6). This is the second stage of mind, when it is guided by the intellect and functions as the firm, discriminating, and determining factor. In a dream state, the mind leaves the physical body and enters the subtle body.

The mind from the subconscious level slowly enters into the state of unconscious level, before getting into deep sleep. It means the *Apsara* has withdrawn from *Annamaya*, *Prāṇamaya* and *Manōnmaya kośas* (ref. ch. 2.2 on *kośas*) and enters into a state of deep sleep, which is viewed as the *Vijñānamāyā kośa*. Here sleep is indicative of a calmer state of mind.

2. THE *KOŚAS*

Kośas as they are called in Sanskrit, are the layers or veils which block the view of God – the ultimate truth. They are the sheath of awareness, consciousness or discrimination. An understanding of *kośas* is essential for the study of *Apsara* sculptures, as her activities are directly related to *kośas* and her state of awareness.

Every human being is not merely a physical structure, but a four-forked entity with four distinct personalities like physical, mental, intellectual and spiritual. These are like layers covering the core, the spirit of man. These sheaths have no separate existence as such but they function coordinatively in every human. They are analysed for the understanding of the self or *ātman*.

Kośas are five in number

1. *Annamaya kośa* – the physical existence of the body, that is alive by the food that is taken.
2. *Prāṇamaya kośa* – the sheath of *prāṇa* or the vital breath (without which body does not exist or move), which confirms the existence of life between the first inhalation and the last exhalation.
3. *Manōnmaya kośa* – the sheath of mind where there is flow of thoughts and emotions.
4. *Vijñānamaya kośa* – the sheath of intelligence – the *buddhi* or intellect – the discriminatory faculty.
5. *Ānandamaya kośa* – the innermost sheath of blissfulness/consciousness.

In every experience, man contacts the world through the media of his body, mind, intellect and consciousness. The physical body is a hutment where mind and intellect dwell. The first two layers are the grossest where the five organs of action, the abstract working senses (*karmendriyas* – the hands, the legs, speech, genital organ and the organ of evacuation) and the five *prāṇas* exist. They are formed and are existing because of the food and vital air that are utilised by the body. The vital air sheath controls and regulates the food sheath; as when the function of *prāṇa* is affected, the body also suffers. This is called the *Sthula Śarīra*, gross body, which is universally common in its function, but differs only in its outward appearance. *Annamaya kośa* works when the *prāṇa* or the vital air is active. It is through the medium of gross body, the individual contacts the outer world of objects, experiences his joys or sorrows, and hence can be linked with the *Jagrut avasthā*.

The third layer is the sheath of mind, which is not a definite organ in the body but stays there as a form of energy. The five sensory organs of perception (the abstract knowing senses are *jñānendriyas* – the eyes, ears, nose, tongue and skin) are active in *Manōnmaya kośa*. It is a powerful sheath that enlivens the activities of the previous *kośas*. A sound mind stays in a sound body. The mind regulates and orders the vital air sheath, which means when the mind is upset, or in shock, the functions of *prāṇa* and food are affected. Mind entertains the thought process of a man with experiences of joy, doubt and the nine basic emotions (*Navarasas*) that are felt and experienced by every human. These emotions are the fundamental aspects imbibed by a living organism. A troubled organism expresses anger and loss of kith and kin is expressed through sadness. This layer is the first part of the subtle body, which is constituted of thoughts. The second part of the subtle body is the fourth layer of intellectual sheath, the *Vijñānamaya kośa*, which judges and determines the course of action to be taken, when the mind is active with emotions. The mind and intellect together are called *Sukṣma Śarīra*, or subtle body. The subtle body differs from individual to individual because of the difference in the texture and quality of mind and intellect. The performance of intellect improves in its clarity and firmness when training is imparted to it, leading to a better control on the wandering mind.

Blissful sheath is the experience of undisturbed state of peacefulness due to the cessation of the agitation experienced in the other states of consciousness. The pleasures and pains experienced are stored in memory, which are called *vāsanās*. The intellect functions according to the stored memory of *vāsanās* and the blissful sheath controls the sheath of intelligence. This sheath is also called the causal body – the *Kāraṇa Śarīra* – because it is the ultimate determining factor that orders the mind, intellect and the consequent behaviour of the physical body.

The following chart simplifies the classification of *kośas* where the individual soul is *jīva*, and the state of oneness with God is referred to as 'AUM'. A represents *jāgrut*, U represents the *svapna* and M represents the *suṣupti* or blissful state. The total recitation of the mantra 'AUM' is followed by brief silence, which is recognised as a state of *turīya* – the perfect bliss. The mantra Aum is chosen because it is the most powerful of all the seed sound syllables, the source of all mantras and a key to realization. 'AUM' is composed of certain letters, arranged in a definite sequence of sound, of which the letters are the representative signs. It represents the self, which is a non-dual state of reality and the supreme. Self is known in four states of waking, dream,

AUM – The Supreme Soul Parambrahman

State of silence between two consecutive mantras as AUM	**5 - Ānandamaya Kośa**	**Turīya Avasthā** (Blissful state) Soul identifies with Parambrahman
M	**4 - Vijñānamaya Kośa**	**Suṣupti Avasthā** (Deep sleep state) Soul identifies with *buddhi* or intellect and withdraws from body and mind
U	**3 - Manōnmaya Kośa**	**Svapna Avasthā** (Dream state) Soul identifies with mind, the subtle body, and withdraws from the body
A	**1 - Annamaya Kośa** **and** **2 - Prāṇamaya Kośa**	**Jāgrut Avasthā** (Awake state) Soul identifies with the gross body

Every individual soul (Jīva) has to cross the five sheets of reality in life to reach the supreme soul, which is otherwise called
Mokṣa

deep sleep and perfect bliss. In the fourth state of perfect bliss or *turīya*, the individual identifies with the supreme who comes from nothing. The parallel words to AUM, which are the sacred mantras sung in different parts of the world, are Omen, Amen, Ameen, etc.

A knowledge of *kośa* in detail is essential to the study of *Apsara* sculptures at Belur temple. In many sculptures *Apsara* identifies herself with her physical body, - so attached to it , decorating it forever, and making sense objects as the source of cognition, which are classified under *Jāgrut avasthā*. But there are some sculptures where the *Apsara* does not refer to her physical body. Her mind is in a state of doubt, regarding the choice between the un-real (temporary pleasures) and real (permanent) source of pleasures. This transitory stage of mind is classified under *Svapna avasthā* as it is a transitory stage between body reference and intellectual activities. The sculptures where *Apsara* is totally engrossed in *Nādayoga* is classified under blissful state or the *Suṣupti avasthā* as here, she bears no references either to her body or the changing moods of mind. It is beyond the pleasures and pains of the physical or the emotional world. *Apsara* figures also come under *Turīya avastā*, where she identifies herself with the supreme soul and merges one with it, with the cessation of the activities of body, mind and spirit. The four pillars in the *Navaraṅga* of the temple has *Apsara* figures, that indicates these four states. The *Apsaras* on the outer walls of the temple depict various activities explaining each state. Every *Apsara* sculpture is analysed for the state of mind, the reason behind her activities and that of the attendants who are with her.

III

Suṣupti Avasthā – A State of Calmness

1. *APSARA* IN *SUṢUPTI AVASTHĀ*

Suṣupti is derived from the root word 'sputa', which means in Sanskrit 'to sleep'. 'Su' is an adverb or adjective used to mean good. *Suṣupti* in Sanskrit means, deep sleep or profound sleep a state of repose. Here sleep is with reference to the mind and not the physical sleep.

Suṣupti avasthā or deep sleep state after the dream state is a symbolic interpretation of the mind which is no longer agitated by the demands of the body or the impulses of the mind. It is totally relaxed from the demands of the gross body. It also explains how *Apsara*'s mind is withdrawing from the outer world and proceeding towards the inner self, as her thoughts and actions are no longer tied to the limitations of the body. From here the phase of self-realisation begins as the mind is stilled and ego is annihilated.

It can be categorised under *Vijñānamaya kośa*, where the intellect – the discriminatory faculty – starts working to channelise the wandering mind into a refined, relaxed and blissful strata. Suṣupti though means deep sleep, does not indicate she is inactive. It refers to her relaxed state of mind, which is relaxing like during a deep sleep stage. Her activities are oriented towards a goal of yoga. It is still a transitory stage before experiencing the total blissful state of *Turīya avasthā*.

Apsara's activities, involving herself with various instruments and singing clearly depicts her involvement in the various stages of *Nādayoga*, with a conscious effort to withdraw from the physical body and proceeding to a phase of meditation on *nāda*. Her awareness now has surpassed the third sheath of illusion – the *Manonmaya kośa* and enters the *Vijñānamaya kośa* as her mind is now governed by the intellect, the *buddhi*, in determining the course of action to be taken for the wandering mind. This state of awareness is co-related with the *Vijñānamaya kośa*, where the intellect penetrates into the realms 'unknown', to investigate, contemplate and comprehend the new discoveries. With this insight, the personality beyond the *Jagrut* and *Svapna avasthās* is elevated, with the thought textures characterised by purity and serenity of *Sāttvikguṇa*.

2. MANIFESTATION OF *SĀTTVIKGUṆA* IN *SUṢUPTI AVASTHĀ*

Human behaviour springs from a record of thoughts called *vāsanās*. The mind reigns over the physical body where thoughts flow ceaselessly. The gross body merely obeys or performs actions according to the commands of the mind. The human body is merely an instrument of thoughts, and actions are nothing but solidified thoughts. It is the difference in thoughts that distinguishes a person from another. The subtle body which stays in the gross body has two aspects – the mind and *buddhi* or intellect. The mind operates as thoughts and doubts. The intellect operates as the discriminating power of judging the right from the wrong and illuminates the judgement with knowledge or intellectual comprehension. When the mind is purified from the agitation of *rajas*, or the evils of *tamas*, intellect becomes steady and more efficient intelligence is manifest. The main characteristic of *Sattvaguṇa* is knowledge (*Jñāna*) gaining an upper hand surpassing emotions, resulting in good *karmas*. The other characters are – purity, equanimity, memory, compassion, faith and love. Ch. 14/6 of *Bhagavadgītā* defines *Sāttvikguṇa* to be stainless, healthy and luminous. *Sattva* brings attachment to knowledge and happiness. Mind under the influence of *Sattvaguṇa* becomes pure, steady, reflecting the consciousness – the self. It is a state of inward peace, enjoying the subtle understanding and intellectual comprehension. The personality transforms to be intelligent and creative in skills, enjoying a perpetual state of joy. In the author's opinion, the *Apsaras* who are engaged in activities with various instruments, indicate a phase of *Sāttvikguṇas* as she is totally involved in music – the yoga with the *nāda*. It is a state of meditation where her mind is in a continuous current on one object, much like the flow of water in a river.

Dhyānam nirviṣayam manaḥ – dhyāna or meditation – is a state of mind wherein there are no *viṣaya* or sensual thoughts. The mind concentrates constantly and intensely on one subject, attaining gradually a state of super consciousness or bliss. Meditation is possible when the mind evolves from *rājasik* to *sāttvik* state as the *sāttvik* intellect draws a distinction between bondage and liberation.

The *sāttvik* qualities are:

1. Thoughts are not self-centred. Attachment to the body is substituted by selfless thoughts, arising by the kindling of *Jñāna*. Actions no longer wait for a reward as the mind is detached from mundane pleasures.
2. *Sāttvik* life is an inspired and an inspiring one. High thinking with elevating experience are the qualities of a *sāttvik* person. *Sattva* means consciousness. When it prevails, time and space are transcended to discover the eternal self.
3. *Śraddhā* – the faith arising out of firm intellectual convictions are the qualities of a person in whom *Jñāna* is kindled. With the blossoming of the hidden talents, he has the desire to gain knowledge – a quality that adds beauty to a *sāttvik* personality. The inner unfoldment reflects as *sāttvik* joy.
4. A *sāttvik* person easily becomes proficient and efficient in skilled art; work becomes a joy and he progresses within, with a capacity to understand the subtle aspects.
5. Personality is purified experiencing a greater share of inward peace and happiness.
6. The person becomes creative by nature. An individual who experiences the thrills of creative moments in life (any independent thinker in the field of arts or science) will not ever like to come down to the passionate world of *rājas* or the dark sorrows of *tamas*. *Sattva* makes a person attached to inward happiness arising from life that is fully and sensibly lived.
7. Knowledge arises from *sattva*. The mind and intellect are conditioned and hence is pure and serene, with least agitation and leads to the rediscovery of the self – the experience of pure wisdom.

The *Apsara* sculptures indicate how by getting rid of the *rājas*, a person is elevated to *sāttvik* level and finally rises to the peak of wisdom with the knowledge of self and becomes united with the supreme soul, enjoying a godly status with godly qualities.

Apsara sculptures also hint how the mind that was so sensitive to external impressions becomes insensitive to worldly aspects and becomes one with the *nāda*/sound, and becomes rapidly absorbed in *cidākāśa* (*citta* and *ākāśa*). In the author's opinion, the *Apsara* where she is depicted as a Goddess Bhairavi (Goddess of *Kriyā śakti*) indicates how an individual, after surrendering to *nāda*, loses worldly consciousness and merges into universal consciousness from individual consciousness like each wave merging in the ocean.

3. *NĀDAYOGA*

Nādayoga is a composite word, comprising 'nāda' and 'yoga'. To understand the essence of *Nādayoga,* it is essential to know what yoga means. Yoga is derived from the root word *Yuj*, which means to unite with the self. When the *Icchā śakti* – the great will, *Jñāna śakti* – the knowledge, and *Kriyā śakti* – the power of actions, are united and are in harmony, it is yoga. In other words, a union of body, mind and spirit, in absolute harmony, resulting in oneness with the self is yoga. Yoga is a system of exercise, which helps the body and mind to be in order, to achieve tranquillity of mind and a spiritual insight. Yoga means the union of self with truth; it is gained through a successful *viyoga* (detachment) from the false. Yoga recommends to get away from finite objects (and its limited joys, which further is the cause of dissatisfaction and sorrow) and enter into a realm of bliss, which is lasting.

"Yogaha chitta vrutti nirodha" – According to Maharsi Patañjali,
yoga is that which locks the movement of mind and thought.

The paths for realising the supreme soul and the meaning of self (*Ātma Jñāna*) is of many ways like *Jñāna yoga*, *Bhakti yoga*, *Rāja yoga*, *Haṭa yoga*, *Kriyā yoga*, *Karma yoga* and so on. *Jñāna yoga* is the path of knowledge. By controlling the wandering mind, paying attention to the inner longing of the soul, through the study of related scriptures and meditating on the subject, one can detach from worldly pleasures and pains and enter into a realm of peaceful and eternal world of bliss. In the process, the personality is transformed from the level of mere existence to a creative personality. In the *Apsara* sculptures of Belur temple, the core theme is based on the philosophy of *Jñāna yoga* and *Kriyā yoga* (*Nādayoga*). Austerities, study of scriptures and self-surrender constitute the yoga of purificatory action, which is *Kriyā yoga*. By constantly engaging oneself in the practice of yoga, the self-controlled yogi disentangles from all material contamination and achieves the highest stage of transcendental happiness. To be aware of one's position in relation to God, that is, to know that soul is part and parcel of the supreme God, is called self-realisation and that is the goal of *Jñāna yoga*.

By an enquiry into what is real and unreal, eternal or ephemeral, one can control the wandering mind and get rid of the *rājasik* and *tāmasik* tendencies. *Nādayoga* is one such path of *Kriyā yoga*, where sound and its manifestations lead a man to the destiny of supreme bliss.

NĀDA

Nāda means the cosmic sound, the deep humming sound like the drone. It is a force of nature and an instrument of God. Etymologically, *nāda* is the sound that is produced by the vibrations of anything. Sound or *śabda* is a form of energy and the source of knowledge. It is elevated as the divine sound or the *śabda Brahman*. The compact mass of energy that resides in *śabda* is called *bindu*, and that which resides in nāda is called *Nāda bindu*. *Nādayoga* is the union of the human soul to the supreme soul through the path of *nāda*. It may be an outward expression of *Āhata Nādayoga*, where the mind gets involved with music heard by the ears, or may be an inward journey of *Anāhata Nādayoga*, where *nāda* is experienced in isolation of sensory organs. The science of sound involves not only becoming aware of audible frequencies, but also frequencies that are inaudible to the ears.

Nāda is from the root word 'nad', meaning to flow. It is classified as divine because it is a stream of consciousness or the flow of inner sound current. The level of sound propagates from grossest to the subtlest. The exploration of consciousness through sounds is *Nādayoga*, and listening to these sounds in all their forms, is the practice of *Nādayoga*. The goal of *Nādayoga* is *samādhi*, a state of equilibrium. The thoughts that create ripples in the mind no longer disturb the mind, when it is under the influence of *Nādayoga*. True peace begins when the reality of soul and its divine nature is experienced, which can happen by a process of concentration. The spiritual realms that is within us can be approached only when we tap within, through meditation, and realise the realm of bliss. *Nāda* is the support through which one can dwell within, elevate to the world beyond, experience the celestial sound and realise the warmth of the inner light.

Human mind easily fixes on sounds that are heard. It gets into the melody and *laya* (rhythm) and the listener gets involved in it. Mind responds well to vibrations at the frequency matching to their own mental resonance. This is called the magic of music as the vibrations of sound relieve the mental stress and soothe the mind. *Nādayoga* is the ancient spiritual art and a science of inner transformations, through sound and tone. Sound has an operative role. The divine energy of *nāda* calms down the suffering heart of all beings. The Vedas and Upaniṣads had more of sound and rhythm, which were used as a source of healing and upliftment. The *samagana* emphasized on harmony between speech, tune and rhythm. A great number of texts are united under the name *Gandharva veda* – the veda of celestial musicians. These texts refer to the metaphysics of the science of sound. *Śabda* or sound is classified into:

1. *Sphota* – the bursting.
2. *Nāda* – the movement, the drone and the force that make the sound blossom.
3. *Anāhata* – the sound from unstruck or the unbeaten origin, which is in a latent form within. It is explained as one's own sound vibrations, close to self, and heard by yogis and seers.
4. *Āhata* – the audible sound that is created by the striking of two surfaces, heard by all humans and animals, that is within the decible and frequency range.

Nāda is a classification of sound. It is the pleasant flow of sound which is perceived by the auditory apparatus, and interpreted by the brain. Meditation is seeing God within. Meditation on sound is a universal path to self-realisation accessible to everyone, irrespective of age, gender or religion. The chant of sacred mantras or the classical music, gives scope for the human mind to move into the realm of melodies and then fix upon the rhythm, which calls for the intellect to get involved and thus enjoys a state of *samādhi*, supreme bliss, or the state of ultimate realisation as the mind gets detached from the physical world.

Sound is the source of all knowledge, for which reason it is called *śabda Brahman*. When the relationship between sound and knowledge is analysed, the fact becomes evident that:

– Knowledge is dependent on language or the *bhāṣā*.

– Language is an evolved expression of group of words.

– Words are evolved of various *śabdas* (sounds) in combination.

– Each sound that is produced from the larynx, is born from the *Prāṇa śakti* – the vital breath force at the navel region, which comes out supported by *īcchā* (will) and *Jñāna śakti* (knowledge). It is expressed as a word, which comes out through the articulation of throat, tongue and lips. So the basic and fundamental unit of speech is *śabda* or sound, which is a manifestation of the vibrations of *nāda* and hence sound is elevated to the status of *nāda Brahman* or *śabda Brahman*. The two evolved forms of speech are executed either as speech (words or *Vāk*) or singing – the music, which is a combined outcome of melody and rhythm. The union of *buddhi* (intellect) with the *nāda* of sound is called *Nādayoga*.

4. *ĀHATA NĀDA* – THE POWER OF SOUND

Nāda is an outcome of vibrations, which is present everywhere. We are not aware of the sound within due to lack of attention. Presently our attention is scattered throughout our body and goes out to the external world through the five senses. When the attention is conserved, focussed and diverted to within, one can experience the inner vibrations, which is called *Anāhata nāda*. When the vibrations are perceived by the exterior ear, it is called *Āhata nāda*. *Āhata* means struck, or beaten sound arising from a known origin.

Āhata is the sound manifested by air vibrations. It is the sound that is heard by the ears, encompassing all that is heard and unheard, within the decibel and frequency range of humans and animals. The deeper we go into the vibrations of sound, the greater is the withdrawal from worldly complexities. The union with the music that is audible to material ears, is considered as an outward expression of *Nādayoga*.

Human mind is always attracted by certain sounds and gets absorbed in it, because sound is the force of nature, and there is a relationship that exists between sound and mind. Mind runs towards the sound and in doing so forgets the external world all together and finds solace in *nāda*/sound. A person who is ignorant of the intricacies of music also stands still, when he hears melodious music. In the presence of rhythmic sound, the mind refuses to think about anything other than sound. After hearing music, it experiences a stage of joy and exclaims that it enjoyed it well and knew nothing of the external world. This proves that it was enjoying a state of oneness with music, feeling refreshed and renewed in energy, like after a deep sleep. This also proves the superiority of the effect of sound on human mind. Mind can easily be controlled by the power of *Nādayoga* as *nāda* entraps the mind and leads the body from gross to subtle level. The *nāda* of mantras or the sacred chants has a profound influence on mind. Mantra means *man* (the mind) + *tra* (to protect). The sound of mantra protects the mind from its aimless wandering. The *nāda* of music has a strong magnetic power to draw human mind towards it. As long as a person is with the cosmic vibrations of sound energy, he enjoys aesthetic pleasure. Once the vibrations stop, the blissful state gradually gets entangled in a worldly state of mind. To enjoy a perpetual state of bliss and tranquillity, one has to undertake the journey towards *Nādayoga*. It is the journey in the pathway of *Nādayoga* that the mind reaches the destination of perpetual state of bliss and tranquillity. The aim of *Āhata Nādayoga* is to purify and harmonise the gross and the subtle bodies in alignment, with their natural vibrations and to bring the individuals to a higher state of awareness.

Wind instruments, stringed instruments and percussion instruments like drums or cymbals have each a distinct, different and particular effect on the physical body. The sound of music which touches the physical plane, affects the nervous system, soothes the senses, enjoys a state of ecstasy and unites one with music, which is a spiritual or *sāttvik* effect. While the mind and intellect are enjoying a state of harmony and oneness with the music, the body sways involuntarily in response to this ecstasy. This sway of body is dance. Human body sways to the melody and rhythm of the music. It is essential to know why the body responds to rhythmic beat. It is because there is a perpetual rhythm in the body, which is a sign of life. It can be compared to the breath, the sign of soul within, the movement of the air, and the rhythm of the breath as inhalation and exhalation to sustain life, which are the unmanifest form of the *Prāṇa vāyu*. The rhythmic beat of the heart and pulsation, is the sign of good health and one's mood depend on heartbeats. This aspect of rhythm that is already existing in the body harmonises with the rhythm aspect of music. This is the reason why music touches the deepest part of man's being, effecting in the unfoldment of the soul.

5. *ANĀHATA NĀDA* – THE VIBRATIONS OF SOUL AND MUSIC

Sufi Hazarat Inayat Khan has explained the metaphysics of vibrations, in his book *The Mysticism of Music, Sound and Word*. According to him, all creations are associated with vibrations, which Hindus have called *nāda*. He who knows the secrets of the sounds, knows the mystery of the whole universe.

The sense of music, and attraction to music is because there is music in the depth of our being. Sound/music is the sensation received by the ears from air. Singing is an outcome of vibrations, of the vocal cord, the source of which is breath or *prāṇa* – the vital energy that is within the body. The audibility of breath manifests as voice, music or speech, which means the primordial form of it lies within. The vibration of this inner music or *nāda*, which is in an un-manifest form is very fine and not audible to material ears; it is one's own sound vibrations that is experienced by the *ṛṣis* and seers. *Anāhata* is totally private, personal and exclusive to the yogi. This is the *Anāhata nāda*, the sound of unstruck music which is only experienced and hence is divine in origin. This becomes audible when the external ears are shut and the realisation of self is in progress. The soul gets into bliss, harmony, relaxation and self-realisation with this *Anāhata* music.

Nāda, the vibrations of the sound, which the material ears can perceive, is manifestation of *Āhata nāda*, which is born by the striking of two surfaces. The origin of vibrations could be either from a natural source or from an artificial source. The cosmic energy is one of the natural sources of vibrations to which the mind responds with good effect. Every vibration as a rule has its own dimensions of space and time. The reach of this is according to the fineness of plane and the starting point. After manifestation, the vibrations get merged in its original source. The intensity of vibrations at different directions produces different emotions, which surfaces out when it is active. This rule holds good to both *Āhata* and *Anāhata nāda*. When the vibration activity is controlled properly, an atmosphere of harmony establishes, expressed as joy or peace.

The soul is an embodiment of mind, thought and body (actions). The harmony between these aspects leads to harmony with self. The soul rejoices momentarily in the comforts enjoyed by the body but it yearns for true bliss, which is overlooked by the body, resulting in a state of disharmony. Every human has to have harmony of three aspects like individual, universal and eternal. Individual harmony is with aspects like harmony between body, mind and soul universal is the harmony between individuals. The eternal harmony is the harmony of conciousness, which means all things and beings live and move together, co-exist, observing harmony and live peacefully (which is remotely controlled by the unseen power). The key for harmony with music lies in the notes of the *rāga* (a musical mode or order of sound). Any one single note, which is beyond the order of that particular mode, disturbs the structure and melody of the tune resulting in disharmony which is not tolerated by the ears. A parallel or a miniature for the law of harmony in universe is traced only in the art of music. Hence, among all the different arts, art of music is considered sacred and divine. The music of both *Anāhata* and *Āhata* uplifts the soul, to unite with the Supreme Bliss. The process involved in focussing the mind and channelising it to the world of music is called *Nādayoga*, which is studied under the branch of *Kriyā yoga* - according to Swami Śivananda.

A yogi under a deep meditation of *Anāhata Nādayoga*, experiences certain sacred sounds, which are recognised as ten different sounds. The *vīṇa* of Goddess Saraswatī, flute of Lord Kṛṣṇa and the *Damaru nāda* of Lord Śiva, are the symbolic sounds which are the source of revelation to *Nāda* yogis.

Nādayoga is the union with the sound, both inaudible and audible. It is the awareness that moves from the outer to the inner realms. The upliftment balances and heals the mind and spirit, which energises the soul. The inaudible or the *Anāhata Nādayoga* can be described as the sound current, the stream of life consciousness, the cosmic rhythmical vibration. All matter is made up of energy, with a sound quality to them. *Anāhata* is the union with the inner sound. A commoner may remain ignorant of this inner *nāda*, in the utter psychological darkness.

Nādayoga or union with sound, for a commoner, is through the *Āhata* (struck or heard sound) and *Vyakta nāda* (that which manifests) and for a yogi, it is through *Anāhata*, the unstruck, unmanifest, soundless sounds. In worship sessions, the blowing of conch, bells and cymbals are considered as sacred sounds to focus the mind. The flute of Lord Kṛṣṇa is symbolic of the sound of the soul (as the vital force does not undergo the manipulation by the larynx), which is the source of all revelation to the yogis, to whom it was revealed from within.

There are ten inner sounds a *Nāda yogi* experiences with *Anāhata nāda*, before merging with the *nāda* of 'OM' – the infinite sound without barriers. This is the spirituality of *Nādayoga*, where one gets attuned to the inaudible sounds, and hears the voice of the inner teacher. It is the union with the *ātman*, the divine, through the mystic spheres of the inner sound, which is attainable only when the yogi can silence the mind to stillness. The sound develops through ten different aspects as the journey progresses inwards, because of its manifestation through ten different tubes or *nādis* of the body and their vibration frequencies, which are audible only to the inner ears and has some significance. It is the gradually increasing activity of meditation, which causes the vibrations to materialise. Each step in their activity becomes distinct from each other.

1. Chin - Sound of silver bells, a sound of awakening.
2. Chin chin - Which is feeble, indicating that there exists something beyond the self.
3. Bell - A sound that alerts the mind towards spirituality.
4. Conch - A sacred sound, the vibrations of which inspire the mind to move in a *sāttvik* way.
5. Stringed instrument - Movement of mind in the gentle graceful melodies, whose audibility is feeble. Spiritually, it is expressed as a vibration that is appealing to the ears.
6. Cymbals - Guides the yogi for the rhythm; when there is sway of the body, they dance in response to the spiritual insight or when the mind is in tune with the melody it overflows as singing or dancing.
7. Flute - When the soul is instigated by divine *nāda*, this sound of bamboo flute shrills in the ears.
8. Small kettledrum - Mind responding to rhythm aspect, for vibrations of high frequencies, and audibility of a higher range.
9. Mṛdaṅga (double drum) - Understanding the rhythmic vibrations of the inner self which is an evolved phase of spirituality.
10. Thunder (sound of ether) - Oneness with the ethereal and highly refined sound. It is the most sacred of all sounds as it is not a man-made sound. It gets manifested in *ākāśa*, the only element of *pañcha tattvas*, which does not get polluted and the sound of thunder gets manifested in *ākāśa*.

These stages are compared to natural sounds like, twittering of insects, sparrows, humming of a bee, flow of running water, whistle of the wind, the roaring of the sea (waves have a rhythm in their sound vibration) and finally the sound of thunder. Yogis have practically experienced these stages of meditation, totally shutting off to the external sounds. These experiences of the stages of oneness with sound is however a very personal feeling. They are compared to the natural sounds like the twittering of the birds at the first stage as it is not a continuous sound. The sound of waves is a continuous process much like the rhythmic beat and movement within the body and hence compared to a stage of meditation. The third stage is compared to the sound of thunderbolt, which is a sudden revelation along with the light of knowledge. The practice of *Nādayoga*, elevates a person to become one with the divine sound. It opens up the currents, resonating with the stream of universal love consciousness, that flows throughout the universe, and our bodies. The *Anāhata nāda* is related to the heart *chakra* and one cannot hear the inner sound until one has progressed in the spiritual path to the level of heart *chakra*. The study of the subject, *Nādayoga*, is different from the practice of *Nādayoga* in reality. The search for the sound in the body may take years or a lifetime of spiritual practice to achive the ultimate union with the self.

In the *Apsara* sculptures of Belur, the tuning of the stringed instrument (tuning of the mind), the effect of the music of flute (soulful music) the oneness with rhythm at various stages, and finally her oneness with the supreme, are sculptured beautifully. The awareness stages of *Anāhata Nādayoga* are linked and projected as stages of *Āhata Nādayoga* in the *Apsaras* of Belur.

6. CONTROL OF MIND THROUGH *NĀDA*

The goal of *Nādayoga* is to lead a human soul back to the silence within. Music is nothing but sculpturing the silence. It is a vehicle to inner bliss. Every student of *Nādayoga* has to control the wandering mind effectively, before embarking on the journey of *Nādayoga*.

Music can take us to the very core of our emotional body. *Nāda* gives an opportunity to make up with the odd behaviour, which does not serve any purpose. This process results in an increase of our own vibration frequencies. Music is one of the most powerful therapy forms through which one can experience the multi-dimensional being that we truly are. Sound serves the purpose of a sharp goad to control *citta*/mind, which roves in the pleasure garden of sensual objects.

Sound also serves the purpose of a snare, to bind the ever wandering/fleeing deer (deer is compared to the mind). Unless the mind is cultured and controlled, the *Indriyās* cannot be controlled. Ancient sages have rightly said *Mana eva manushyāṇām, Kāraṇam bandha - Mokṣayah* (*Nārada Upaniṣad*). Meaning, mind alone is the cause for man's release and bondage. Mind is the seat of all emotions and feelings. Intellect is the discriminating faculty judging the right from the wrong and real from the unreal. Mind is also a seat of impulses and feelings which is common to all living creatures. Mind is defined as a flow of thoughts, and the banks of the river is compared with the intellect which guides and directs the flow of water. When the banks are not firm, the water runs amok. So too when the intellect of a human is not firm and determined, mind functions as it wants and gets tossed hither and thither by the vicissitudes of circumstance and environment. The intellect governs the mind which remains firm, only on training imparted to it.

Every aspirant has to prepare himself to understand the purpose and goal of any form of yoga and especially *Nādayoga*. The first and most important demand is the control of the wandering mind. Any amount of religious practice or worship session, with mantra or tantra, will not be fruitful, until the mind is applied with concentration in it. The person whose mind is under the control of his intellect is a blessed person to whom any path of yoga bestows the aspired result. *Manō-nigraha* or concentration comes with personal effort, which is indispensable for *Nādayoga*. Even though *nāda* has the power to draw the human mind towards it, it calls for active participation of the subtle mind (mind along with intellect) by the seeker, like it is in any other branch of *Jñāna* or *Kriyā yoga*. After a successful practice of *Manō-nigraha* (controlling the wandering mind, which can be compared to B.F. 6a), one has to precondition the mind to understand the purpose and goal of *Nādayoga*. They are like four essential pillars, called *Sādhanā chatuśtya*:

1. *Nityānitya vivēka* – The mind has to be matured enough to differentiate between the real and unreal (*māyā*) source of happiness. It is the ability to discriminate between the right and the wrong path, between the permanent and non-permanent source of bliss called *viveka*, for knowledge without *viveka* is not fruitful.
2. *Bhoga virāgya* – It is understanding the *sāttvik* support for a better spiritual life. It is also a realisation of renunciation, highlighting the benefits of renouncing worldly pleasures, for the attainment of a perpetual blissful state of mind. One has to prepare to shake off the wordly pleasures, for they are just the sources of momentary pleasures, satisfying the sense organs, and not the means of bliss.
3. *Śama-dama* – This means calmness of the mind, withdrawal from the storm of emotions and passions, related to mind and body. The qualities like anger, lust, greed, jealousy, and pride are like obstacles between the human and the supreme soul. Unless and until these obstacles that enhance the feeling of thirst and hunger for pleasures are cleared, it is impossible to experience a blissful state of mind, attaining *Sat sampatti*, the six kinds of inner wealth.
4. *Śraddhā* – It is the aspect of faith, backed up by effort, sincerity and devotion to understand and assimilate the contents of the scriptures. The aspirant of *Nādayoga* has to have perseverance and not get disturbed by base level achievements, negative thoughts, or emotional restlessness, which manifest as obstacles in achieving the goal of yoga. As described in *Bhagavadgītā* (Ch. VI. 24), yoga is to be practised with an eager and decisive mind. To practise with an un-despairing heart is the simple secret for the highest success in *Nādayoga*.

All the Upaniṣads have prescribed these four qualifications to make one fit, to get into the path of spirituality.

Nādayoga/music is elevating, inspiring, strengthening and invigorating to mind. It vibrates in memory and thus is a therapy too, as it soothes the brain and relaxes the nervous tension. Music is a series of harmonious vibrations, that are electrical in nature and hence affects the emotions also. Music steers the mind to one point quickly and helps to commune with the lord. Music is elevated to the status of *nāda Brahman* and *Samaveda* is full of music.

7. *KUṆḌALINĪ CHAKRA*

Nādayoga employs *nāda* or resonance not only for easing out all the problems connected with the mind and consciousness but also for raising one's level of consciousness, through various subtle psychic centres in the body called *chakras*. The human body has seven levels of functioning. On each level, the energy moves in a particular characteristic way. Yogic tradition connects the *Anāhata nāda* to *Anāhata chakra* and to the movement of *Kuṇḍalinī*. In *Nādayoga*, the concentration is on these deeper and inner sounds, moving from the outer to the inner realm, moving from the awareness of outer world to the inner sounds. In this form of meditation, music of *Āhata nāda* that falls on the outer ears, gently eases the mind into a relaxed state, advances into concentration and focuses the mind into one location, and leads to the understanding of *Anāhata nāda*. When the *Icchā śakti* and *Jñāna śakti* (the great will and the power of knowledge) are focussed, this meditation is highly enjoyable and comparatively an effortless form of meditation. In the process, every part of the body and every thought gets purified and balanced by the sounds that the mind is focussing on.

This transformation of the mind from gross to subtle level is compared to the movement of *Kuṇḍalinī śakti*. *Kuṇḍalinī* is the latent magazine of cosmic power or *śakti* that resides in every human body called *Kuṇḍa* – the pot. There is much hidden potential in every human being. On activation, it blossoms, bringing out all the strength, and God-given talents that are inherent within, which is natural, original and genuine. It is comparable to the activation of the divine core within, which builds up the inner strength, equipoise, keeping one peaceful, cheerful perennially. This supreme force of energy is visualised as a serpent coiled into three-and-a-half loops, and lying motionless in a dormant state, irrespective of age, sex and gender. The three coils symbolise the *Icchā*, *Jñāna* and the *Kriyā śakti*. The cosmic power of energy manifests in three mighty forces, visualised as these coils of the snake.

1. *Icchā śakti* is the great will, which moulds the object that is formed within.
2. *Jñāna śakti* is the power to know, the power of knowledge, which illumines the mental formation of the object that is moulded within.
3. *Kriyā śakti* is the force of power to act. It is a fight of consciousness riding on the mind.
4. The half coil is the power of creativity (the outcome of the three forces). Any action of creativity is backed by will and knowledge of action.

This *Kuṇḍalinī śakti* is considered as divine and godly power, which does not respond to any amount of worldly riches but moves only on spiritual practices or some disciplines of yoga that train the body, mind and intellect. Once awakened from the sleeping state, *Kuṇḍalinī* serpent power tears open the layers of *māyā* (illusion) enmeshing it, and ascends upward in the body to unite with the supreme power Brahman – the ultimate truth. *Kuṇḍalinī śakti* is called as the awakener of pure knowledge. It is an abstract visualisation and philosophical phenomenon, the movement of which cannot be traced in the physiological body, but can be studied by the evolution of thoughts and actions of the person.

The *Kuṇḍalinī śakti* has to pass through seven areas of spinning energy called *chakras*. *Chakras* are the nerve plexus, associated with a specific number of nerves called 'yoga nāḍīs', which are concentrated on certain regions of spinal canal of vertebral column. These seven *chakras* as are called:

1. *Mūlādhāra* – situated at the pelvic floor
2. *Svādhisthāna* - situated between navel and genitals
3. *Maṇīpura* – situated at navel region and above it up to the breast bone tip
4. *Anāhata* – situated at heart region
5. *Viśuddha* – situated at throat region
6. *Ājñā* – situated between eyebrows
7. *Sahasrara* – situated at the crown part of the head.

The four stages of sounds and the divine descent of *nāda Brahman* like the *Paravāṇi*, *Paśyanti*, *Madhyama* and *Vaikhari* (ref. Ch. 3.8, Part II of this book) are specifically compared with the ascent of *Kuṇḍalinī śakti*, or the ascent of awareness in a yogi.

1. & 2. *Mūlādhāra* and *Svādhisthāna chakra* – The *Para nāda* or the primal subtle sound is visualised to be at the *Mūlādhāra chakra* as *Nāda bindu*, where it is in an un-differentiable state as it does not stir or produce vibrations at audible frequency. Both the *Mūlādhāra* and *Svādhisthāna chakras* are compared to the state of *Para nāda*. *Mūlādhāra* is represented by a flower of 4-6 petals which corresponds to the vibration of 'yoga nāḍīs' in the physical body.

3. *Maṇīpura chakra* is compared to the state of *Paśyanti* at the level of navel. It is experienced by the yogis as observing or visualising the sound. It is the navel region probably because the baby first tears off at navel, from dark and non-movement state, to a visual state of world, which in turn means the yogi is introduced to the form of music. The stage of expansion of knowledge, which is associated with the *Maṇīpur chakra*, after the interest in music is kindled is indicated by study of scriptures and guidance by a Guru. The activity of 'yoga nāḍī' is represented through ten petals.

4. *Anāhata chakra* or the heart *chakra* is compared to the *Madhyama* state of 'Nādayoga', which means middle or intermediate state. It is the sound of the heart (just the melody and the rhythm of a tune, and not the words of tongue). Psychologically, *Anāhata chakra* is the state when one gets into the capacity of loving another soul or anything, which means the mind is set on it with intelligence from the previous stage. It is also explained to get into flashes of knowledge, as the mind observes the glow of melody and rhythm, which makes a person intuitive by nature. Air is the element associated at heart *chakra* in *Madhyama* state. The sound physically descends from the non-audible to an audible state, with a hearing range of frequency. In heart is situated the *Jñānalōka*. *Anāhata chakra* is represented with a flower of 12 petals. The activity of 12 'yoga nāḍīs' is associated with *buddhi* or the intellect.

5. *Viśuddha chakra* is associated with *Vaikharī* stage of *Nādayoga*. The fifth *chakra* is located at the laryngeal plexus, nerve centre at the throat pit. *Viśuddha* means clean which means *nāda* is clearly audible at a hearing range, which comes out through larynx (voice box), tongue and mouth. It is the dwelling place of Goddess Saraswatī – Goddess of the power of knowledge. Speech or singing is also the gateway connecting the physical body to the spiritual thoughts. Psychologically, a human while singing (according to the path of *Nādayoga*) believes in God. The gratitude and devotion to God is articulated through the faculty of speech, which is associated with his eyes seeing the power of God, and ears hearing the mysterious sounds. Hence *Vaikharī* stage, at *Viśuddha chakra*, is the stage of perceptual knowledge of sound, the divine sound conveying its meaning to the mind. The mind at this stage is devoid of worldly desires and is in a calm, relaxed, and peaceful stage, which is fit for the advanced, deeper contemplation and meditation. The person, backed up by his *Icchā śakti* (will) and *Jñāna śakti* (knowledge) gets into the stage of action, the *Kriyā śakti*, and expresses as creative skill. The *Viśudha chakra* is associated with the element of sky, to the capacities of the infinite nature of purity and vastness of the sky, which is compared with the *Vaikharī* stage of *Nādayoga*.

The sound or *nāda Brahman* has descended from, transcendental to visual, mental and intellectual stages of articulation, which is also compared to the embryo, the first leaves, buds and flowers of a plant. The four stages of sounds are drawn parallel from *Mūlādhāra* to *Viśuddha chakra*. *Viśuddha chakra* is represented with a flower of 16 petals, which means the vibrations of 'yoga nāḍīs' are the highest.

* The Belur Cennakēśava temple *vimāna* had sixteen corners, which the author believes to be the representation of the sixteen petals of *Viśuddha chakra*. Physically and psychologically, a human is elevated as *śuddha* or pure, at this level of awareness. This is the gateway connecting the physical body to the spiritual thought. Purity of thought for every devotee was the aim of King Viśnuvardhana. With this vision, the Hoysala ruler elevated the psychological status of his subjects.

6. *Ājñā chakra* has two petals as compared to *Viśuddha chakra*, which is represented by 16 petals, the most active state of 'yoga nāḍīs'. Hence *Ājñā chakra* means moving to the inner zones with concentration at the region of *bhru madhya* (between the two eyebrows, which is the seat of the soul). It represents the control of intellectual perception, intuition and comprehension.

The mind is under perfect control and the person is transformed into a visionary by nature. The abstract ideas are experienced here. The spiritual activities are linked to a state of pure awareness. [In the *Apsara* sculptures, it is probably indicated by the three male artists playing small drum, flute and big drum, indicative of the *Apsara*'s advancement in her meditation on *Anāhata nāda*]. The figure where the man is playing on the flute (B.F. 11) has an idol of Kṛṣṇa at the base, which suggests the 'Nāda yogi', at this stage of awareness, experiences, the cosmic sound of flute through his inner ears. Focus on *Anāhata nāda* steadies the mind, gives contact with the current of sound and light within, and leads it to the final stage of *samādhi* at *Sahasrara chakra* – the world beyond.

7. *Sahasrara chakra* is the seventh and the highest psychic centre, visualised above the crown of the head and hence called crown *chakra*. The union with the supreme soul, *Parambrahman* takes place here. It is conceived as a stage where ignorance and illusion (*avidyā* and *māyā*) are not existing, and the person is at the highest point of spiritual advancement. The person is liberated from the veil of *māyā* and is in a free state of mind without any binding or pulling towards material comforts. In this state, the self or *ātman* unites with *Paramātmā* (*param* + *ātmā*) – the supreme soul. The power of knowledge is limitless, total self-awareness and a non-dual state of universal joy is experienced here. The *Icchā śakti* of *Mūlādhāra chakra* and *Jñāna śakti* of *Anāhata chakra* reflects as *Kriyā śakti* – a creative phase with a casual body. The yogini attaining the status of goddess is indicated in *Apsara* sculpture (B.F. 9 and 22) as a goddess with a crown and holding a *khatwanga* (skull mace), *kapāla* (skull bowl) in hand which are the aspects of Lord Śiva to indicate oneness with him. Her powerful gait of moving forward is suggestive of *Kriyā śakti* in action. The mini skulls which adorn her crown are indicative of the sacred letters of the Sanskrit alphabet, which is indicative of her command over the language (of *Vaikharī* state). This is the ultimate state of *Nādayoga*, the merging of *Jīvātmā* with *Paramātmā* to become one whole.

* In B.F. 25, the *Apsara* indicates the positions of the *Mūlādhāra chakra* in her left hand, and *Sahasrara chakra* in her right hand. The dwarf attendants indicate the playing of flute, *mṛdaṅga*, and singing. In totality it is *Saṅgīta* which is the recital of *vādya*, *gīta* and *nṛtya* (dance). It is a beautiful representation of the path of *Kuṇḍalinī śakti*, through the *Āhata Nādayoga*. The four stages of *nāda*, and the seven *chakras* are analysed in relation to the activities depicted in the *Apsara* sculptures.

8. THE FOUR STAGES OF SOUND

Around 24 *Apsara* sculptures are analysed for depicting the various stages *Āhata Nādayoga*, which are correlated with *Vijñānamaya kośa*. Hence, it is required to know the four stages of *nāda*/sound to appreciate the sculptures representing their involvement with music.

Nāda is sound. Sound, supported by the capacities of will and knowledge, evolves as words or speech (*vāk*), which is the source for knowledge or *Jñāna* in the universe. Hence *nāda* is also called *nāda Brahman* or *śabda Brahman*. The manifestations of sound are four, from the highest to the lowest sound frequencies. When the four physical manifestations of sound/*nāda* are correlated with the psyche of awareness levels, indicating oneness with *nāda*, it is elevated as 'Nādayoga'.

Para is the transcendent sound beyond the comprehension of senses. It is heard only at a higher level of consciousness. *Para nāda* has the highest sound frequencies, so high that it has no vibrations and is a still sound. It is the pure energy and unmanifest sound. *Para* stage is indicative of the mind listening to the distant divine sound of *Paravāṇī* to which *Apsara*'s mind is attracted. This indicates the stage of concentration to hear the *Paravāṇī*, as focus is always cultivated.

Stages of *Nāda* and *Nādayoga*

- *Para* – Primordial sound (focus and concentration)
- *Paśyanti* – *Svādhyaya* – Expansion of knowledge
- *Madhyama* – Mind and intellect – Meditation on sound
- *Vaikharī* – Speech – Evolved form

Paśyanti stage is followed by concentration on *Paravāṇī*, a visualisation of sound like hearing music in dreams. This occurs when all the external sounds disappear, and a ringing sound of cosmic origin is heard. This is compared to *Svādhyaya* or the study of scriptures, which is depicted in an *Apsara* sculpture. This is a sacred stage of expanding one's knowledge about a subject or *Nādayoga* – a path in which *Apsara* is intending to proceed.

Madhyama is the intermediate stage, a mental sound, where mind and intellect are in combined activity. The mind is first tuned to *nāda* and it moves to explore the melody of music. This stage is depicted through *Apsara*'s involvement with the stringed instrument. The second stage is her involvement in rhythm, where the intellect guides. It is the stage of absorbing the *laya* or rhythm, which is expressed through her involvement with various types of percussion instruments. This also is the stage of *Anāhata chakra*, through *Āhata nāda*. There are many graceful dancing postures where the grace of body movement unites with the rhythm (*tāla*) and depicted as graceful rhythmic dance movements. The rhythm that is understood is shown in her foot, which she is tapping to the rhythm.

Vaikharī is the fourth stage, where the sound frequencies are lower and hence audible, modified, heard and felt through the senses. It is an evolved stage of speech, where *Apsara* is singing. It is a phase of *Saṅgīta* where she is involved with melody (*vādya*, like flute) and rhythm (*tāla*). Singing is an evolved form like speech, in the stages of *Nādayoga*.

This is followed by a depiction of three male figures playing instruments like flute and *mṛdaṅga*, which suggests two things. Listening to the art of others for refinement in one's musical knowledge or it may be viewed for the capacity of hearing *Anāhata nāda* – the divine sounds of kettledrum, flute and big drum. This represents the higher level of meditation in *Nādayoga*.

The next stage of total union with *nāda*, which elevates one to the state of godliness, where *Apsara* is united with the supreme soul through *Nādayoga* and she is depicted as a goddess, will be discussed later.

Even though *Apsara* appears in the same costume in all sculptures, her mind is not focussed on her appearance (as seen in *Jāgrut avasthā*), which is a proof that she is withdrawn from the gross body. She is associated with an instrument to show that her thoughts are channelised to the field of music.

When the four stages of *Nādayoga* are compared to the movement of *Kuṇḍalinī śakti* of awareness, it can be viewed as:

Paravāṇī stage - *Mūlādhāra* and *Svādhisthāna chakra*
Paśyanti stage - *Maṇīpura chakra*
Madhyama - *Anāhata chakra*
Vaikhaṛī - *Viśuddha chakra*
Contemplation of *Anāhata nāda* - *Ājñā chakra*
Union with the supreme soul - *Sahasrara chakra*

A SYNTHESIS OF NĀDA – THE SOUND

	1 Four stages of the sound	2 Manifestation in the body	3 Plexus or chakras	4 Nature of the sound	5 Manifestation of the sound	6 Analogy	7 Bracket figure numbers	8 Representation in the sculptures.
1	Paravāṇī avyakta nāda (sound in subtle form)	Prāṇa – the breath, the seat of the sound (first manifestation of the voice)	Mūlādhāra and svādhisthāna	High frequency, still sound, with no vibrations	Transcendental undifferentiated sound, non-audible	(1) Embryo of the seed (2) Foetus in the womb (3) Latent heat in the fire wood	27, 4 and 2	Parrot is the symbol of paravāṇī. Approach of paravāṇī in figs 27 and 4. Concentration on paravāṇī, Fig. 2.
2	Paśyanti	Mind goaded by icchā śakti, runs towards the sound, along with the subtle inner vision	Maṇīpura (at the navel region)	Visual manifestation of seeing the colour and form, sound energy is in agitation.	Ultrasonic sound; audible for yogis.	(1) First leaves (2) First call of the baby after birth. (3) Friction of the fire wood	28	Study of the scriptures as svādhyaya.
3	Madhyama	Predominence of jñāna śakti, mind is governed by the intellect, but expressed as mime language.	Anāhata – the region of the heart.	Sound heard only as melody and rhythm.	Audible, but not evolved	(1) Buds which are yet to gain colour and fragrance (2) Cooing of the baby or the murmering sound (3) Smoke before the fire	(1) 14, 25, 29, 30 (2) 32, 24, 10, 8, 13 (3) 38, 19, 40	(1) Figures with stringed instruments (2) Percussion instruments (3) Dance postures
4	Vaikharī (gross form of sound)	Kriyā śakti – the power of creativity of speech, is expressed through the larynx – supported by the icchā and jñāna śaktis.	Viśuddha, larynx, throat and mouth	Sound heard as speech or singing. Lower limit of frequency and hence audible	Evolved phase of sound as speech, words, and sentences	(1) Blossom (2) Fully evolved speech (3) Full form of fire	12 and 20	Lady singing
			Sahasrara chakra	Nādayoga	Oneness of individual sound with the param brahman		9 and 22	*Apsara* depicted as a goddess, with the aspects of Lord Śiva

Paravāṇī finds manifestation in the *prāṇa, paśyanti* in the mind, *madhyama* in the *indriyas*, and *vaikharī* in the articulate expression. Articulation is the last, grossest manifestation of the divine descent of sound energy. These four stages of sound are viewed as the divine force of Goddess Lalitā (in the 81st stanza of *Lalita Sahasranama*) who is present in the minds of every devotee as,

Para pratykchiti rūpa paśyanti paradevatā.
Madhyama vaikharī rūpa bhakta manasa haṃsikā.

A major class of *Apsara* sculptures are associated with *Suṣupti avasthā* where she is totally engrossed in music, which are compared with the four different stages of *nāda*, that are *Para, Paśyanti, Madhyama* and *Vaikharī.*

Para is manifested in the *prāṇa*, the vital breath. *Para* in Sanskrit means remote or beyond, anything like the highest object. They are like root ideas or germ thoughts that can be compared with the awakening 'chin-chin' sound of small silver bells of the first stage of awareness in *Nādayoga*. *Para* is the vital breath, the primordial form of the divine voice, as voice is a manifestation of breath, which becomes audible and meaningful after it undergoes a process through the organs of voice. It is considered as the voice of silence, the voice of *ātman* – the divine self. *Para* is the highest manifestation of sound energy, which is beyond the reach of ordinary consciousness. It is the subtle form of sound energy with such high frequency that it is a still sound without vibrations. The concept of *Para nāda* is an abstract theme and in *Apsara* sculptures *Para nāda* is represented as a parrot, on which the *Apsara* is concentrating. *Para nāda* can be compared to the sound that is present with the foetus in the womb or can be compared to the embryo of a seed. Parrot is an analogy for speech. Next to human, probably it is the parrot which can speak some words and hence it is visualised in Hindu iconography, for primordial of speech – the *Para nāda*. Even in the days of *Yajurveda*, the parrot was tamed for it is described as uttering human speech. A goddess holding a parrot means she is the controller of the vital breath – the *prāṇa* – which manifests later as spoken language or knowledge.

Paśyanti is the second stage of the divine descent of sound, which can be visually experienced. *Paśyanti* is the mental manifestation of sound energy, where the organs of phonation are not active, but the letters are pronounced mentally. It is like seeing or observing sound mentally. A person with a subtle inner vision can experience this second stage of sound, which can be compared to the alerting sound of a big bell or an inspiring sound of a conch that leads to a *sāttvik* way. Will or the *Icchā śakti* plays a role at the *paśyanti* stage. The will to know and expand one's knowledge about *nāda* is the visualisation of *nāda*. It is like seeing the form and colour of Lord Śiva or Nārāyaṇa mentally as we chant the sacred names silently within with closed eyes. It is a stage of agitation as the mind struggles to know about it. In subtlety, it is lesser than the *Para nāda* and hence can be conceived as ultrasonic sound vibrations, which can be deciphered by people with inner vision. *Paśyanti* sound in manifestation is compared to the first cry of the baby as it is born or the first two leaves of the sprout, which is with a stage of agitation. In *Apsara* sculptures, it is indicated as a lady holding palm leaves in the act of studying scriptures and focussing her concentration on the expansion of knowledge. *Paśyanti* stage is like the plant being watered by mind; the mind is totally set on *nāda*.

Madhyama is the third stage of *nāda*, for which heart is the seat. *Madhyama* means middle in Sanskrit, and according to the stages of *Nādayoga* awareness, it can be compared to the gentle and graceful movement of sound emerging from the stringed or wind instrument. Sculptures showing *Apsaras* engrossed in playing several instruments probably indicate the state of *Madhyama*. It is an unexpressed state of sound (as expression of sound as voice occurs in the next stage), which is not totally evolved and hence indicated as instrumental music where only melody is heard and not the words. The seat of sound is the heart and not the tongue. *Madhyama* is compared to the cooing voice of an infant in which speech is yet to evolve or the stage of buds, which is nurtured by *buddhi* or intellect, but the colour and fragrance is yet to come out. The frequency of *Madhyama* stage is in an audible stage to normal ears and hence categorised as the first stage of gross sound. *Madhyama* stage of *Nādayoga* involves the activity of intellect, which is indicated as *Apsara* playing different stringed instruments for melody and percussion instruments of rhythm.

Vaikharī is last stage of the descent of divine sound which manifests as speech or voice, expressed through the voice box, tongue and throat, where the theme of the song or the intentions of the mind is conveyed clearly through speech. It is the fully evolved stage of *nāda*, the *Para vāk*, which is audible to everyone and hence a gross sound with lower frequency limit. It is compared to the evolved form of speech or singing act of humans, or the blossoms of the plant whose colour and fragrance are conveyed to the world. In *Apsara* sculptures, it is expressed as the lady singing. In *Nādayoga* awareness, *Vaikharī* is compared to the evolved phase that is full of peace and gratitude overflowing as words that are backed up by mind and intellect which means, her music has the involvement of both melody and rhythm.

The subtle and unmanifest sound of *Para* and *Paśyantī* state is called *Avyakta nāda*.

The sound or *nāda* that manifests as gross is the *Vyakta nāda*, expressed in stages of *Madhyama* and *Vaikharī*.

9. DEPICTION OF THE FOUR STAGES OF *NĀDAYOGA* IN *APSARA* SCULPTURES

The *Apsara* sculptures in *Nādayoga* can be classified as the following:

1. Hearing the *Para nāda*, the primal sound which is indicated as a parrot with the *Apsara*. In the psychological domain, parrot is like an analogy for the love or attraction for *nāda* or music, without which oneness with *nāda* never happens.
2. *Svādhyaya* or the study of scriptures for expansion of knowledge – *Paśyanti* stage.
3. In the *Madhyama* stage I, tuning of her body and mind are expressed as *Apsara* with different stringed instruments exploring the capacity or the movement of mind.
4. In *Madhyama* stage II a phase of *Laya yoga* where she is one with rhythm or *laya* is indicated in the *Apsara* sculptures with a variety of percussion instruments. The gradation goes by a small kettledrum (like *budabudaki*), medium size drum or *mardala* and a big drum like *mṛdaṅga*.
5. In *Madhyama* stage III, she is one with the melody and rhythm, and the physical body participates in this harmony which is expressed through dance as an expression of joy.
6. A *Vaikharī* stage where she is singing with the cymbals in hand. This is an evolved phase of peaceful state of mind, the melody – uniting with rhythm and speech – an overflow of joy through the articulation of the phonetic organs.
7. Hearing the divine sounds of *maddala*, flute and big drum in her meditation – a mental conception of hearing *Anāhata nāda* (this is classified as *Anāhata* as she is not physically involved in playing the instrument, which means she is experiencing the sound).

Among the 42 *Apsara* sculptures, three are male figures (B.F. 18, 11 & 36) in which a young man is playing a smaller version of kettledrum. A slightly older man is playing on flute and an older looking man is on the big drum. These three probably represent the three stages of *Anāhata Nādayoga* a yogi can conceive when he is at different stages of concentration (indicated by the age representation of the figure) at the *Ājñā chakra* (the brow *chakra*). These figures indicate the concept of hearing the mystic divine sounds whose origin is transcendental.

8. B.F. 9 & 22, and 41, represent the *Sahasrara chakra* of *Kuṇḍalinī* awareness where the *Apsara* is elevated to the status of a goddess, wherein her *Kriyā śakti* (creative skill) is at a peak backed up by her interest (*Icchā śakti*) and knowledge (*Jñāna śakti*).

When the yogi is deep into meditation, he experiences the cosmic sound of small drums, *vīṇa*, flute and finally hears the loud sound of the percussion instrument *mṛdaṅga* through his inner ears. The *mṛdaṅga* is held by the attendant figures on either side of the *Apsara* represented as goddess, in B.F. 22 & 9, which suggest the *Anāhata* sounds the yogi can conceive mentally at this level of awareness.

In B.F. 25, the *Apsara* indicates the first and the last of *chakras*, the position of *Mūlādhāra chakra* in her left hand and *Sahasrara chakra* in the right. The dwarf attendants indicate the playing of flute, *mṛdaṅga*, cymbals and singing. In totality it is *Saṅgīta* which is a recital of *vādya*, *gīta* and *nṛtya* (dance); it is a beautiful representation of the arousal of *Kuṇḍalinī śakti* through *Nādayoga*.

The four stages of *nāda* and the seven *chakras* are analysed in relation to the activities depicted in *Apsara* sculptures.

10. ANALYSIS OF *APSARA* SCULPTURES IN *SUṢUPTI AVASTHĀ* AND THE STAGES OF *ĀHATA NĀDAYOGA*

A. First Stage of *Nādayoga* – Focussing the Mind on *Para Nāda*

Para nāda or the *Paravāṇī* is the transcendental sound, which is the primal sound of *Nādayoga*. It is an un-differential sound, which can be conceived by the mind only on concentration. Concentration is preceded by a focus on a sound. This primordial sound, which are like root ideas or germ thoughts, is the first manifestation of the 'chin-chin' sound in *Nādayoga* that draws one's attention. *Paravāṇī* can be compared to a state of mind when its focus is shifted to *nāda* or music. The love or focus on the art of music in a commoner needs to be nurtured and tended, as it has a tendency to fly away from an uncongenial atmosphere. This *para* sound is symbolically represented in *Apsara* sculptures as a parrot. (Even many sculptures of goddesses hold a parrot in the right hand which may suggest the primordial *Para nāda*.) There are in total four sculptures in the state of focus on *para* sound which show stages of *japa* or first level of meditation on sound.

After the parade of thoughts and capturing the mind, the human mind needs to be channelised by the intellect to one field of knowledge. These set of four sculptures indicate how *Paravāṇī* comes closer to a person when the mind is in a noiseless state (free from agitating thoughts). When the state of silence is at its highest intensity, the *Paravāṇī* comes closer and closer and ultimately it will be like a tamed parrot sitting willingly on the hand of the yogi. This hints that the seeker of *Nādayoga* has focussed his attention on *nāda* (the subject of sound or music). As soon as the yogi (*Apsara*) comes to a state of no thought, the divine *Para nāda* is heard automatically. This is indicated in the *Apsara*'s association with a parrot which is sitting on her left hand or on her shoulder.

B.F. 4

A bird is sitting on the lower part of the *Apsara*'s right arm and is hesitantly moving towards her. Any noise (disturbance of mind) will make the bird fly away. The *Apsara* is also indicating an effort to hold the bird – the *Paravāṇī*. In her left hand she holds a bundle of palm leaves (which is being opened by the attendant). This is a stage of meditation or *japa* where the study of scriptures or the guidance of Guru (a teacher) will guide the human mind on how to concentrate. The dwarf attendant to her left, appears to be watchful in trying to safeguard the concentration of her mistress. In the beginning, concentration will not be an easy process. The mind often passes through a state of parade of thoughts. Hence, here the bird is very hesitantly sitting at the lower part of the hand.

B.F. 27

The *Apsara* is holding a bird in her left hand and appears to say something (like, 'why do you want to fly away'?) through a gesticulation made by her right hand. This represents the second stage of *japa* where she has captured the *Paravāṇī* – the parrot – which needs to be goaded to be with her fearlessly. The attendant to her left is offering a fruit for a parrot which indirectly suggests the aspect of concentration needs some goading to make it stay comfortably can be compared to the specific place and posture required for *dhyāna* or meditation.

B.F. 2

The bird *Paravāṇī* is sitting on the left hand fingers of the *Apsara* and it looks like she is trying to understand what the bird is saying. Her mind and hearing is totally focussed on *Paravāṇī*. The bird needs to be goaded still to remain freely with her. This is indicated by the dwarf attendants who are offering fruits and corn to the bird and persuading or tempting the bird to stay there. The *Apsara* appears more at ease with the bird and vice versa than the B.F. 4. This is the third stage of concentration on *Paravāṇī*.

The abstract theme of focussing the mind on germ thoughts is very difficult to be represented in sculptures, where it can easily be misinterpreted. The Hoysala artists and sculptors have mastered the art of conveying the toughest theme of philosophy in a very artistic way through the *Apsara* sculptures. When compared to the state of *Kuṇḍalinī śakti*, the *Paravāṇī* stage represents the *Mūlādhāra* and *Svādhisthāna chakras* of *Kuṇḍalinī chakras* as the *Kuṇḍalinī* has just awakened from the resting or sleeping stage.

B.F. 39

The *Navaraṅga* pillar suggests a phase where the bird (*Paravāṇī*) is fearlessly sitting on her left upper arm and playing with the necklace of the *Apsara*. This is the intimacy that is existing between a student of *Nādayoga* and the primordial sound. The dwarf attendants on either side

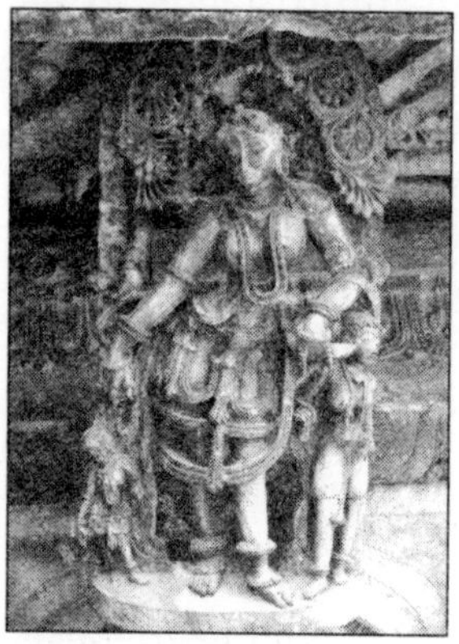

B.F. 4. *Apsara* with a bird on her right arm

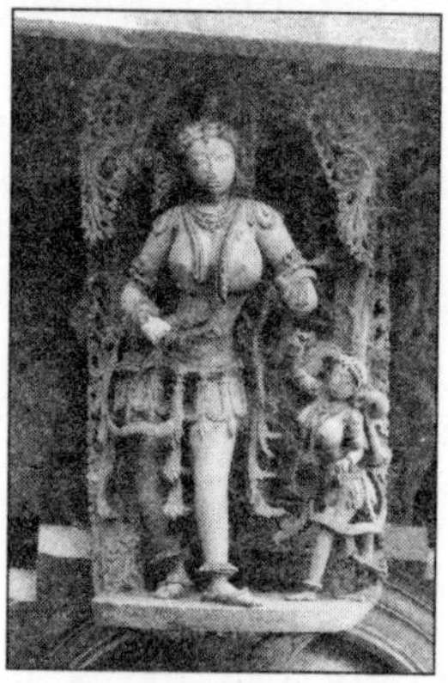

B.F. 27. *Apsara* with a parrot, encouraging her pet parrot to speak

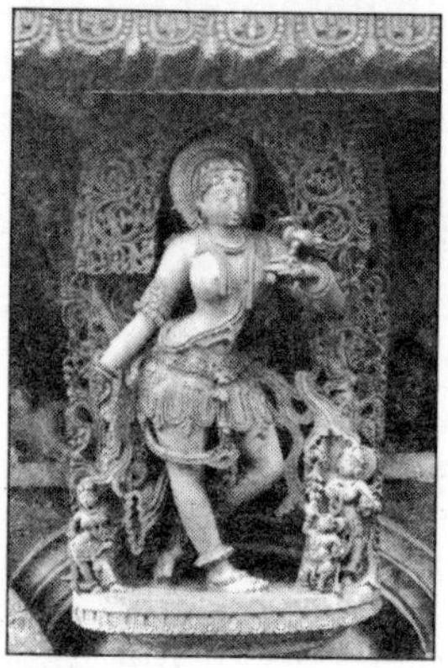

B.F. 2. *Apsara* with a parrot

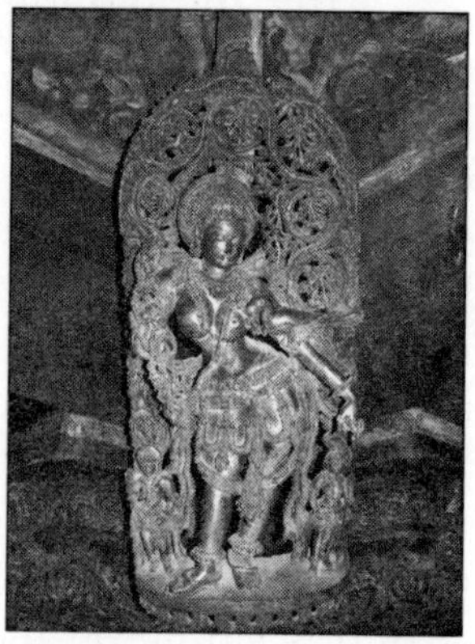

B.F. 39. *Apsara* with a parrot (on the *Navaraṅga* pillar)

are quiet, guarding their mistress so that she has no disturbance while meditating due to noise nor are they tempting her with jewellery as seen in the previous chapter. Here the bird needs no goading, or an offer to stay with the lady. It is happy to sit and play with the *Apsara* – a final state of focussing on *Paravāṇī*.

B. Second Stage of *Nādayoga* – *Paśyanti*: The Visualisation of Knowledge – *Svādhyaya* - B.F. 28

Paśyanti is the visualisation of sound. It is a state of agitation as the mind struggles to know, similar in experience to the expansion of knowledge. Will or the *Icchā śakti* plays a significant role. The will to know and expand one's knowledge about *nāda* is visualisation of sound, much like silently chanting the name of Rāma or Kṛṣṇa with closed eyes and trying to picturise mentally the form and colours of the deities. *Apsara* is holding palm leaves (scriptures) in her left hand and *jñāna mudrā* in her right hand. *Jñāna mudrā*, where the tip of the forefinger touches the tip of the thumb (fingers are damaged in the sculpture), is held at the time of *dhyāna* or meditation. It helps in concentration, relaxes the mind from agitation and sharpens the memory and brain. *Svādhyaya* or expanding one's knowledge is at three phases:

1. *Śravaṇa* or hearing. The knowledge that is gained by listening to a teacher or Guru (*Apsara* displays *śūnya mudrā*[1] in her left hand, which is indicative of enhancing the hearing faculty).
2. *Manana* - Remembering the knowledge that is learnt (her right hand *jñāna mudrā*[2] is indicative of this).
3. *Dhyasita* - Practising (seen in sculptures with instruments).

The two attendants on either side are quiet, guarding the lady so that she is not disturbed in her meditation. They are holding a fruit (or may be corn, indicative of food) in one hand and *cāmara* – the fan – in the other hand to indicate that the *Apsara* has crossed the sheaths of *Annamaya* and *Prāṇamaya kośas* (ref. ch. II. 3, of part II), and has entered the *Manonmaya kośa*, where her interests are shifted from ego or self-reference to the field of knowledge. Philosophically, distancing away from *Annamaya* and *Prāṇamaya kośas* mean entering into a realm of spirituality where the focus is on the inner spirit. *Apsara* holds the scriptures near the navel region of *Maṇīpura chakra* (ref. ch. III. 7) which indicates her level of awareness to be beyond her body, and her interest for knowledge is kindled. The guidance from a Guru and a constant study of scriptures are factors that guarantee success in *Jñāna yoga*, as they are the sources of communion with the tutorly deity. The student of *Nādayoga* has to observe the proper understanding of his study and of *japa*, the repetition of the knowledge that is perceived, which is called practice in the field of music. This *Svādhyaya* stage is compared to the level of *Maṇīpura chakra* of awareness, in the arousal of *Kuṇḍalinī śakti* through *Nādayoga*. It is a stage of agitation, where the sound is trying to emerge out as knowledge.

According to the *Bhagavadgītā*, knowledge is the highest treasure in the world. The fire of knowledge burns all *karma* into ashes and nothing is more purifying than spiritual fire. Knowledge is the perfect path, which leads to yoga or self-realisation. *Rajoguṇa* is replaced by *Sattvaguṇa* in a person at this stage of awareness. *Apsara* shows a desire to gain knowledge. Her internal stabilisation and concentration, which is symbolically expressed by her hand gesture of *jñāna mudrā*, tells that her mind is now opposed to sensuous desires. There is no limit to the power of human mind when the desire for knowledge is kindled. The more concentrated the mind is, the power of absorbing the knowledge goes higher. *Sāttvik* activities add beauty to a person as the inner unfoldment reflects as *sāttvik* joy. *Citta* or the mind, that is absorbed in *nāda*, no longer longs for sensual objects.

C. Third Stage of *Āhata Nādayoga* – *Madhyama*: An Exploration

The mystery of sound is mysticism, the harmony of life is religion, the knowledge of vibrations is metaphysics, their analysis of atom (units of music) is science and their harmonious grouping is art. Music is the art of arts and science of all sciences, which is like a fountain of all knowledge, a divine art.

– Hazarat Inayat Khan

In the *Madhyama* stage, the awareness according to the movement *Kuṇḍalinī śakti*, is compared to *Anāhata chakra*. The *Anāhata chakra* represents a stage of the meeting of the female and male *Śakti tattvas*, where the mind and intellect are in combined activity. The melody is visualised as a feminine *śakti* and rhythm is a masculine *śakti*. *Madhyama* stage of unevolved sound, and the awareness of *Nādayoga* in the middle state, are studied in the following phases, and correlated with *Apsara* sculptures holding instruments.

1. Tuning of the body
2. Tuning of the mind
3. Exploration of the melody or *Nādānusandhāna*
4. *Laya yoga*
5. Dance – an expression of *Joy*.

Sattvaguṇa dominates in this stage of awareness. In sculptural art, musicians and musical instruments often symbolize peace and love.

I. Tuning of the Body

B.F. 14

Apsara is holding a stringed instrument which looks like a *laghu kinnarī* – a smaller version of the *Rudra vīṇā* (*brihat kinnarī*). She holds a plectrum in her right hand and probably checking the tension of the strings for the best sound production.

Vīṇā in yogic concepts is compared to our *Śarīra* (body). The strings are compared to the nerves. If the strings of our mind are too loose (*Tamoguṇa* is dominant), they produce a base and a unmusical sound, which is compared to dull, lazy and negative thoughts. If they are too tight (*Rajoguṇa* is dominant), they produce a squeaky or unpleasant sound and compared to stressed, tensed, worried and unhappy state of mind. When the strings of our minds are tuned right (*Sattvaguṇa* is dominant), the sound production is at its best, which is compared to a happy, blissful state of mind. This sculpture is carved with a theme not too loose, not too tight just right.

Tuning of the body, is like a commitment, a determination, that disciplines the body in the early stages of the practice of yoga. Once it is established, it becomes a way of life and the progress of awareness comes naturally as the life systems gets balanced.

According to Purāṇic stories, the *Rudra vīṇā* was created by none other than Lord Śiva, who had used the nerves as strings. Since it was a masculine instrument with powerful sound, his consort Pārvati came out with *Saraswatī vīṇā* which could be used by commoners as it was not too hard to play like *Rudra vīṇā*.

Apsara's face clearly expresses a state of calmness and concentration, which is required to tune a *vīṇā* or any other instrument. The dwarf figures who are playing percussion instruments and *tāla* indicate that the *Apsara* is in *Nādayoga*. The sculpture is indicative of the fact that the mind is negated from negative thoughts and is cultivated and attuned to a meditation on *Nādayoga*.

II. Tuning of the Mind

B.F. 13

Apsara is plucking the strings of a *tambura*. Even though the instrument *tambura* is missing, the position of her hands indicates that she is holding a *tambura* and plucking the strings with her right hand. The sound of *tambura* is like *Japa yoga* for a student of *Nādayoga*. It focusses the mind into contemplative mood. Once the body and mind are tuned, the progress of awareness happens naturally. Plucking the string of a *tambura* is a very effective mental discipline which helps the student of music to focus or concentrate on the meditation of music. An interesting feature in B.F. 13, is the presence of a lizard and a bee in the background amidst the leafy and tendrillar carvings. According to the concept of *Nādayoga*, the yogi or the student hears divine sound of *nāda* like ultrasonic sounds, which are not audible to the normal ears. Only a student of *Nādayoga* can conceive the divine aspect of this sound (which is heard like the humming sound of a bee) which has the capacity to transform the agitated, *rājasik* state of mind to a *sāttvik* and contemplative state. It makes the student deaf to the external sounds. The lizard and cricket are creatures which can conceive and act on ultrasonic sounds which is used just as analogy to compare with the sound of *tambura*, which transforms only the person who is interested in music. This special capacity of harmonising with the tonic note is hinted in the lady playing on *tambura* and concentrating her mind inwardly to respond to the further deeper or higher sounds of *nāda*. (This sound is compared to the sound of silver bells, which the student of music hears as the first stage of awareness, in *Anāhata Nādayoga*).

For the devotees, who cannot understand the intricacies of philosophical thoughts hidden in this lizard figure, they can still admire the great artistic skills and capacities of the sculptor, who has managed to carve a lizard and a jackfruit amidst intricate leafy and tendrillar work.

Sattvaguṇa dominates at this stage of awareness. The perceptions of *Jñānendriya* and *Karmendriya* are focussed. Sensitive and *sāttvik* intellect can discriminate and judge clearly about the good and the bad. The focus and concentration which is depicted here, is practised for stopping the modifications of the mind, and holding the mind on one form for a longer time. This condition is experienced only when the body and the mind are prepared by purification (cessation of negativity) and by making the senses fine.

Purandara dasa, the father of Karnatik style of Indian music, has explained the significance of a *tambura* player in one of his compositions in Kannada language.

Tamboori mitidava bhavabdi daatidava, meaning a *tambura* player who can harmonise with the drone or resonance of the instrument has overcome the existing layers of worldly complexities.

III. Exploration of the Melody – Nādānusandhāna

B.F. 30

Apsara is playing a stringed instrument which looks like present day *gettu vādya*. The front resonator (or the bulb of the instrument) is broken. The body of the instrument is long with a snake motif at the other end. She is plucking the strings with a bamboo blade in her right hand and in her left hand she holds a smaller blade to move on strings.

'Anusandhāna' in Sanskrit means 'investigation or exploration'.

Apsara is exploring the aspect of melody. In *Nādayoga*, after the mind is tuned and set initially, it moves into the world of melody exploring the beauty of *nāda* (which is compared to *alāp* in classical music where the beauty and qualities of a *rāga* (melody) are brought out). This phase proceeds to the act of absorbing *laya* rhythm. Melody is visualised as the feminine *tattva* of the power of *nāda* and compared to the mind, before meeting with intellect.

Apsara reflects the *sāttvik* qualities, *śraddhā* or deep interest backed up by faith, arising out of firm intellectual convictions, when *Jñāna* is kindled. She exhibits the desire to gain knowledge. Her thoughts are not self-centred. Attachment to her body is now substituted by selfless thoughts and are focussed in the path of *Nādayoga*.

The melody of *anāhata* sounds are like mystic sounds heard by a yogi at this phase. When the mind moves enquiring about the melody of mystic sounds, it is called *Nādānusandhāna*. This is always after the *japa* or the tuning of the mind, as it purifies the *nāḍīs* – the channels through which astral currents pass in our body. B.F. 30 indicates a picture of what *Nādānusandhāna* is, as she is meditating on the melodies of *nāda*.

B.F. 29

Apsara is holding another variety of stringed instruments resembling the present day *swaramaṇḍal* or *santoor*. It is a shallow wooden box with vertical row of strings held by posts for tuning. Beads are inserted in the strings for fine-tuning. In the left hand, she holds a mallet, made probably of bamboo or wood, to strike the strings. This instrument tunes the mind to a particular melody (*rāga*). The dwarf figures on either side play instruments like flute and cymbals, which indicate the involvement of *Apsara* in *Nādānusandhāna* through *āhata* sounds. The aspect of her meditation and total involvement in *nāda* is clearly indicated through the figure to her right side where an artist is playing on the flute.

IV. Absorbing the Intricacies of Rhythm Pattern – Laya yoga

Mind which is focussed on *nāda*, enjoys the melody and quickly enters into a state of *laya* (rhythm) establishing its unity (yoga) with the rhythmic vibrations. An important feature of *laya* is its capacity to infuse energy, stimulate and enliven music. This stage is also called *Dhāraṇa* in *Nādayoga* which is a phase of intense and perfect concentration of the mind on rhythm, accompanied by complete abstraction (*Pratyāhāra* or withdrawal) from everything pertaining to the external world of senses. Of all the musical instruments, the drum is the most primeval means of communication, its percussive sound travelling to the heart and by extension suggesting the ability to communicate with supernatural forces. The small drum and the big drum symbolises the creative and the destructive power of Lord Śiva – as the sound of big drum was associated with thunder, the symbol of destructive force. Drumming was widely used to achieve the states of ecstasy.

The *sāttvik* mind which is pure and devoid of all agitation, experiences a bliss, becomes proficient in art and skills, and becomes creative by nature. The *Icchā śakti* (great will) and *Jñān śakti* (knowledge) are very active at this stage as rhythm is based on calculations where intellect plays a role.

B.F. 33, 8, 10, 24 are the sculptures in which the *Apsara* is in total union with the sound of rhythm, which are depicted in succession of the size of the percussion instrument.

In B.F. 33, the *Apsara* is beating a small drum called *Budabudakai* which looks like the *damaru* and holds another instrument called *Chitike tāla*, which is used to give the time beat. Both represent her stage of getting absorbed in *Laya nāda*.

* This sculpture is probably a demonstration of the 'Tāla avadhana' or the art of exhibiting the attentiveness, skills and capacities of the artist in a music recital where different rhythm patterns are reckoned at the same time. She is demonstrating a specific *tāla* with the '*Chitike tāla*'

with the right hand, a speedier or a different *tāla* pattern with the 'budabudakai' with the left hand and indicating a different pattern with her foot. The attendants are with a different type of percussion instrument to which the *Apsara* has to synchronise and she is also depicting a dance posture. Such a demonstration requires intence practice, concentration and accuracy which are of academic interest. It also depicts her through oneness with *laya* – the rhythm.

In B.F. 8, *Apsara* is totally engrossed in beating a slightly bigger hourglass drum called *murujā*. She is beating the drum with a small stick (*kōṇa*) in her right hand. Her oneness in *Laya yoga* is expressed in *Indriyās* and the whole body responding to the rhythm of sound. She has absolutely no relation with the external world and is in perfect peace within herself. It is a state of *Suṣupti avasthā* of deep sleep state where she is in deep joy being one with the sound of rhythm (*Laya yoga*). Her *sāttvik* joy derived from divine art is clearly expressed on her face which indicates that music and rhythm are felt rather than heard, and the whole body responds to the rhythm. *Apsara* depicts the subtle path of understanding the source of lasting joy.

In B.F. 10, *Apsara* is beating a bigger drum called *maddala*, which is hung from her left shoulder. She is hitting the instrument with a stick in her right hand and her left hand is inserted in the straps to adjust the tension and tune the instrument. Her blissful smile reflects the blissful state of mind, even though physically she is in an active state. The mind and intellect are perfectly conditioned. She looks pure and serene with rediscovery of self-experiencing pure wisdom.

In B.F. 24, the *Apsara* is engrossed in playing a percussion instrument. The instrument is now missing but her hand position clearly indicates her playing a big percussion instrument, which may look like the instrument played by the attendants on either side. Her face exhibits a blissful state of mind and enjoying a creative state of her skills, which is accompanied and acquired by deep concentration and meditation on *Laya yoga*.

This also explains why there are so many sculptures of *Apsaras* dancing with percussion instruments in various temples of India. It represents a stage of meditation, seeing God within. When the mind gets into oneness with the sound of laya (the mind hears the sounds of *Anāhata nāda* depending on the intensity of concentration in their meditation), the whole body responds to this divine *nāda*, as all the *Indriyās* (5 *Jñānendriya* + 5 *Karmendriyas*) participate in the joy of conceiving the *nāda*. These temple sculptures where *Apsaras* are dancing with *mṛdaṅga* are symbolic of their sway of body to the rhythm and sound of *Anāhata nāda*. Here she appears to be a truly happy person, an introvert, where all her desires have dwindled and she is happy within herself.

V. Dance – An Expression of Joy

B.F. 25, 38, 19, 40, 21

Dance is the sway of the body, a motion, the sign of life, in response to the nature of vibrations. When this movement is set to music, it sets both the performer and the onlooker into a movement of spirituality. Hence, dance is a sacred art for which reason Hindu gods are represented in different poses, all having certain meaning and philosophy. Since dance is an integral part of the *Apsaras* of Belur, the definition of dance had to be considered.

These five sculptures depict the dancing postures of *Apsara*, which is an expression of her joy on getting united with the melody and *laya* aspects of *nāda*. Music is *nāda Brahman*. *Bhāva* (disposition of the mind), *rāga* (melody) and *tāla* (rhythm) are the three constituents of the concept of *Nāda laya*, which leads to *nāda Brahman*. These are expressed as *nṛtya*, *vādya* and *gīta* that make up *Saṅgīta*, which is offered in the service of God.

Music stimulates, energises and invigorates the whole system of the body. It affects the emotions and arouses the impulses to action. Hence dance, fundamentally is the form of physical expression of the ecstasy of joy, when the mind is one with melody and *laya*. In other words, when the subtle body is one with the *nāda*, the gross body (in which the subtle body resides) involuntarily responds to the music with complete integration. Body movements reflect the inner state of the human and also open up the emotional process in the mind. This response may differ from individual to individual, as these movements initiate sub-conscious psychological activity. The sway of body is natural and not guided by the intellect. It is a spontaneous expression of the body when the mind overflows with joy and devotion, on uniting with *nāda Brahman*. Tune and rhythm produce an inclination for dance, which further is a graceful expression of thoughts and feelings without uttering a word.

- Even though dance, the physical expression of joy, is not discussed under the various stages of awareness in the meditation on sound – *Nādayoga* – it enjoys a status here, when we define what 'dance' is. Dance is an instinctive expression of the life force, when one feels united with the cosmic energy of unseen forces. It became the earliest form of theatre, translating religious dogma into expressive movement. Dance in its root concept is the sway or movement of the body when the mind and intellect are in union either with the melody or rhythmic vibrations or both. Hence, dance can be classified as a response or outcome of the physical body when the mind and intellect are attuned to the vibrations of sound. Since mind and intellect reside in the body and also respond with an expression of joy to the vibrations of sound, dance can be studied under *Madhyama* stage of sound and also as an expression of the body at the mid-level awareness of *Nādayoga*.
- When the sway of the body is codified to prescriptions, it is classified as folk or classical dance, which is an outcome of the conscious effort by the artist.

In B.F. 25, *Apsara* is indicating the *Satchakra nirūpaṇa*, probably a demonstration of the *Kuṇḍalinī śakti*, the path of the latent energy, from the *Mūlādhāra* to *Sahasrara chakra*, through *nṛtya*, which is danced to the melody of flute, rhythm of cymbals and *mṛdaṅga*. Her left hand indicates the position of *Mūlādhāra chakra* and right hand above the crown part of her head indicates the position of *Sahasrara chakra*. This figure demonstrates how one can awaken the *Kuṇḍalinī* powers through oneness with dance and music.

B.F. 38 and 19 depict the aspect of grace in dance. The graceful movement (female *tattva*) and vigorous movement (masculine *tattva*) are classified as *lāsya* and *tāṇḍava* aspects in dance, which are based on the execution of movements following the intensity of sound vibrations. B.F. 38 and 19 are the depiction of graceful movements.

B.F. 21, 25 and 40 depict vigorous movements of *tāṇḍava* aspect. In the sculpture, B.F. 25, she is dancing with the accompaniment of flute, *mṛdaṅga*, and cymbals (*pada*, singing the words) to interpret the involvement of melody, rhythm and words in Indian dancing. It is a representation of *Gandharva Kalā* – dance that was performed to the sound of melody, rhythm and *pada*. In B.F. 21 and 40, it is only the rhythm instruments to which she is dancing vigorously. Dancing is a phase of deeper meditation which is an expression, after meditation on melody and rhythm. *Laya yoga* is the key that attempts to unlock the hidden energy reserves that is latent or hidden in human nervous system, which may manifest as dance.

Naṭarāja, the lord of dancing, represents the *Laya yoga* phase. Lord Naṭarāja signifies the union with the cosmic rhythmic vibrations and its continuum. Rhythm is identified as the male force of nature, depicted through the vigorous mode of the execution of dance movements. Here, the dance, dancer and the medium are inseparable, corresponding to the creator, creation and action into one. This perfect union sets not only the performer into action, but the whole world swings into action. Hence *tāṇḍava*, the dance of Naṭarāja, enjoys a unique place in Indian philosophy.

D. Fourth Stage in *Nādayoga* – *Vaikharī*

B.F. 12 and 20

Vaikharī is a faculty of speech – the evolved form of *Nādayoga*. The divine sound, which is conceived as *para*, the vital breath, emerges out at *Paśyanti* backed up with knowledge, and manifests into an audible but unevolved stage at *Madhyama* and is expressed as both evolved and audible in the form of speech or singing in *Vaikharī*. Speech is the creative work of *Kriyā śakti* by the articulation of tongue and voice box which is always supported by *Icchā śakti* (will) and *Jñāna śakti* (knowledge). Hence, *Vaikharī* is the evolved state of *Nādayoga*. *Kuṇḍalinī śakti* is activated at *Viśuddha chakra* or the region of throat, which is like a gateway to commune with the supreme soul. It is a bridge connecting the physical body to the spiritual thoughts. Every word that comes out, undergoes all these procedures which are hardly analysed in daily life.

Highly interesting and most popular among the forms of *Nādōpāsanā*, is *Saṅgīta* (music). *Saṅgīta* may be classified as *prēyas* or *srēyas*. *Prēyas* is that which is immediately pleasant and *srēyas* that which leads to the eternal good of man, like self-realisation. *Saṅgīta* or *saṅkīrtan* (devotional music expressing gratitude to God), which is depicted in B.F. 12 and B.F. 20, depicts their enduring oneness in *nāda*, the *srēyas* aspects. When an individual or group of people chant or sing, the vibrations produced benefit not only to the singer but also those in the surrounding area listening to it. Group chanting or duet, as seen in B.F. 12 was not only a means of passing the knowledge but an easy way of mass communication. *Apsara* is beating cymbals enjoying the rhythmic vibrations along with melody and words in her music. Her blissful expression and poise clearly indicate that her heart has mastered the art of *Nādayoga*. Her eyes and gentle smile are indicative of a blissful state that she is enjoying after visualising God. She is in *Tapo loka* as *Viśuddha chakra* or throat region is attributed to *Tapo loka* and heart to *Jñāna loka*.

Vocal music is considered to be the highest form of art for it is natural. The effect produced by instruments which is merely a machine, cannot be compared to human voice, as voice comes direct from the soul in the form of breath and has been brought to surface through the medium of mind and the vocal organs of the body. Voice has all the magnetism which the instruments lack and it is nature's ideal instrument upon which other instruments are modelled. When music is sung and instruments are played simultaneously, it produces different frequencies of vibrations at the same time, the combined effect of which produce a good effect on the listener.

Music has three stages of ecstasy in union with the Lord. They are:

1. The heart of devotee is filled with love, admiration, gratitude and becomes capable of visualising the form of his concept or ideal of devotion.
2. The second aspect is a higher aspect of union, with the beauty of the ideal, irrespective of form. The song in praise of ideal character, helps for an overflow of the love of the devotee, activating the divine core within, from which flows the perennial stream of peace and tranquillity.
3. The third stage of ecstasy is the union which is beyond limitation of name and form, virtue or merit, with whom the union is constantly sought and whom the soul has finally found. This joy is unexplainable.

This ecstasy or union with the ultimate truth is the goal of music.

11. CONTEMPLATION ON *ĀHATA* AND *ANĀHATA* SOUNDS

B.F. 18, 11, 36

There are three sculptures of male artists playing on drums and flute amidst *Apsaras*. These three can be viewed from *Anāhata* and *Āhata* perspectives. In the advanced stage of *Anāhata*

Nādayoga, called 'mukta', a human is freed from all states and thoughts. This is a state where the spiritual sight becomes fixed, without any object to be seen. The yogi of *Nādōpāsanā* can contemplate on sounds, at the centre of forehead between the eyebrows which is called *Satya loka* and the awareness, according to the arousal of *Kuṇḍalinī śakti*, is at *Ājñā chakra*. A yogi in deep meditation on sound, hears the sound of kettledrum, then the sound of flute, and lastly, the big drum like *mṛdaṅga* or *pakhāvaz* compared to the thunderbolt, at an advanced stage of *Anāhata Nādayoga*. Thunderbolt, philosophically, is the sound born in *Ākāśa* or the space, being understood as vibrations of the cosmos. Thunderbolt is vibration with flash of light, which is explained as a connection between the outward events and the inner events. Light is symbolic of *jñāna*, resulting out of the deep meditation on *nāda*. *Jñāna* is therefore believed to be a discharge of energy, not by chance but in accordance with intelligent causation, revealing a varied phenomenon of life around us.

The stages of intensity of meditation are represented in the age-wise representation of male artists. This is the probable explanation for the male sculptures being present amidst the *Apsaras*.

From the *Āhata* perspective, listening to art and music of others, result in the expansion of one's knowledge of *nāda*. A student of music can switch over to *Satya loka* of visualising God, when he is totally concentrated in hearing divine music. Here, *Āhata nāda* takes the human from gross to subtle levels.

NOTES AND REFERENCES

1. *Apsara* is indicating a *yoga mudrā* called *śūnya mudrā* with her left hand as she is holding the scriptures. According to the principles of *Mudrāvijñāna*, *śūnya mudrā* results when the middle finger touches the base of the thumb and the thumb gently pressurises the middle joint of the middle finger. This *mudrā* helps to correct or enhance the hearing capacities.
2. In her right hand she displays *jñāna mudrā*, where the tip of the forefinger touches the tip of the thumb. This *mudrā* helps in improving concentration, which is essential in remembering the knowledge acquired.

IV

Analysis of Apsara Sculptures in Turīya Avasthā – A State of Bliss

B.F. 22, 9 AND 41

Turīya avasthā is theoretically represented as a state of *samādhi* (deep meditation). This stage indicates a human transformed to godly status, by the highest spiritual and intellectual activity. It is a state of bliss that comes after the realisation of truth. Union with God can be explained as the soul getting into a pure state, reflecting the godly characters of perpetual bliss, where even the flashes of *māyā* fail to make an impact. God is again a concentration of positive energy, the creative power, who is beyond the reference to self and the power, who has concern for others, to relieve them from the clutches of *māyā*. His actions are oriented towards the destruction of *avidyā* (ignorance) and *māyā* (illusion) which are depicted as demons, getting destroyed by Hindu gods and goddesses. In Vedānta philosophy, they are addressed as *Kāraṇa śarīra* – the causal frame, or the inner rudiment of the body. A yogi in *Turīya avasthā* becomes creative in capacities, which is a godly capacity.

Apsara is depicted like a goddess with a crown, but with two arms symbolic of a human in divine status. In B.F. 22 and 9, she holds the mace (weapon) – the *khatwanga*, with a skull head, and in the right hand she is holding an object that may be a *khaḍga* – a small knife or a *kapāla* or a piece of flesh, which is difficult to identify – all indicating that she is fond of flesh and blood indirectly hinting that she is the destroyer of love for flesh and form – a form of *māyā*. She looks terrifying and is proceeding forward. It may be the representation of Goddess Manōnmani, who has a large face and carries a *khaḍga*, and a weapon. She is said to terrify her enemies (ignorance and *māyā*) and bestow comfort to her votaries. She is a form of Kālī. In Hindu iconography, Goddess Kālī is represented in a calm and benevolent state – as Pārvatī, the benign goddess or in a 'raudra' state, one who is terrifying to negative qualities like demons as Kālī or Durgā, the dynamic aspect of the goddess.

Apsara here is a symbolic depiction of a divine state because her ego and impulses are totally dissolved. It is a state attained by one's own effort. She looks terrifying as she has conquered her enemies *avidyā* (ignorance) and *māyā* (illusion). She is carved in a powerful rhythmic gait (indicated by the sound of big percussion instruments) as she is an embodiment of *Kriyā śakti* (creativity), which is progressive by nature. According to the Śiva *tattvas*, this *Apsara* sculpture can be compared to the feminine form of Udyama Bhairava – one who has risen up to godly status, by her self effort in realising the truth.

Apsara's crown part of the head is elevated, which is an insignia or a symbolic representation of virtues in Indian art. It is gained by the enlightenment, through *Jñāna* and wisdom. The *Kuṇḍalinī śakti* of awareness is at its highest point. The *Sahasrara chakra* is a state of her oneness with the Supreme Soul and the ultimate truth – the Śiva. This state of oneness with the supreme soul is indicated by an elevated bump on the head, which is decorated by a crown, to indicate her supremecy.

The various mini skulls on her crown, with which she is adorned, are symbolic representation of the Sanskrit words which is again an expression of *Jñāna śakti*. (Skull is an abstract representation of emptiness where there is the cessation of the six negative qualities. Positive energies like *Jñāna* fills in an empty space.) She is the personification of the great will for knowledge (*Icchā śakti*), knowledge (*Jñāna śakti*) and *Kriyā śakti* – the dynamic power of action. She represents the stage of enlightenment.

In B.F. 41, she holds *jñāna mudrā* in her right hand, which is a *mudrā* of concentration. She wears a crown, symbolic of her virtues, enlightenment and an elevated status. She is in a dancing posture; the four attendants are also with instruments. *Apsara* is depicting her oneness with *nāda*; her constant concentration upon *nāda* has made her free from waking, dream or sleep state. She is above that – as her true self, one with *nāda Brahman* and hence depicted as a goddess. This state of realisation is called *Jīvan mukti*.

As detailed in *Lalita Sahasranama* (Phrase 898, 901, 902, 903), *Apsara* in *Turīya avasthā* in B.F. 41 can be compared to -

Vīra goṣṭi priya – a goddess who is fond of the advanced *upāsaka* (mediators) of *Mahākāvyas*.
Nāda rūpiṇī – mother of *śabda*.
Vijñānakalana – knower of self-knowledge.
Kalya – creative, healthy and creator of bliss.

The transcendental intuition according to *Mandukya Upaniṣad*, is a state where neither the internal world (physical domain) nor the conscious of the external world (objective), will effect the state of mind. With such a realisation, the yogi attains not only complete wisdom, freedom, detachment but also gets identity of the self with all the creatures of the world. She is the inspired one and inspiring one to the society and a source of joy. Her eternal knowledge and intensified love of knowledge, leads to expanded sharing and service of knowledge. She is experiencing *mokṣa* an unconditioned bliss, which is vastly different from pleasure. She is in yoga, in absolute harmony with *nāda Brahman*. At this state she rejoices within, is happy within, and illumined within (of the self) acquiring a divine status attaining the beautitude of God.

B.F. 1

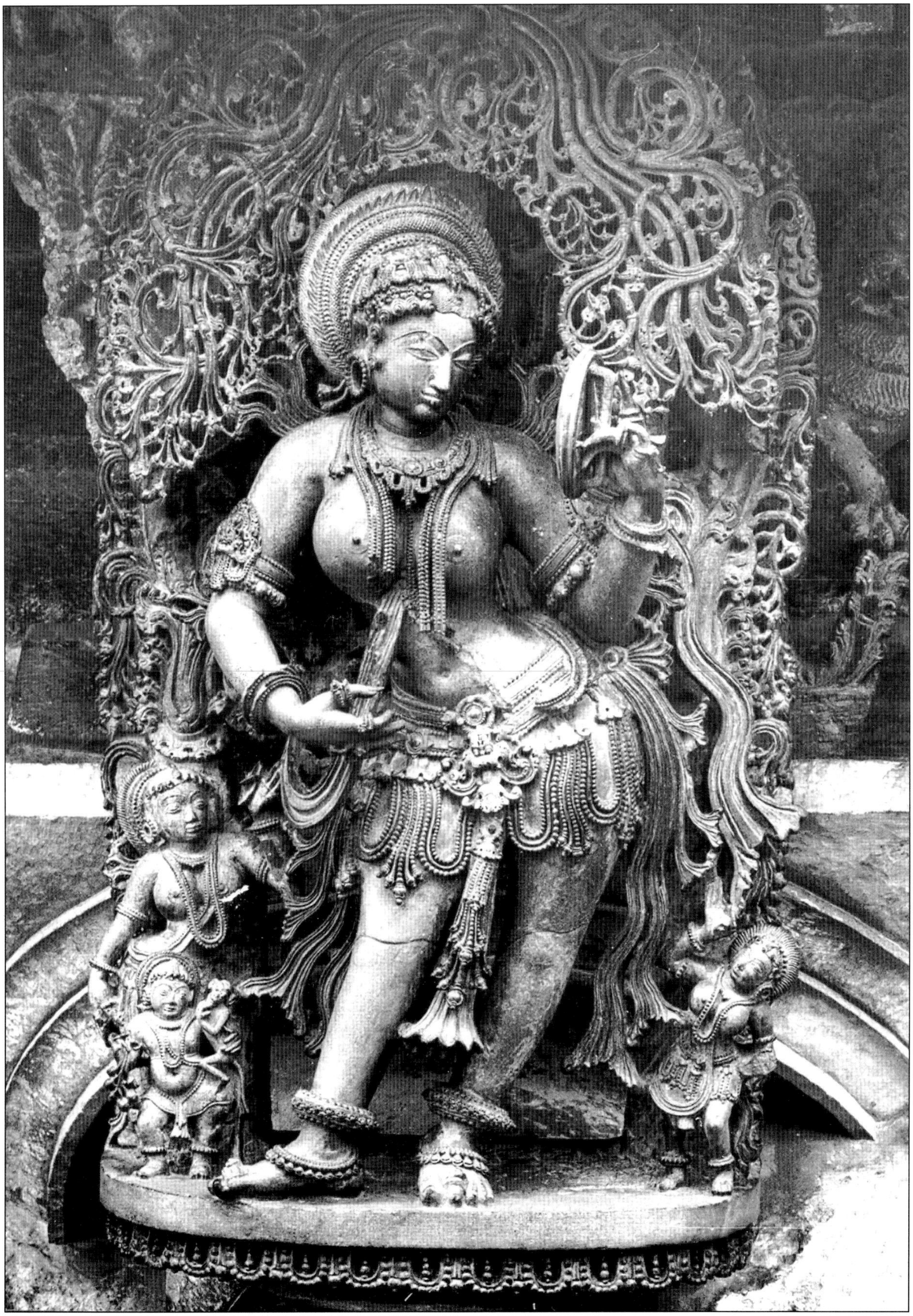

Pl. VII. B.F. 1. *Apsara* admiring her charm in a mirror

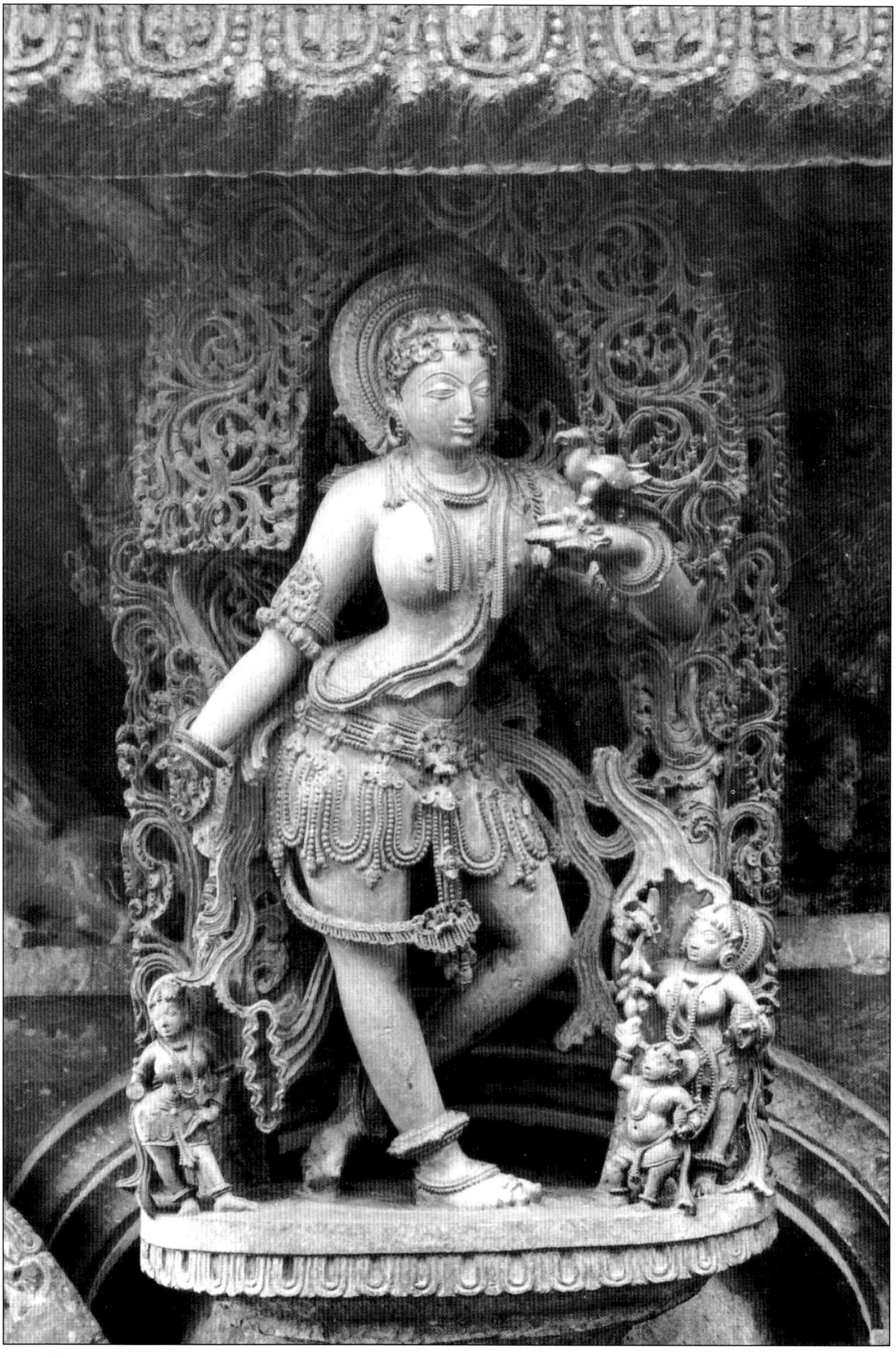

Pl. VIII. B.F. 2. *Apsara* with a parrot

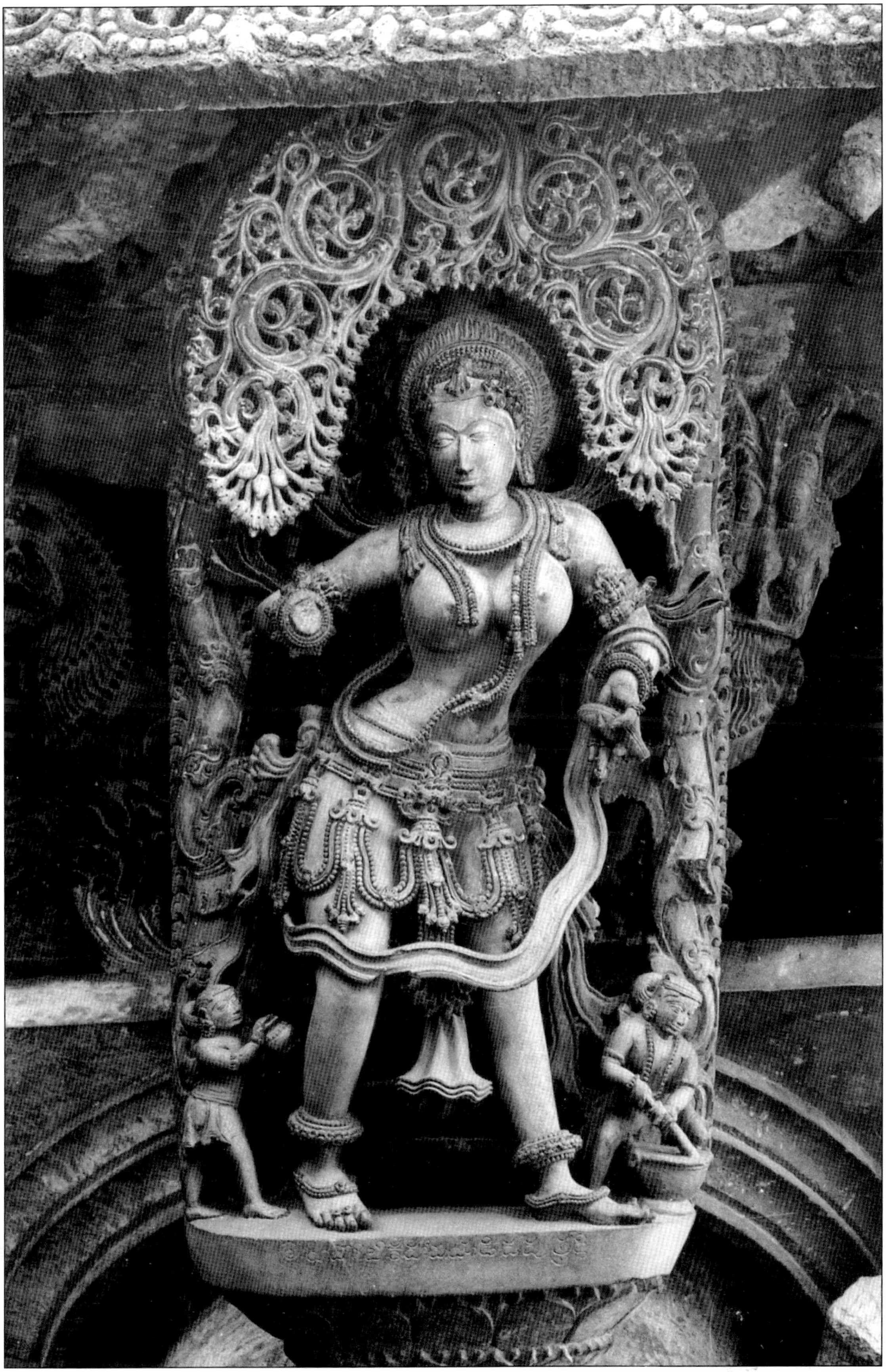

Pl. IX. B.F. 3. *Apsara* playing the game of water

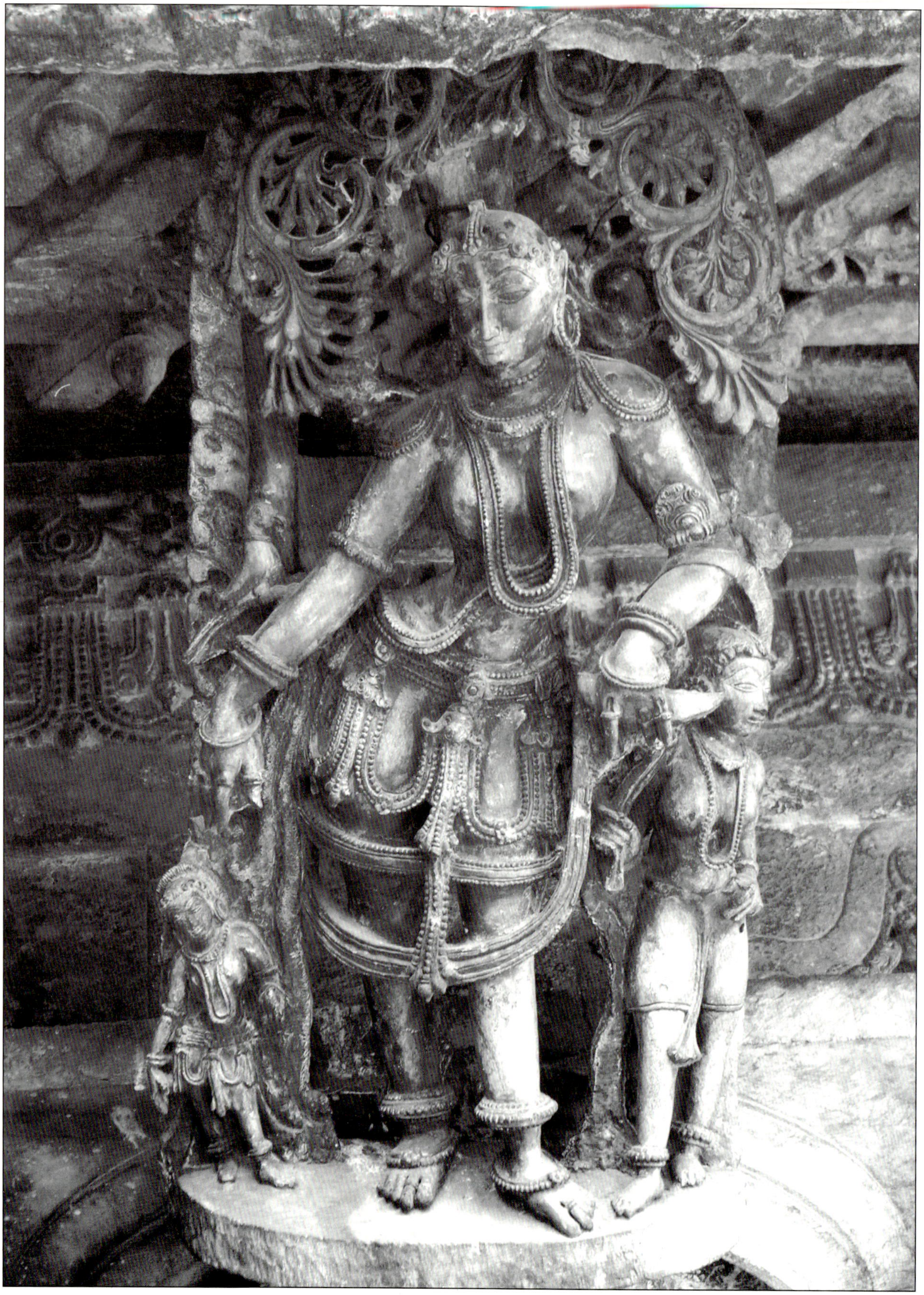

Pl. X. B.F. 4. *Apsara* with a bird on her right arm

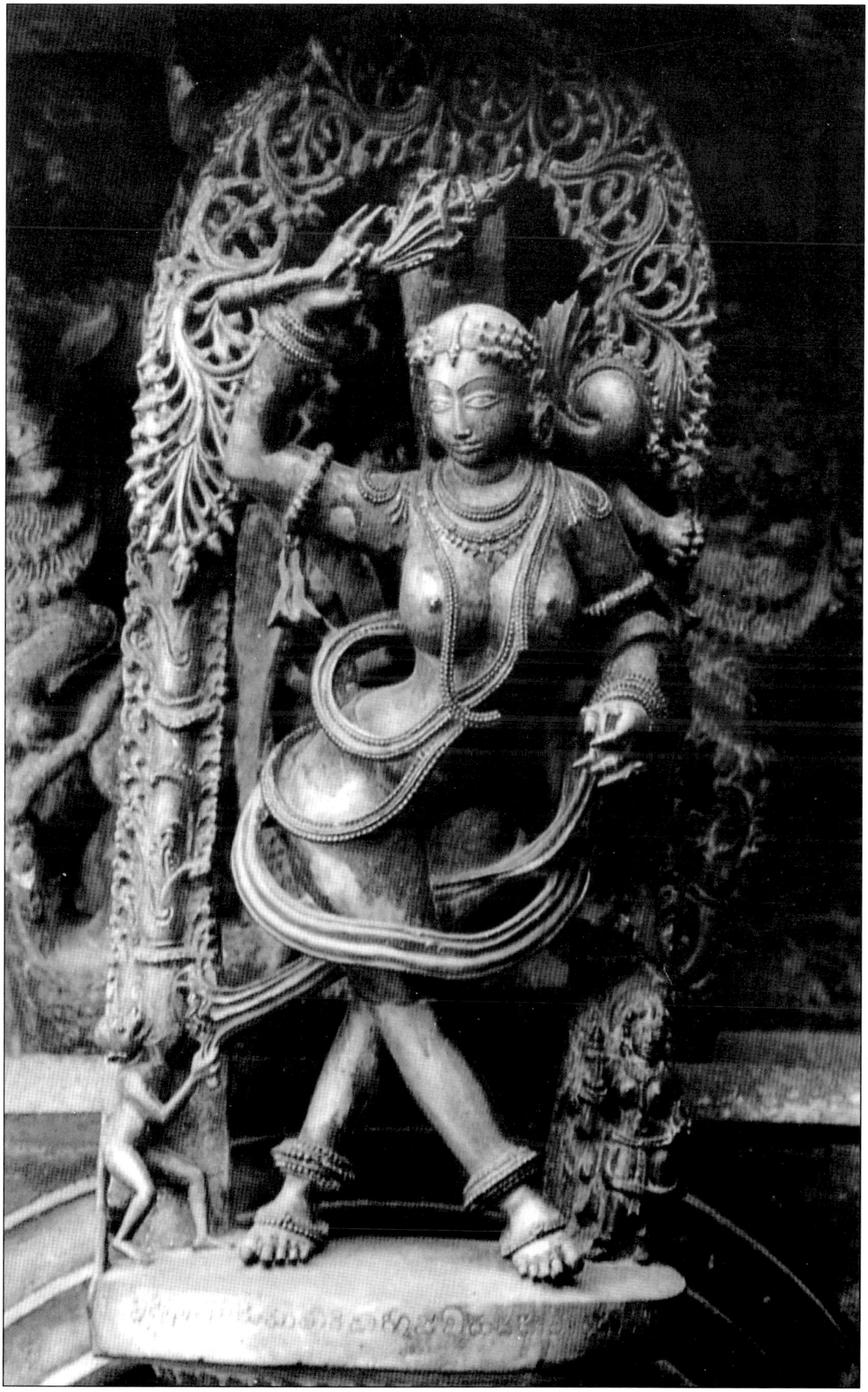

Pl. XI. B.F. 5. *Apsara*'s encounter with the monkey

B.F. 6

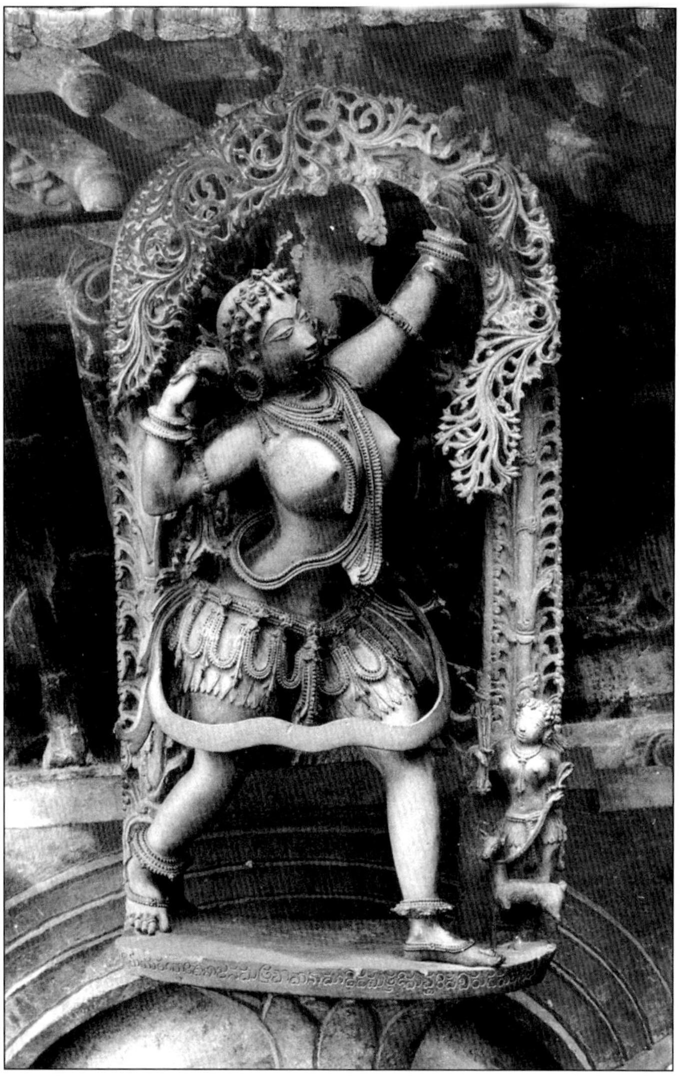

Pl. XII. B.F. 6. *Apsara* as a huntress

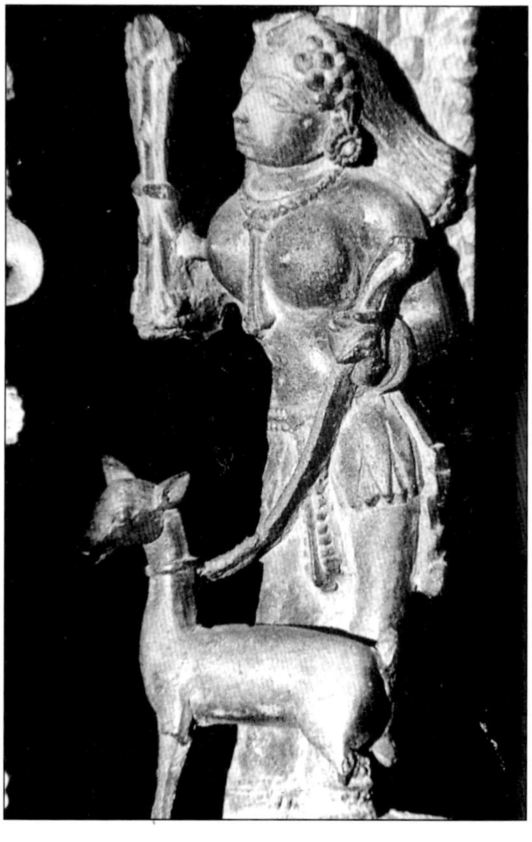

Pl. XII. B.F. 6a. *Apsara*'s attendant Śilpinī, with a trained deer 'dīpa mṛga'

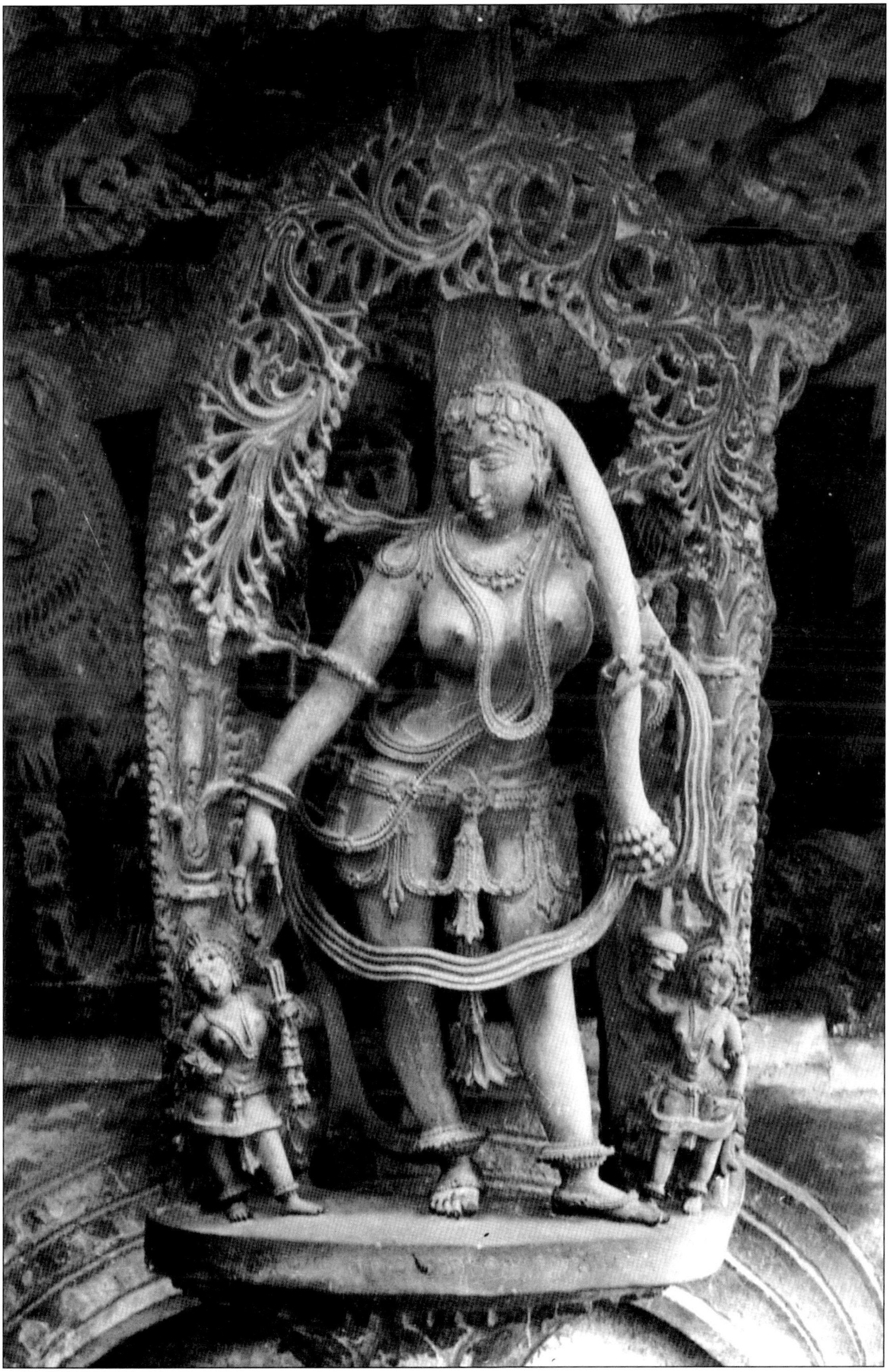

Pl. XIII. B.F. 7. *Apsara* displaying her hairstyle, with a pearly hairnet

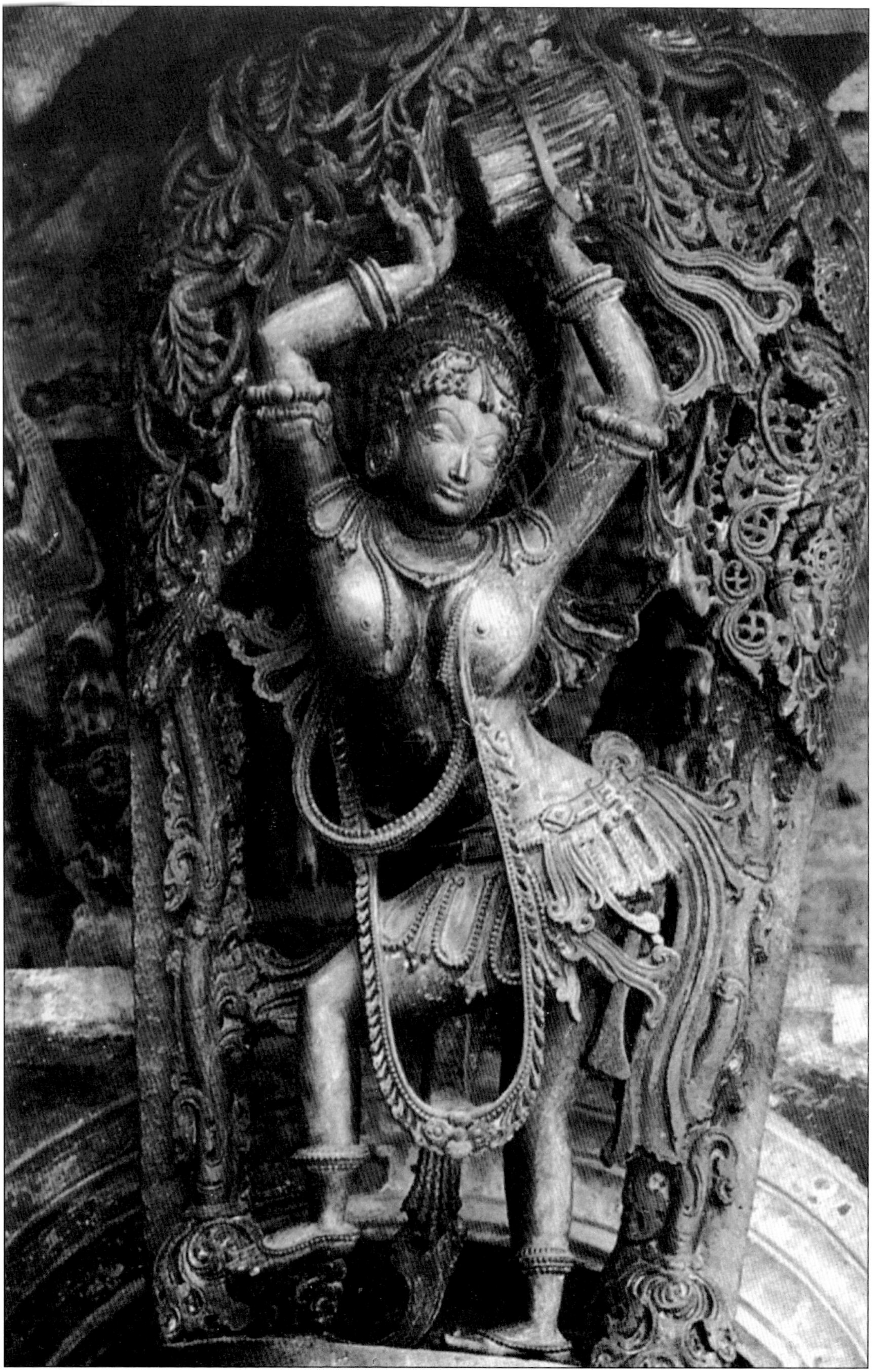

Pl. XIV. B.F. 8. *Apsara* playing a percussion instrument

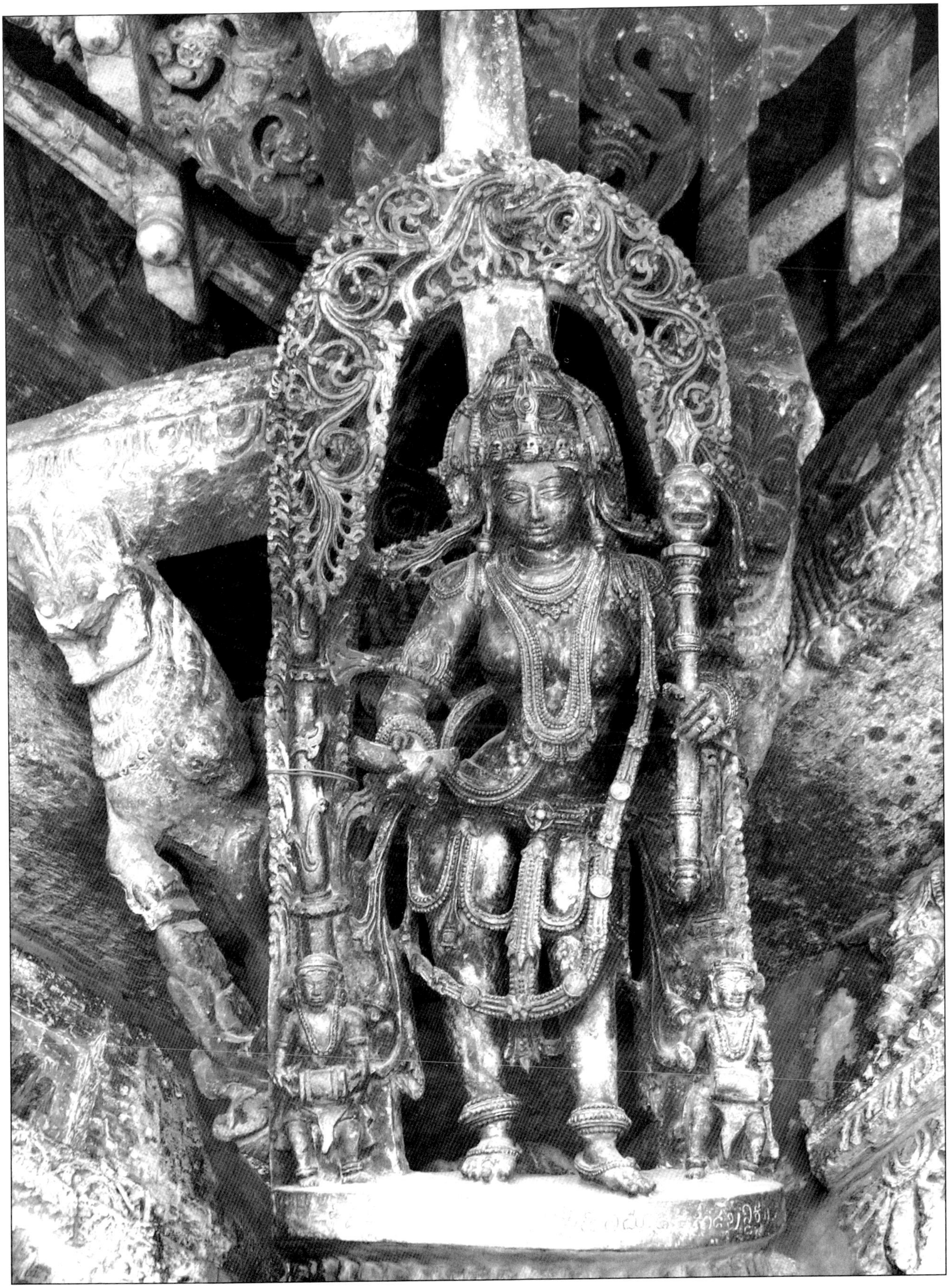

Pl. XV. B.F. 9. *Apsara* appearing as Bhairavī

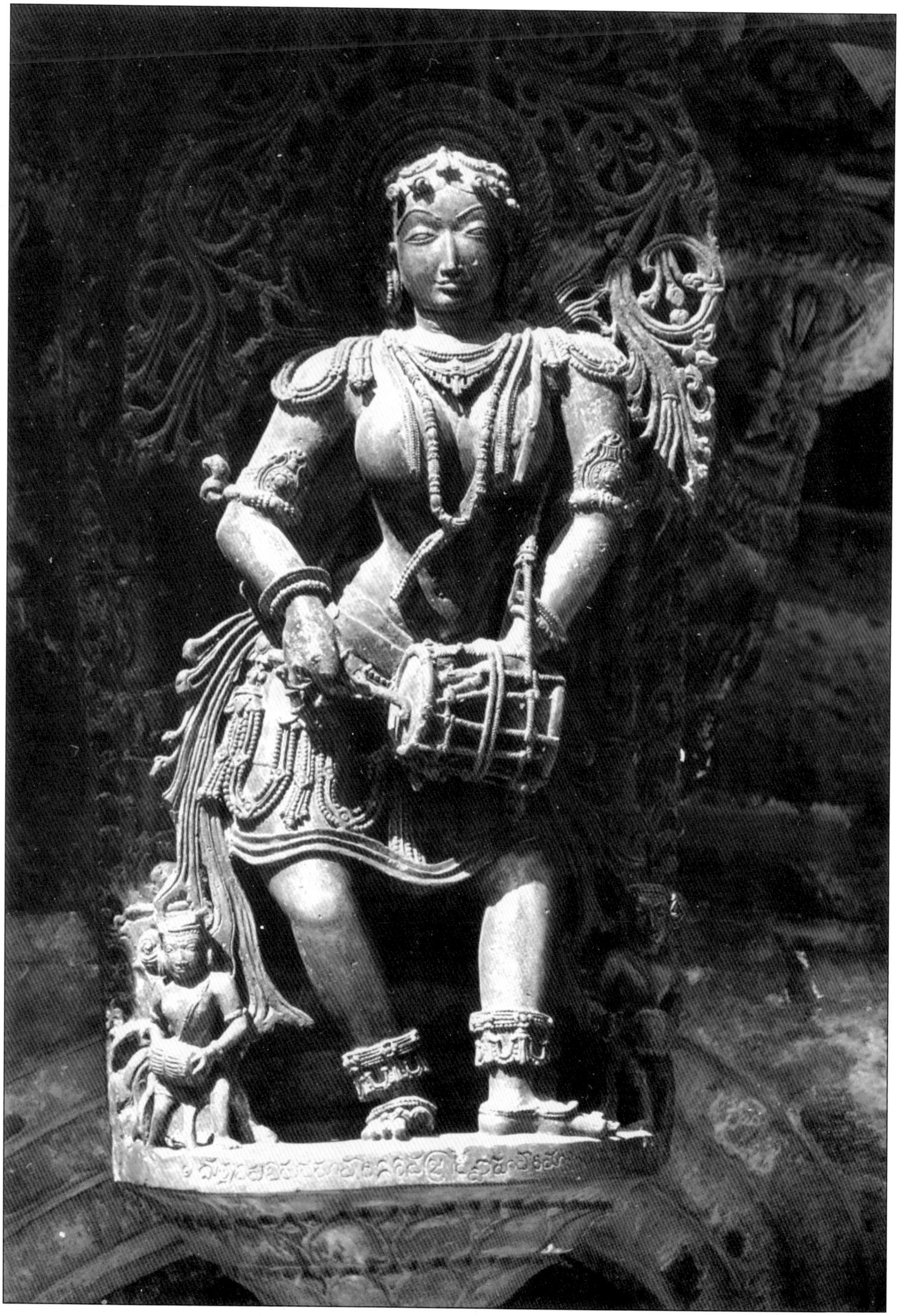

Pl. XVI. B.F. 10 *Apsara* playing a percussion instrument

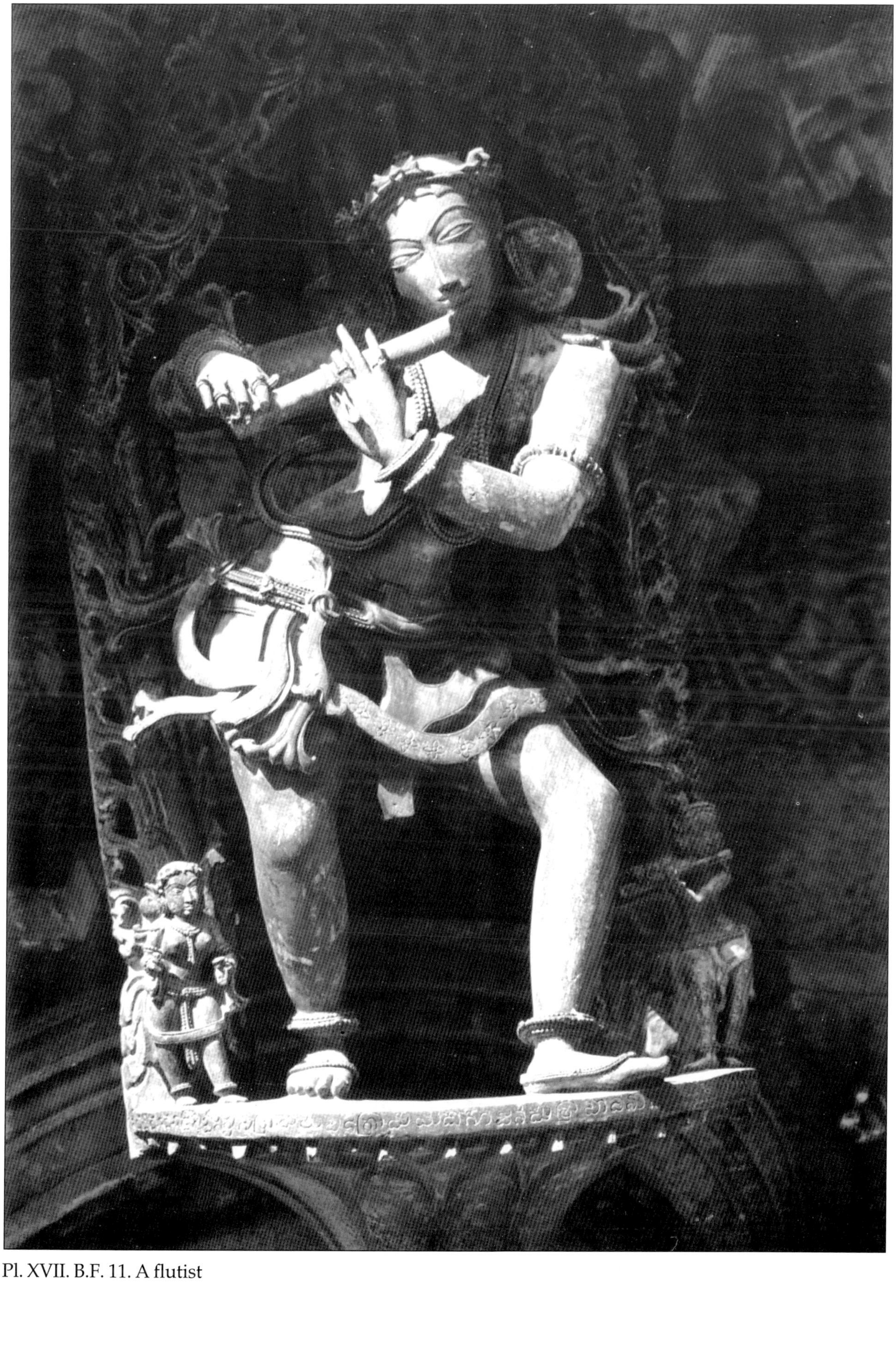

Pl. XVII. B.F. 11. A flutist

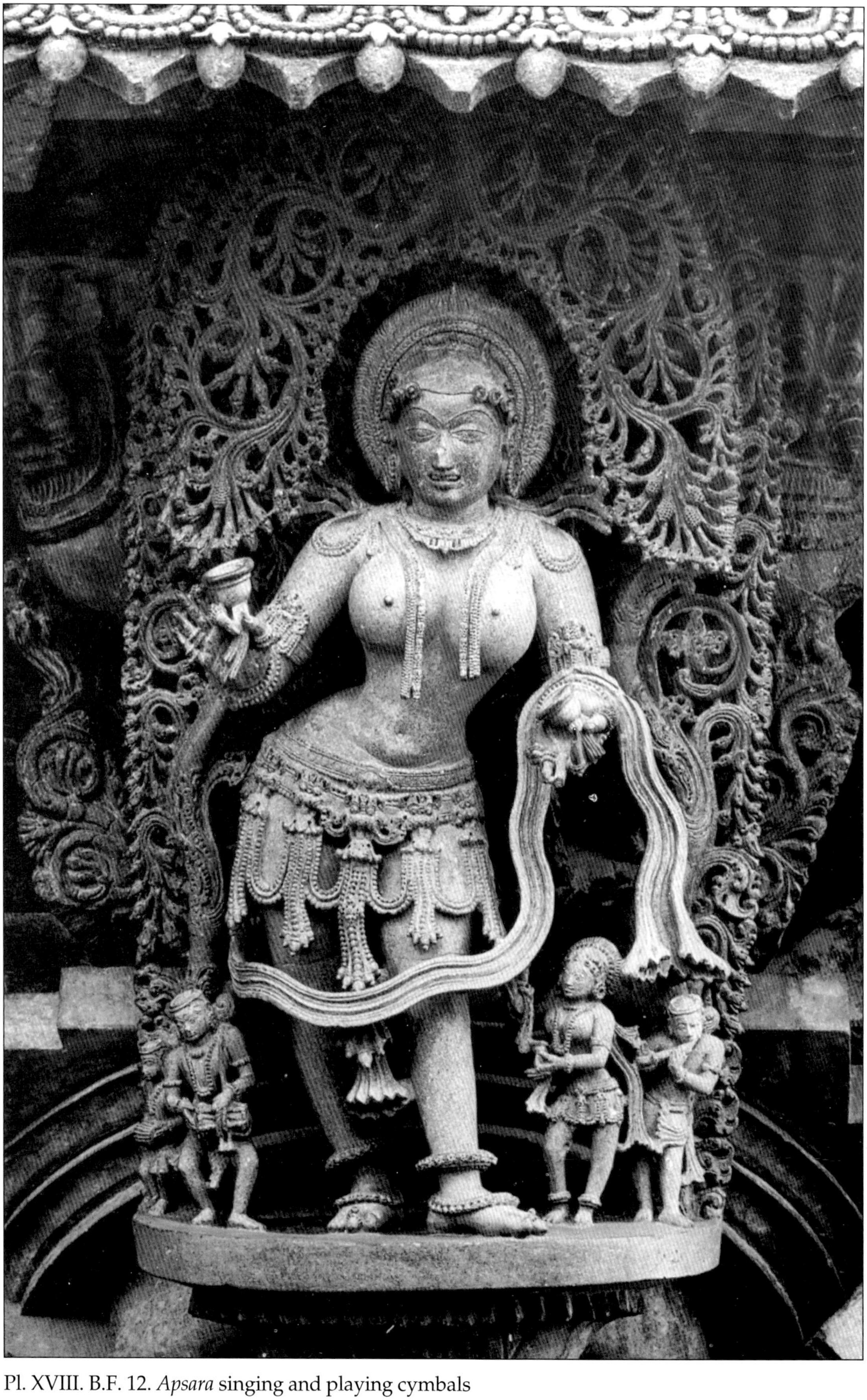

Pl. XVIII. B.F. 12. *Apsara* singing and playing cymbals

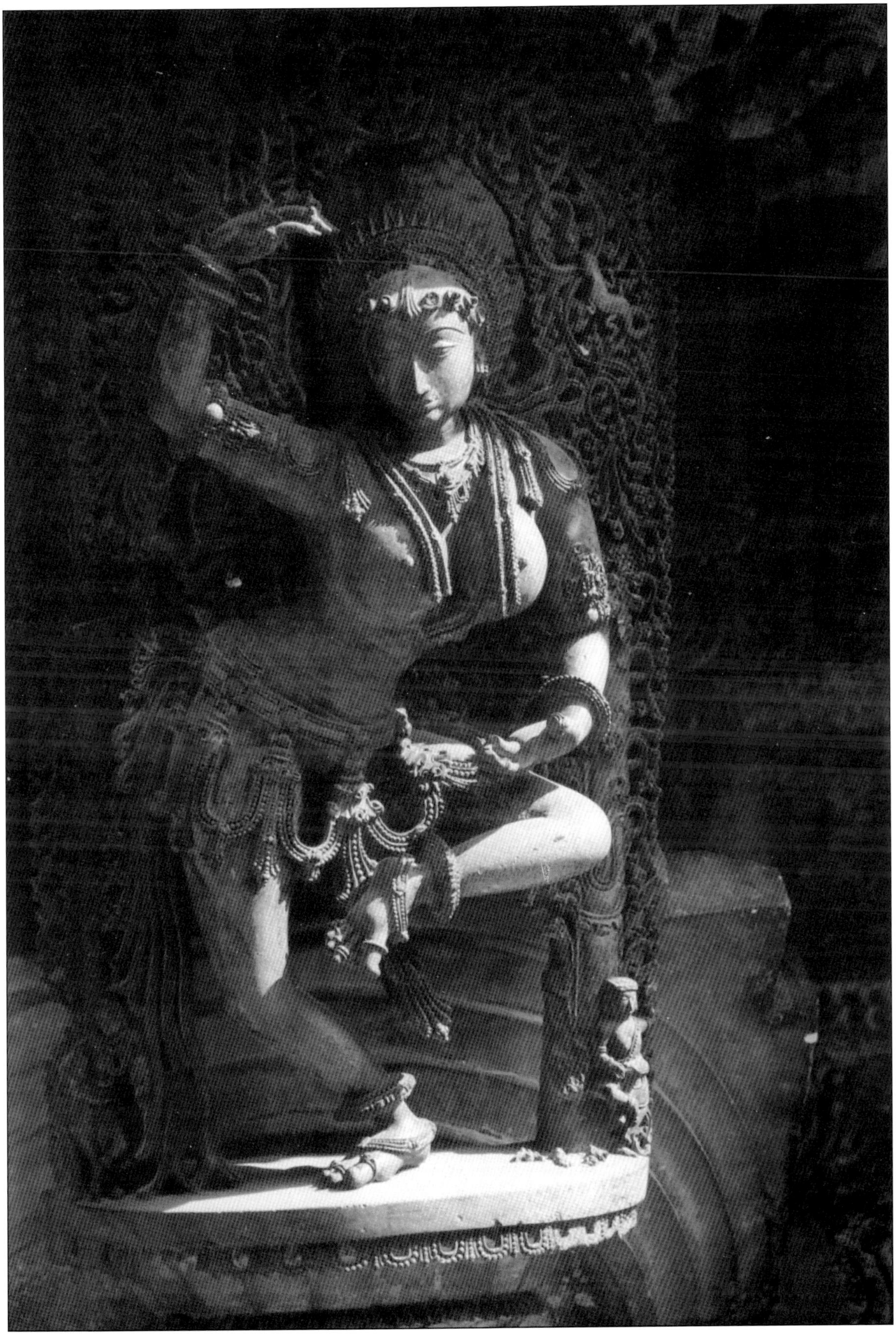

Pl. XIX. B.F. 13. *Apsara* tuning the stringed instrument *Tambura*

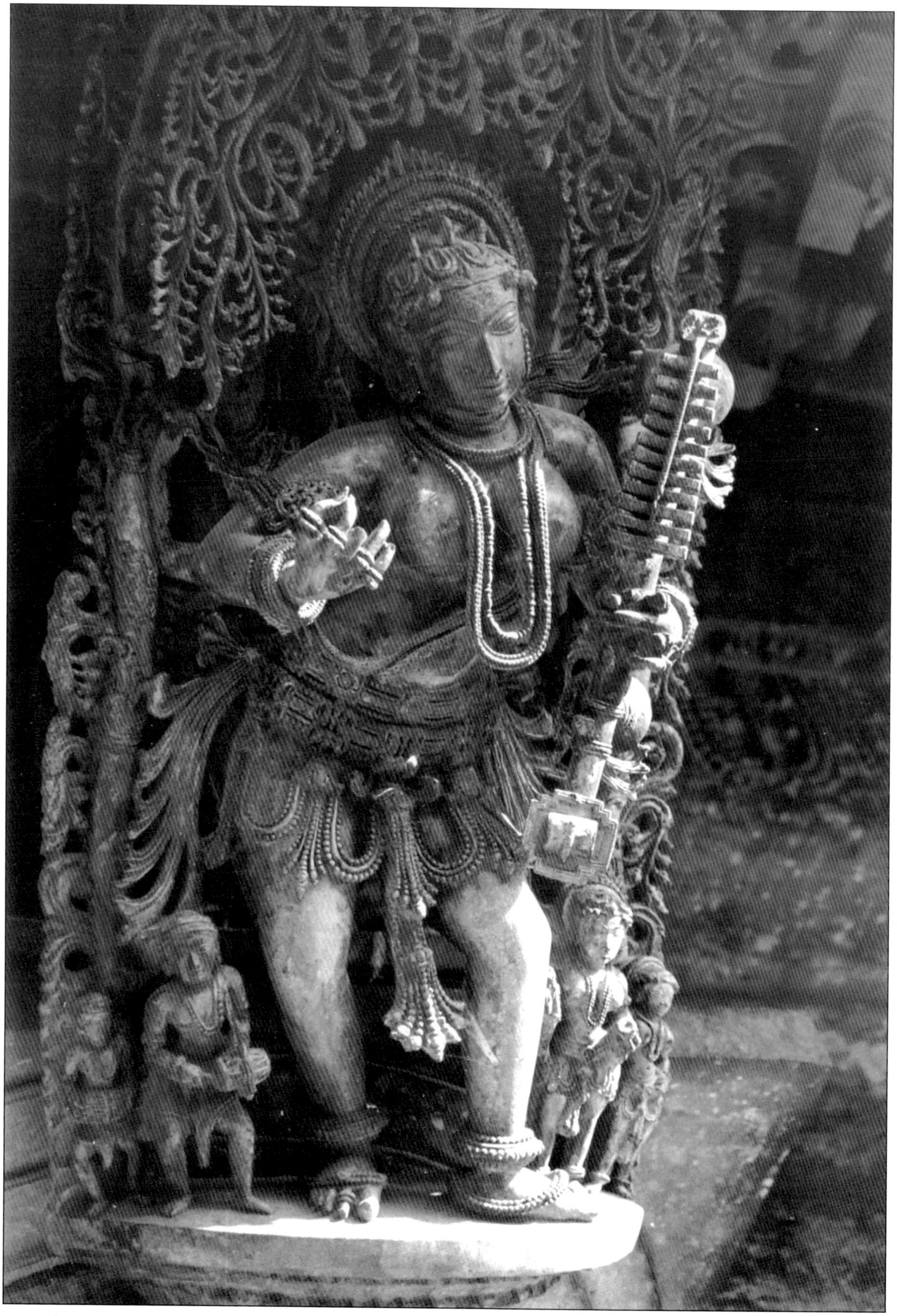

Pl. XX. B.F. 14. *Apsara* tuning the stringed instrument

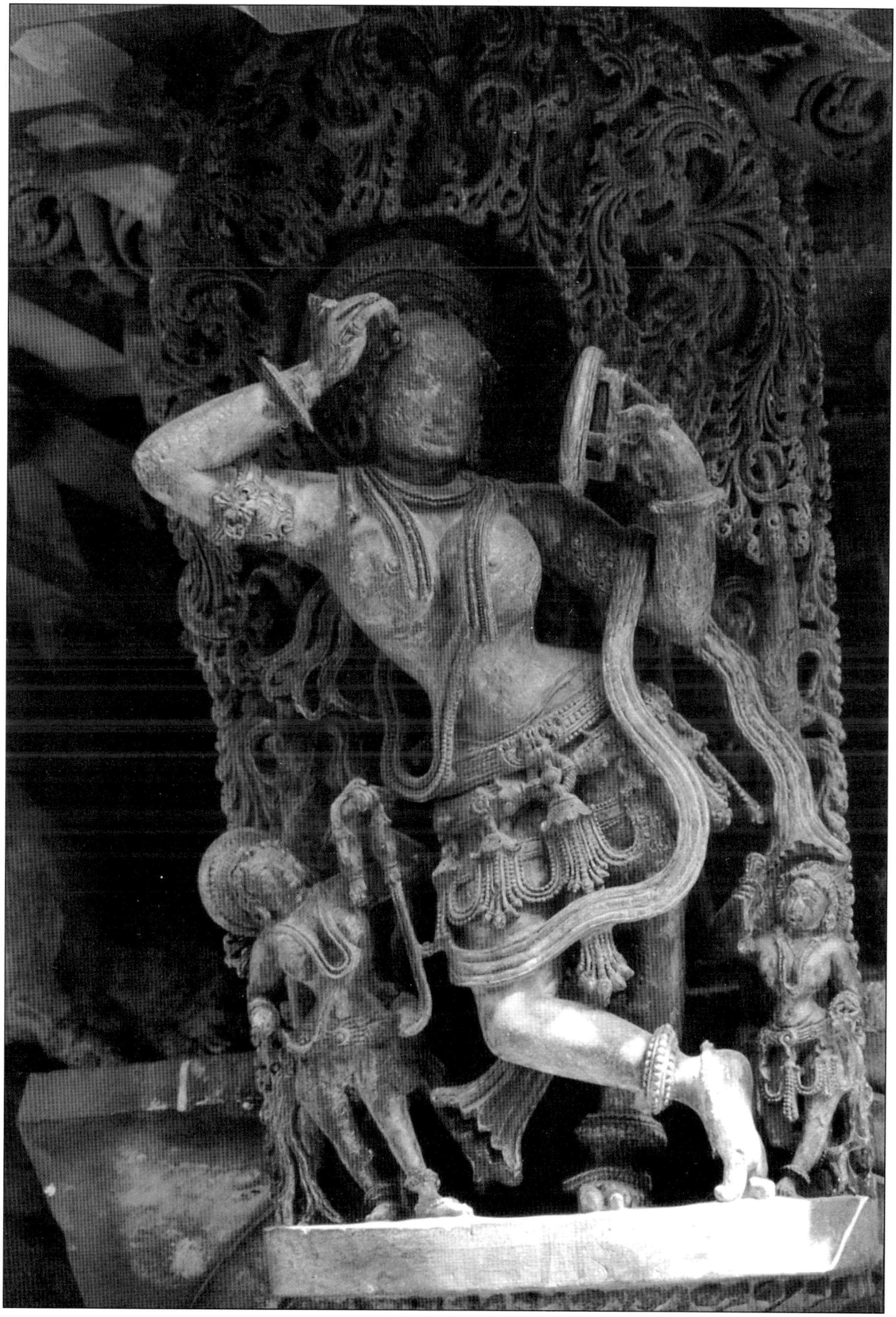

Pl. XXI. B.F. 15. *Apsara* admiring her charm in a mirror

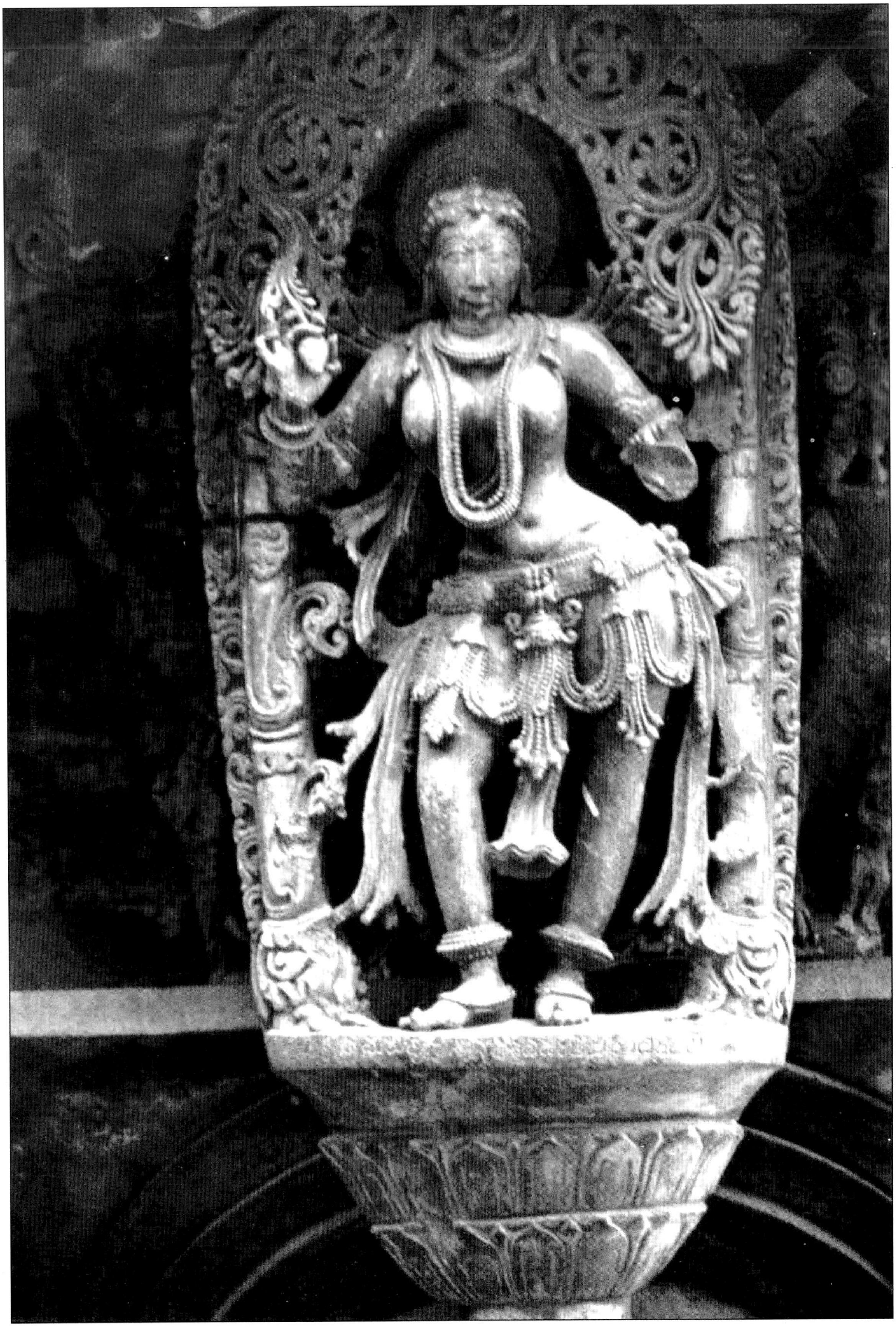

Pl. XXII. B.F. 16. *Apsara* in a garden

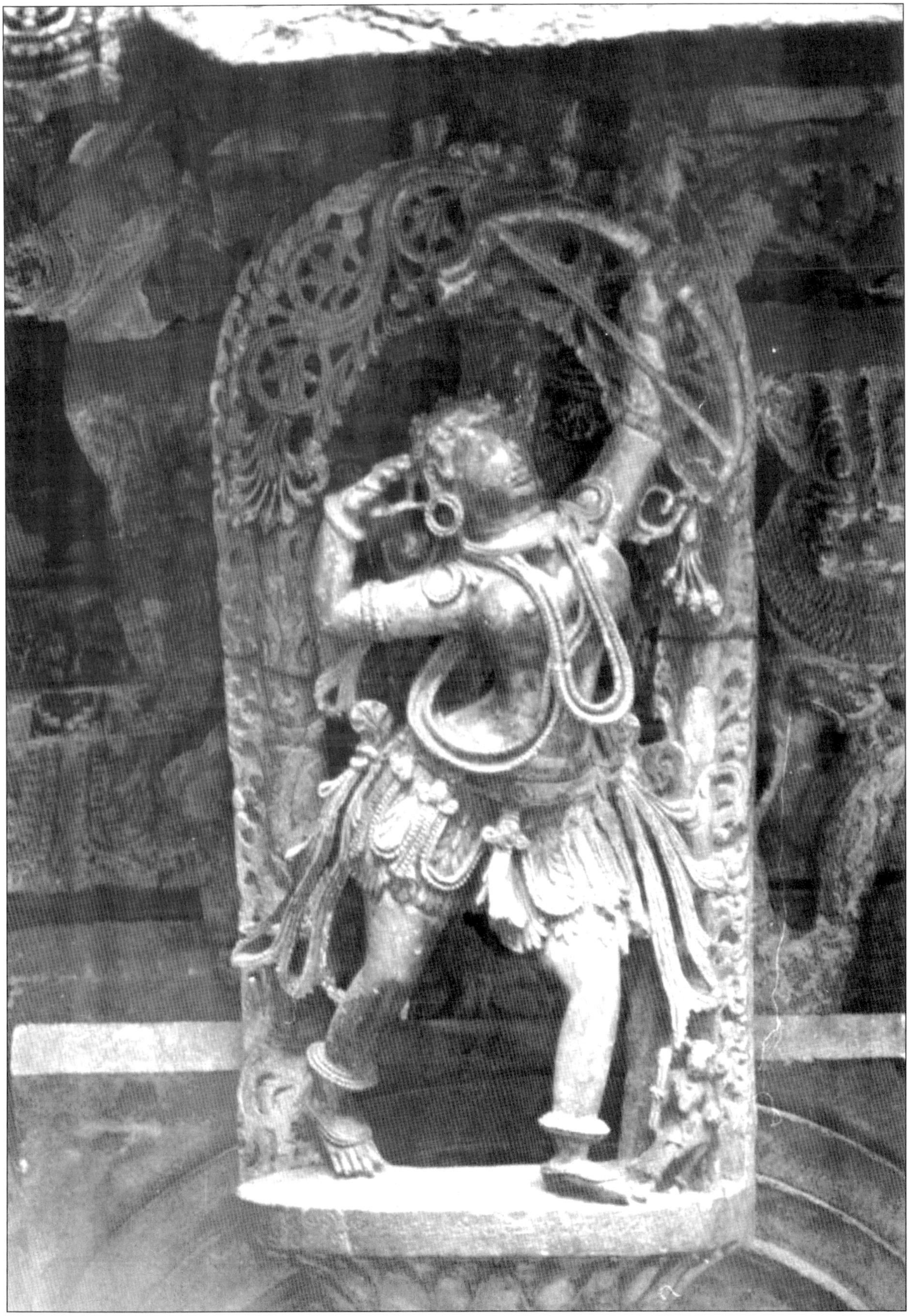

Pl. XXIII. B.F. 17. *Apsara* as a huntress

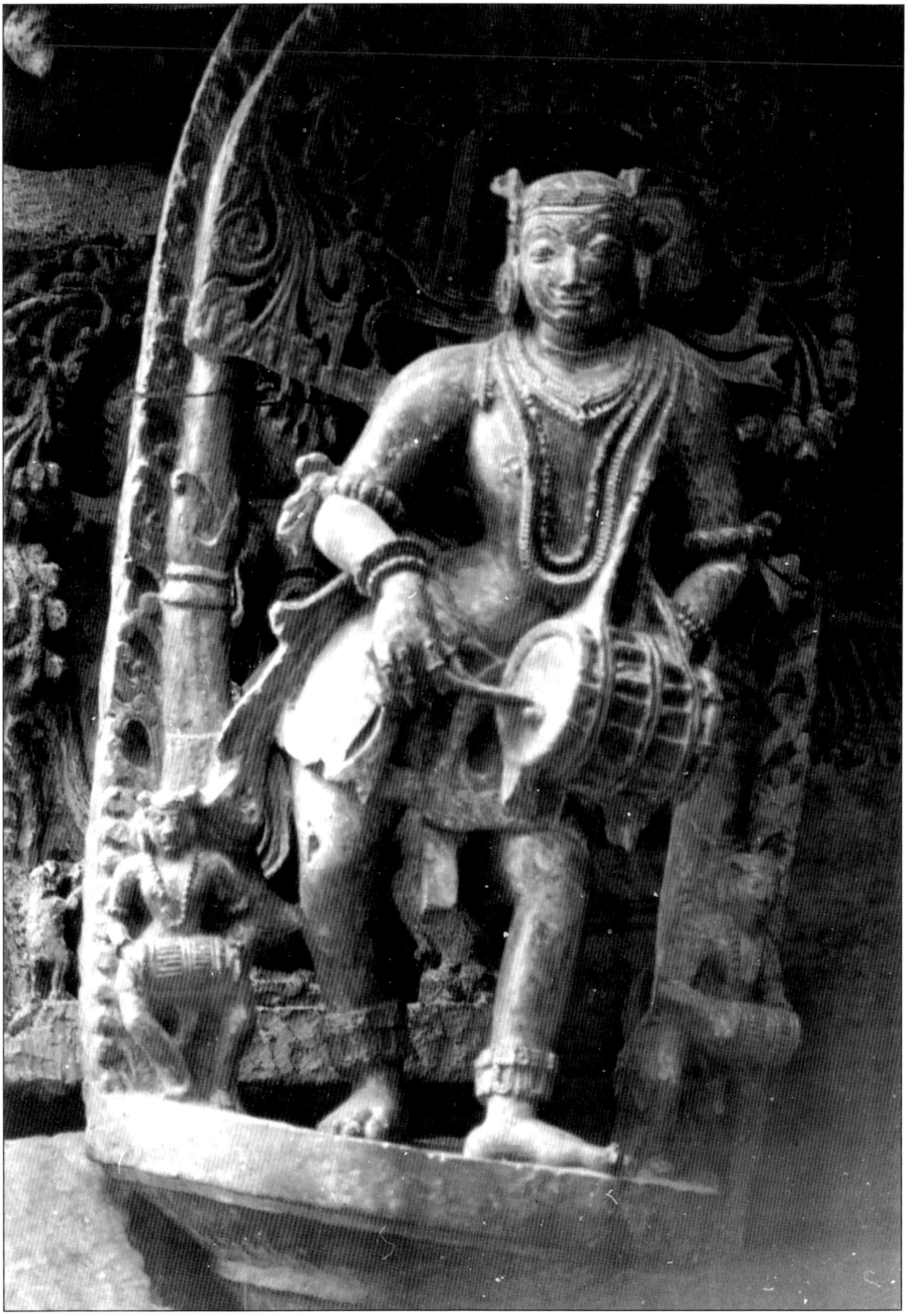

Pl. XXIV. B.F. 18. A drummer

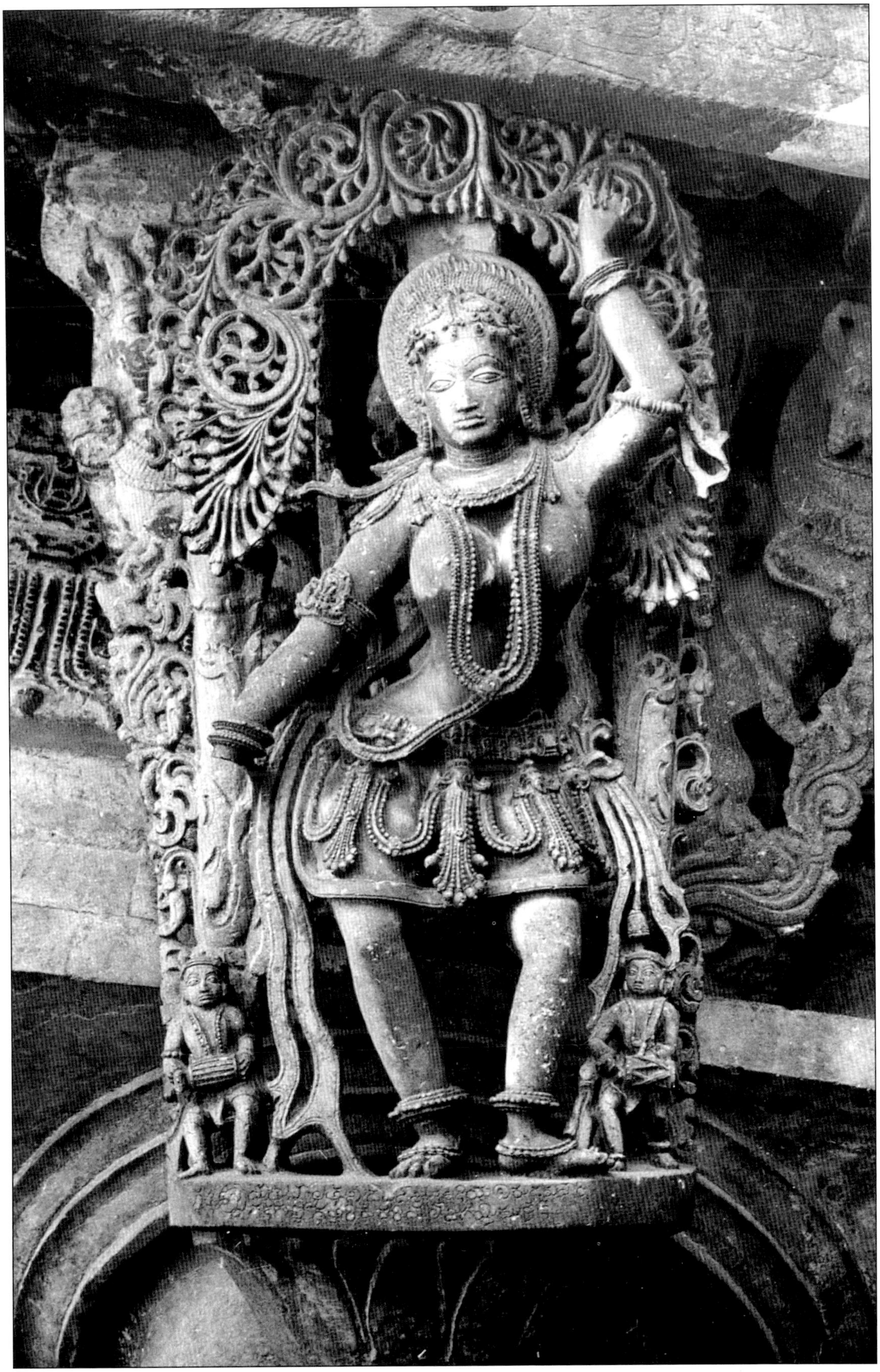

Pl. XXV. B.F. 19. *Apsara* in a graceful dance movement

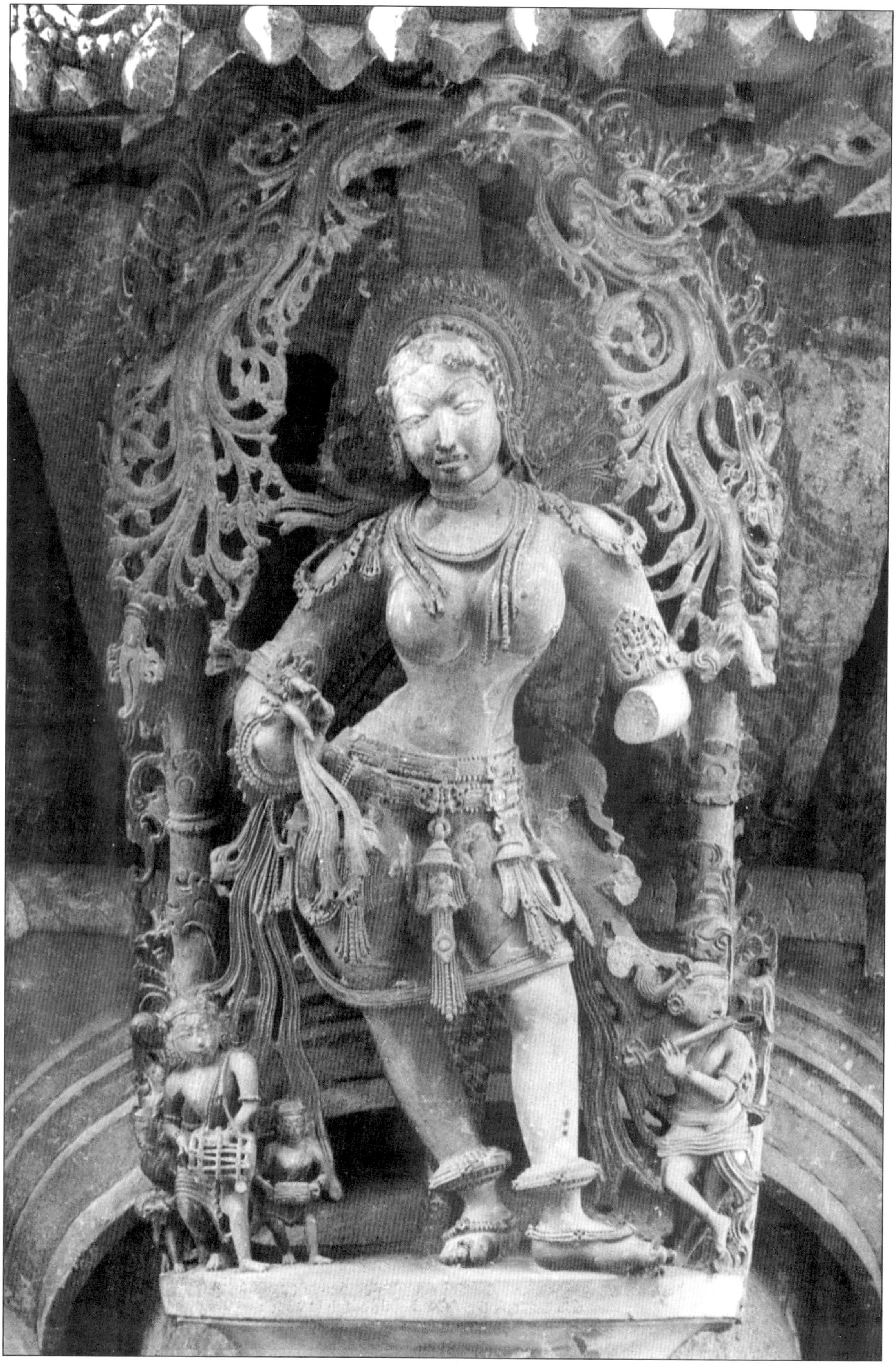

Pl. XXVI. B.F. 20. *Apsara* singing and playing cymbals

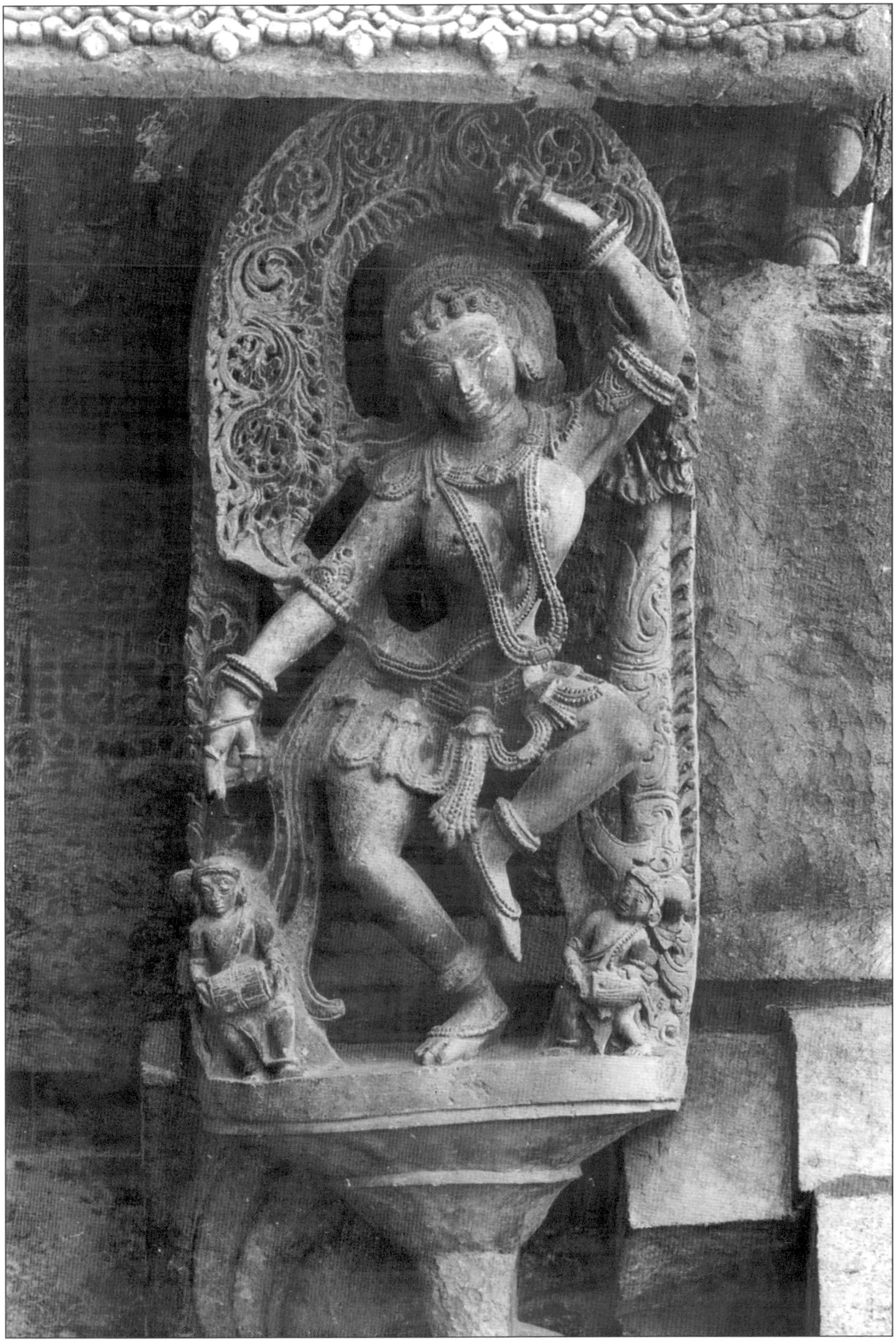

Pl. XXVII. B.F. 21. *Apsara* in a graceful dance movement

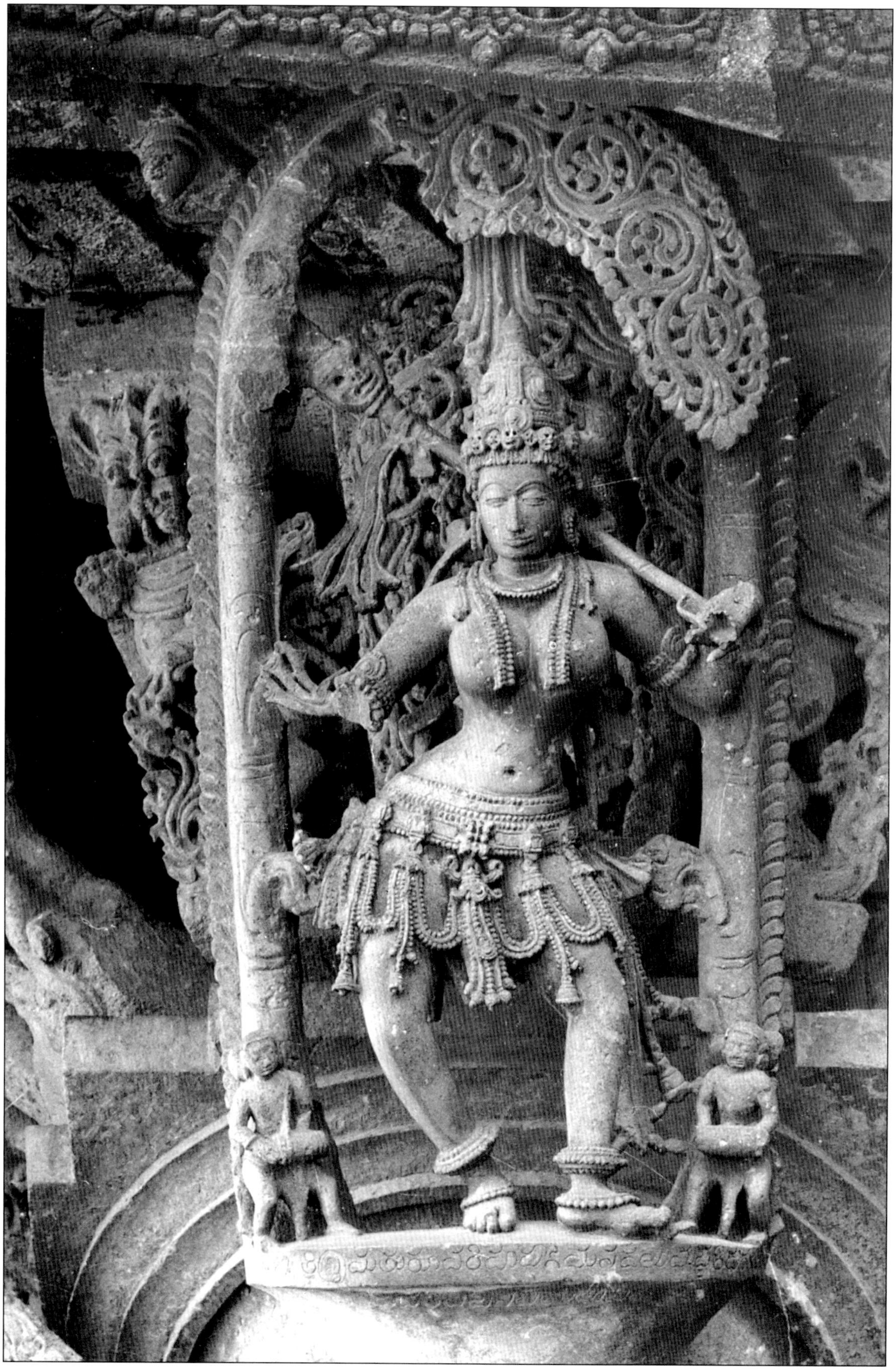

Pl. XXVIII. B.F. 22. *Apsara* appearing as a Bhairavī

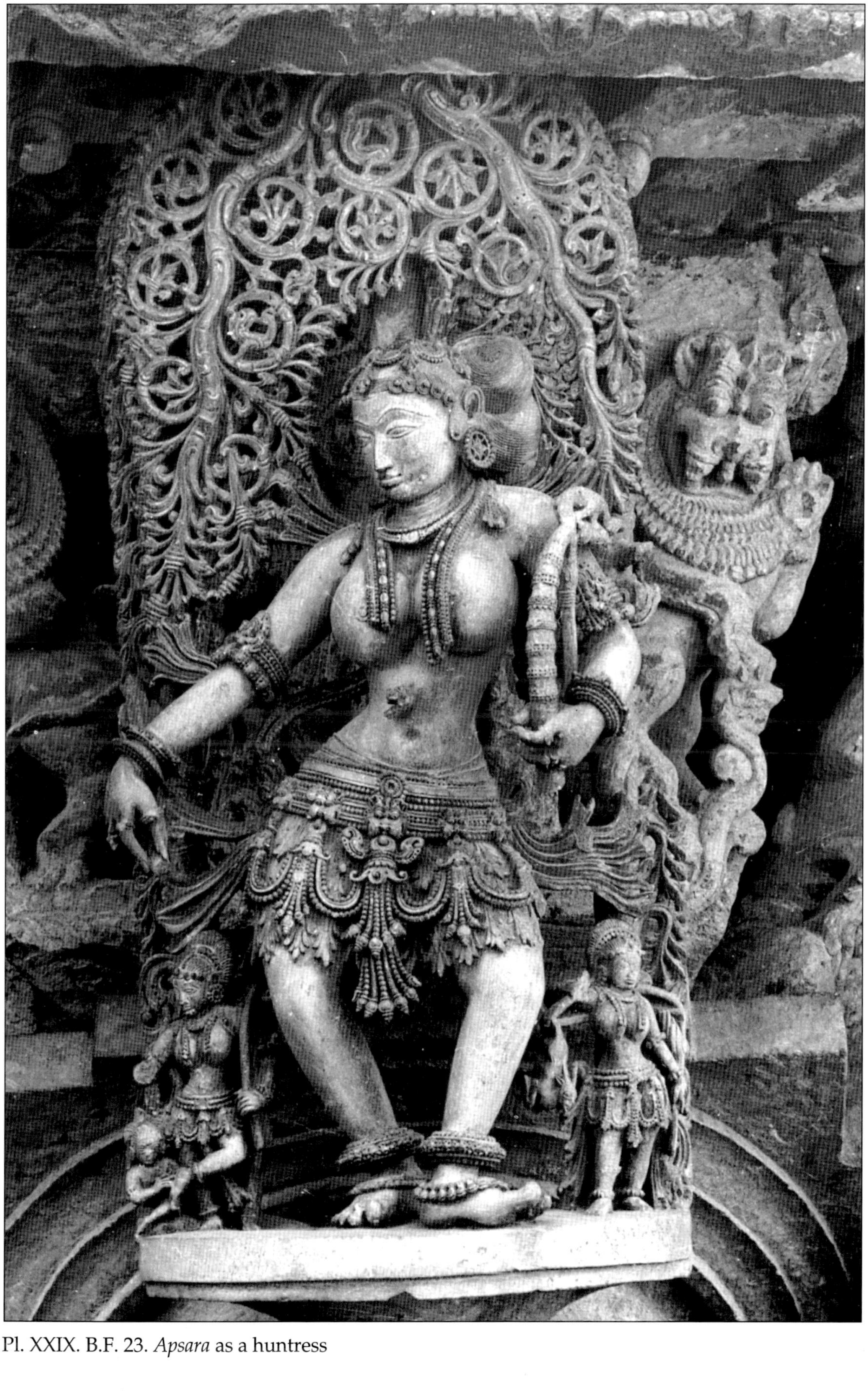

Pl. XXIX. B.F. 23. *Apsara* as a huntress

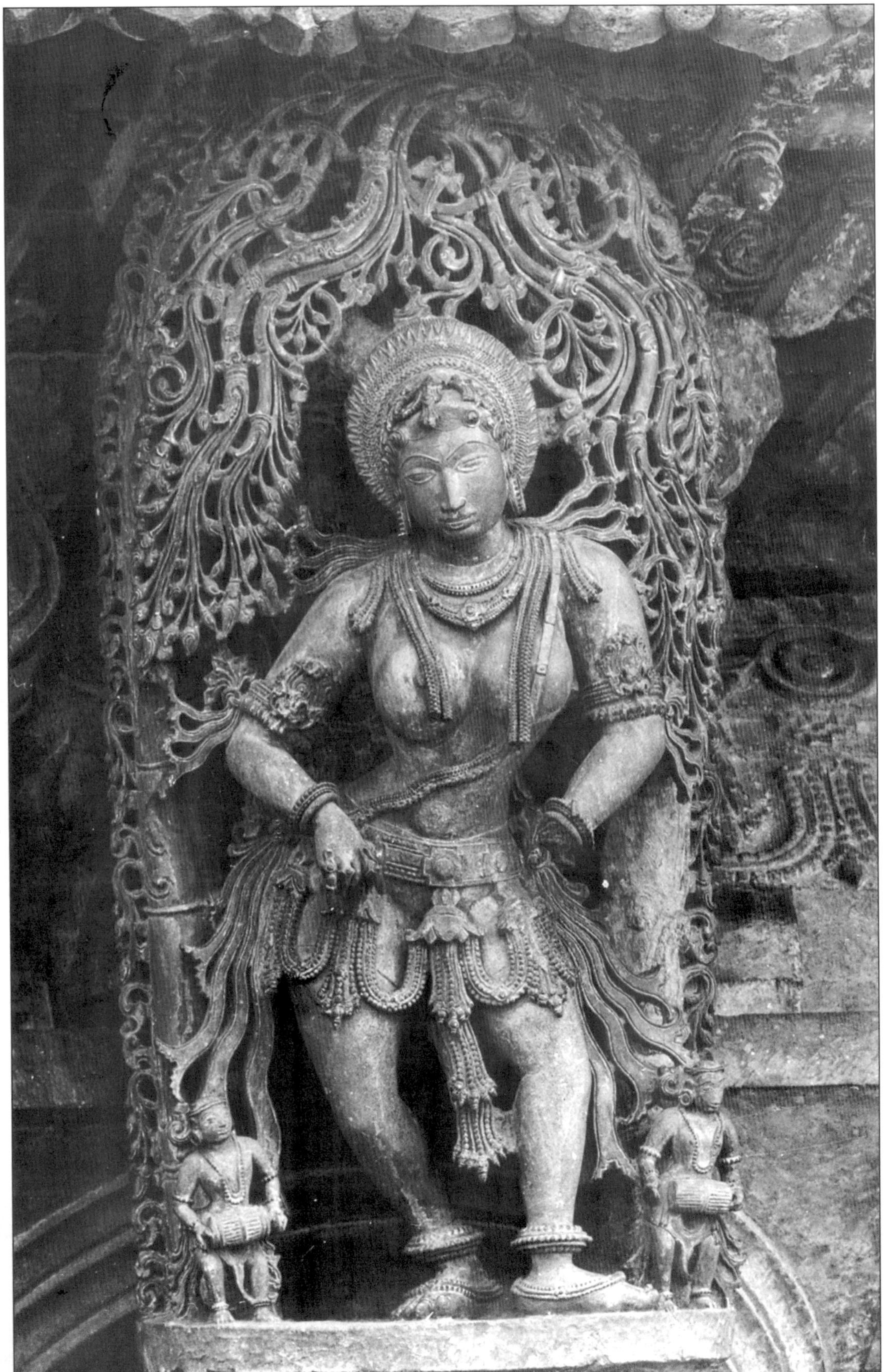

Pl. XXX. B.F. 24. *Apsara* playing a percussion instrument

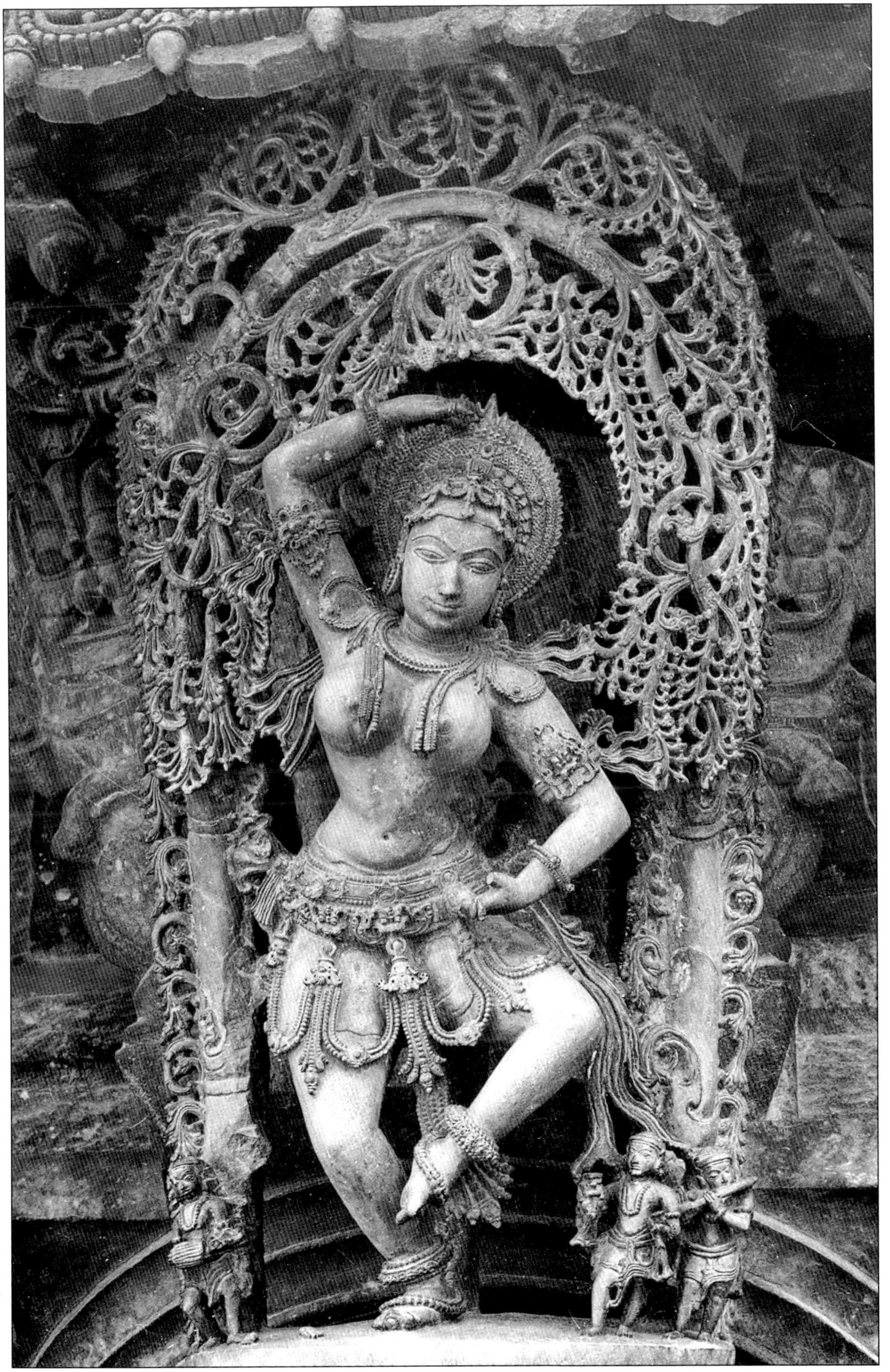

Pl. XXXI. B.F. 25. *Apsara* in a vigorous dance movement

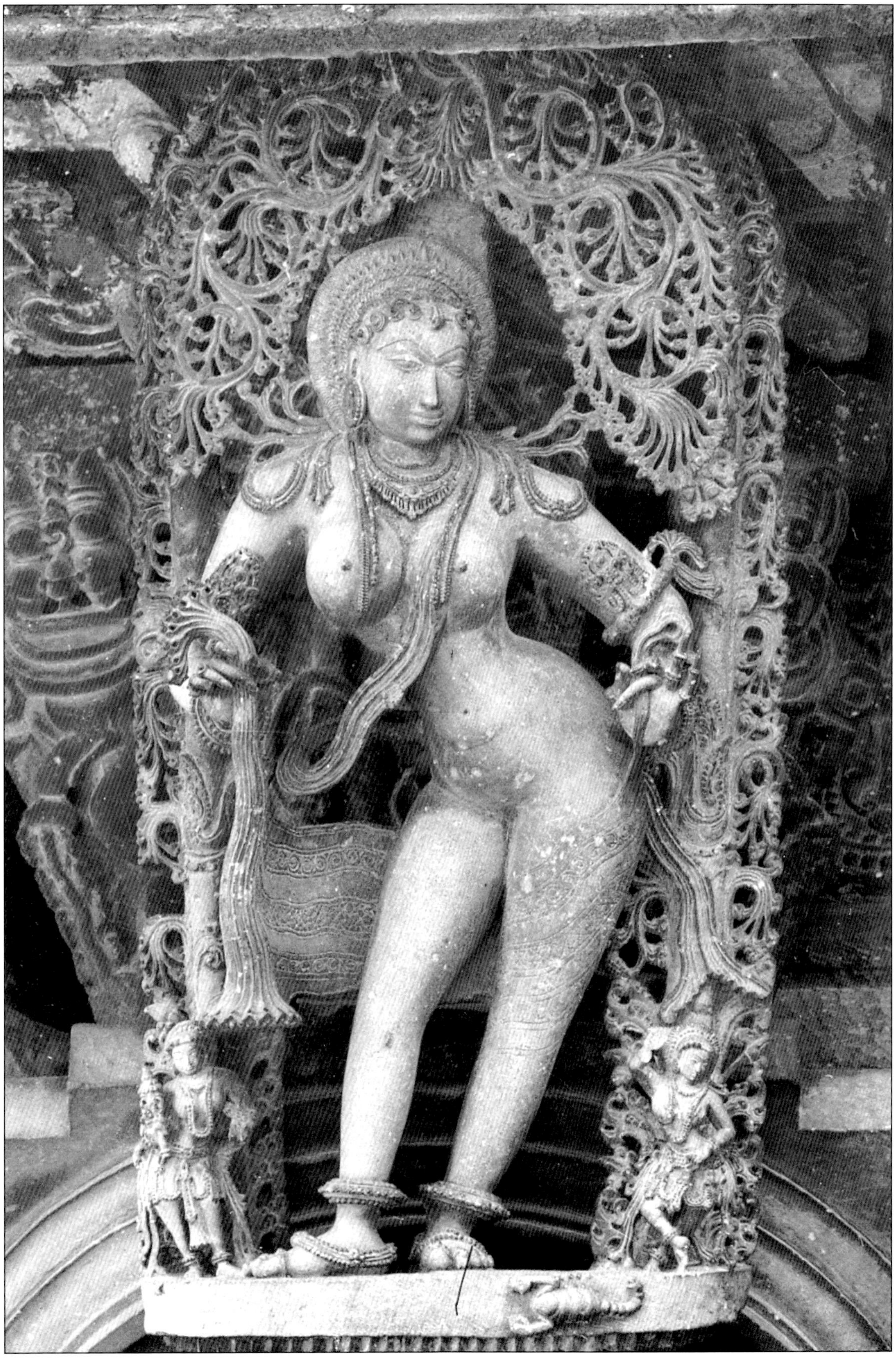

Pl. XXXII. B.F. 26. *Apsara*'s encounter with a scorpion

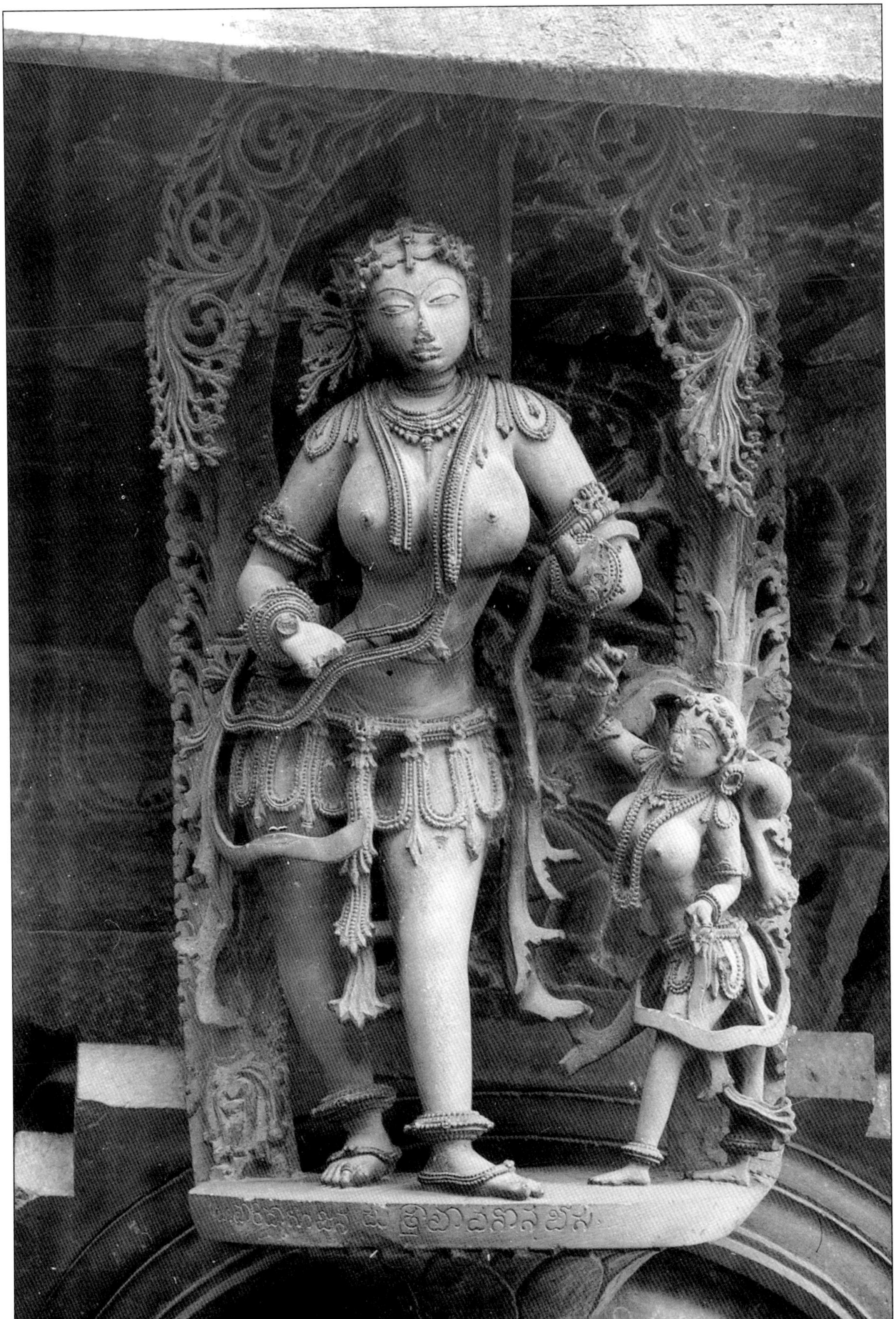

Pl. XXXIII. B.F. 27. *Apsara* with a parrot, encouraging her pet parrot to speak

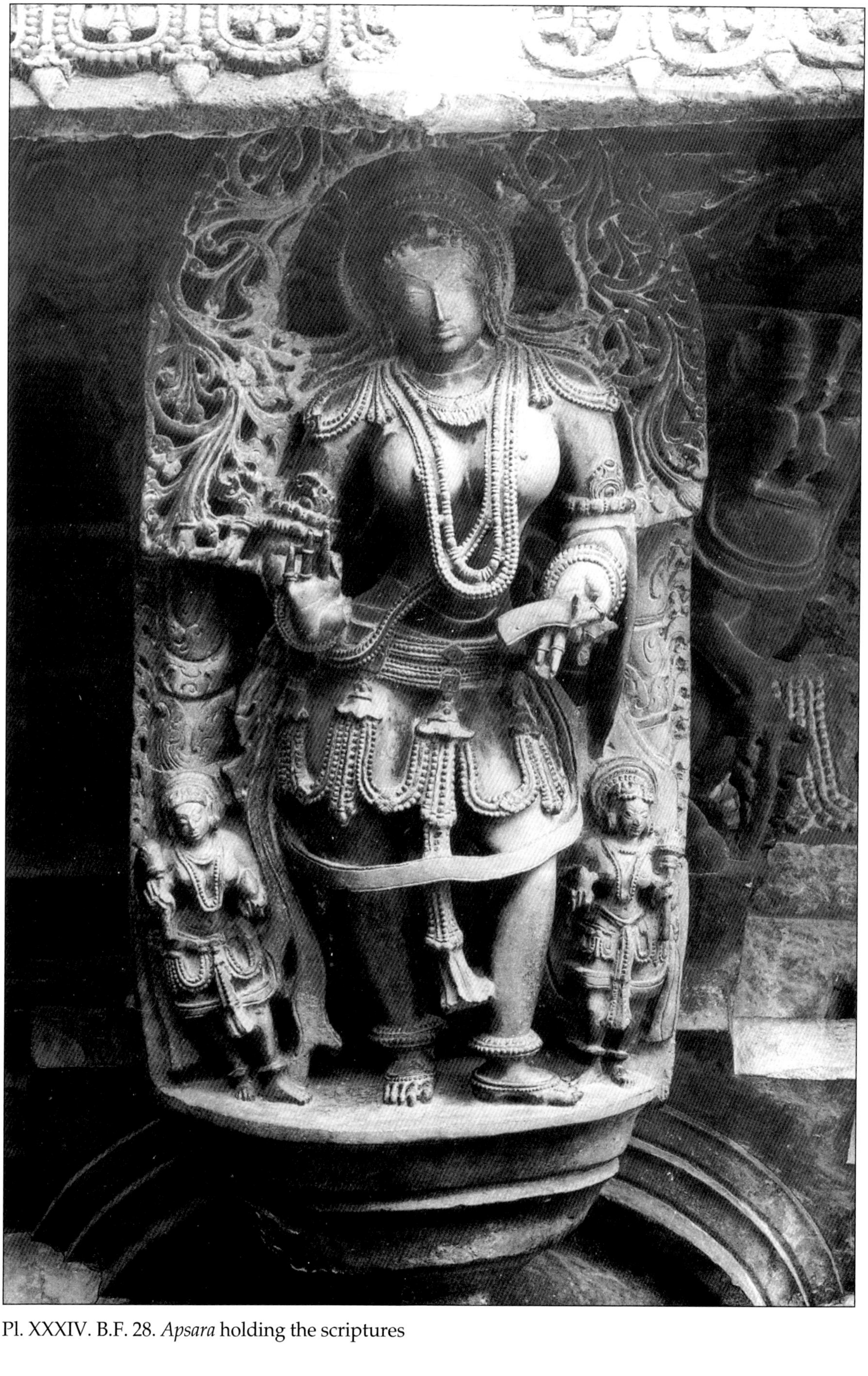

Pl. XXXIV. B.F. 28. *Apsara* holding the scriptures

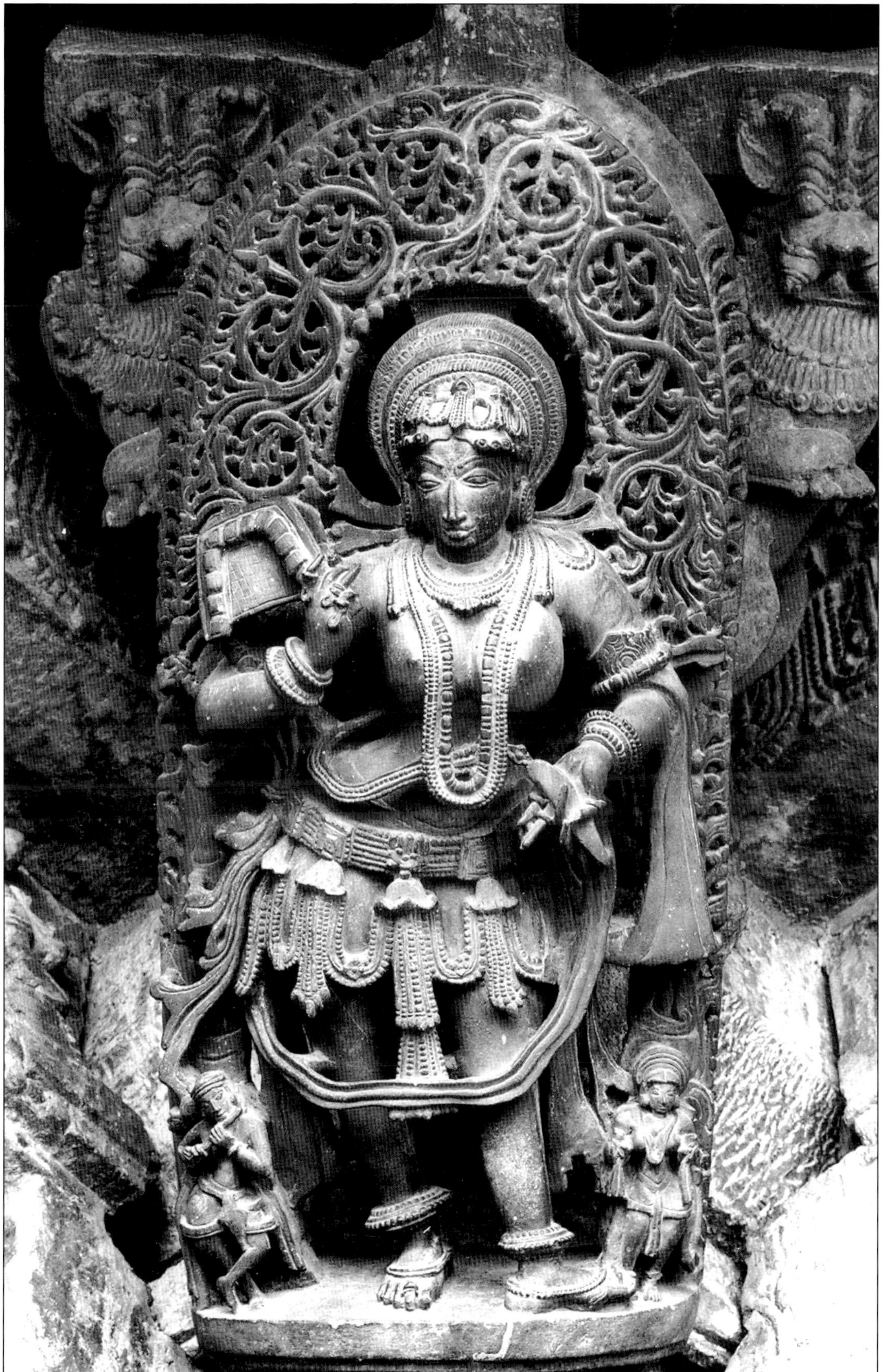

Pl. XXXV. B.F. 29. *Apsara* with a stringed instrument

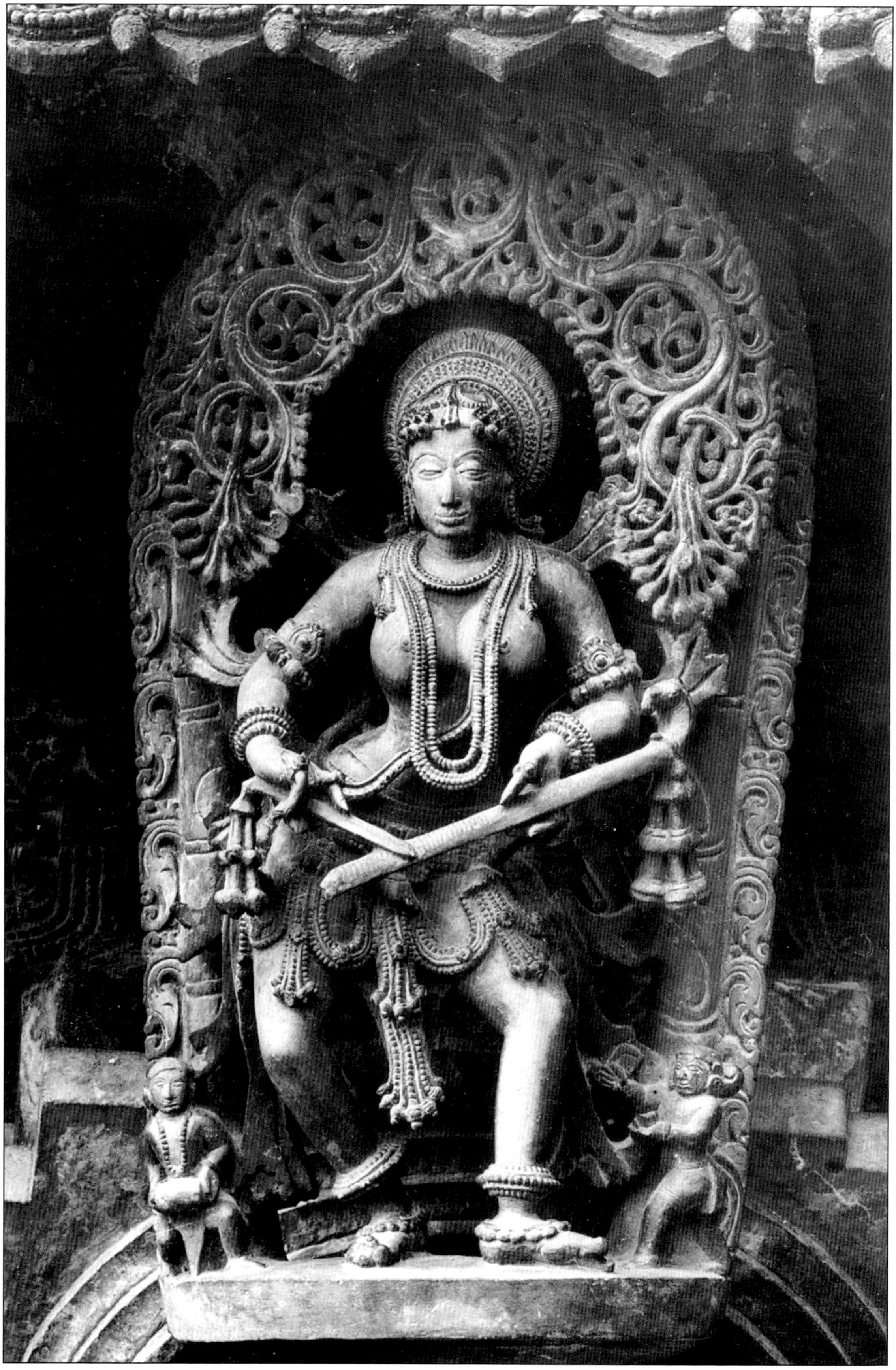

Pl. XXXVI. B.F. 30. *Apsara* playing a stringed instrument

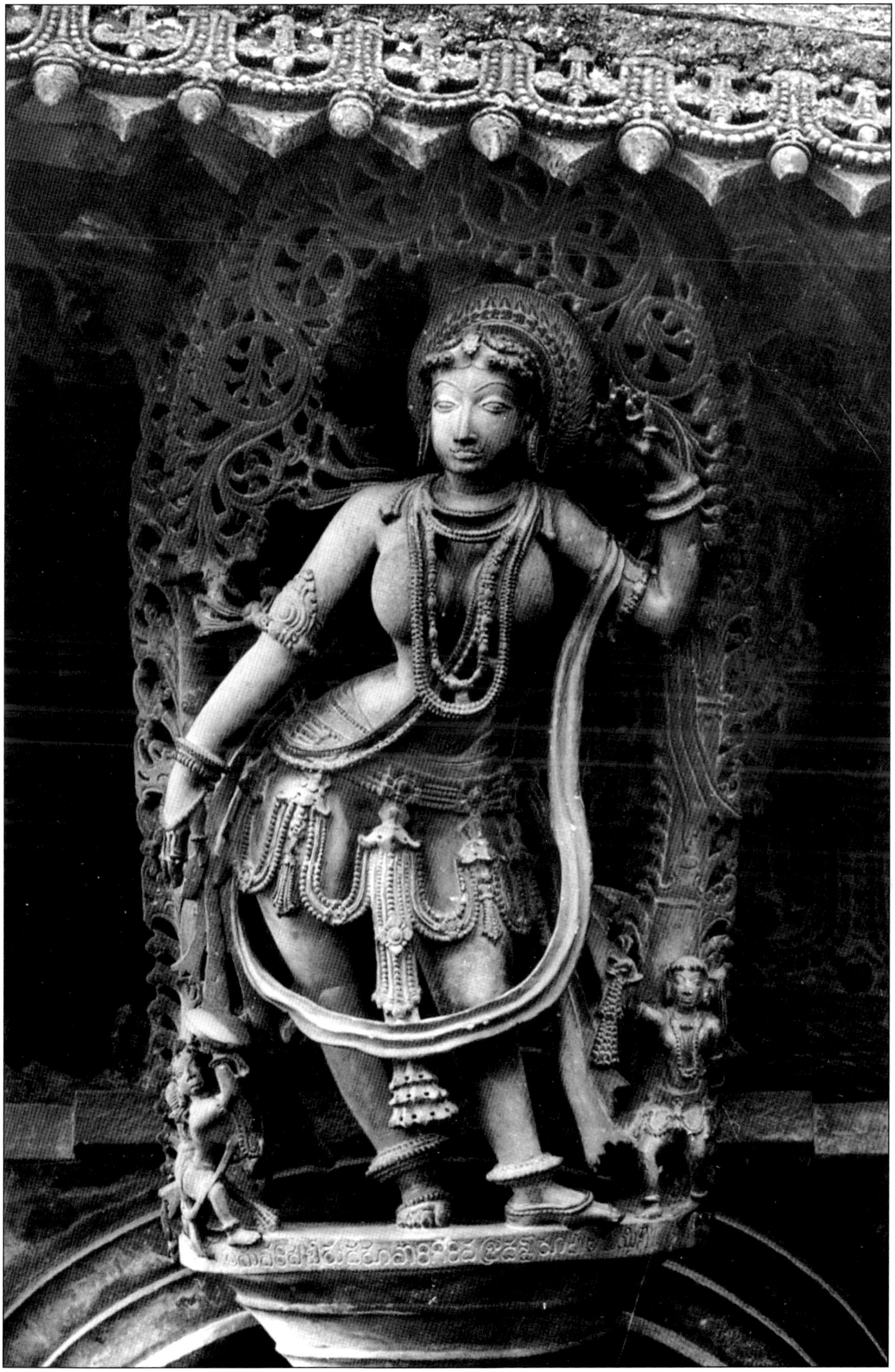

Pl. XXXVII. B.F. 31. *Apsara* adorning herself with a floral ornament

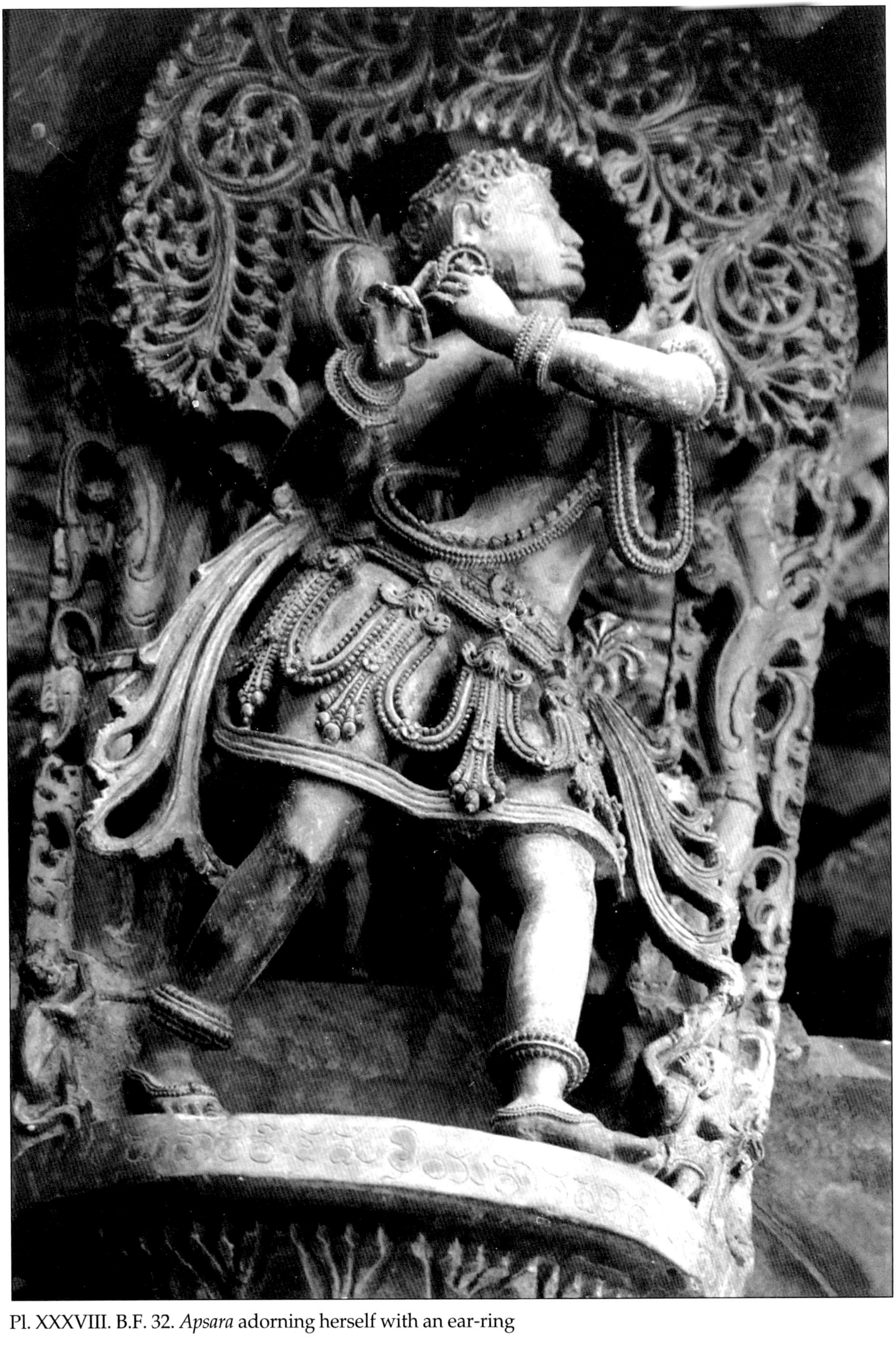

Pl. XXXVIII. B.F. 32. *Apsara* adorning herself with an ear-ring

B.F. 33

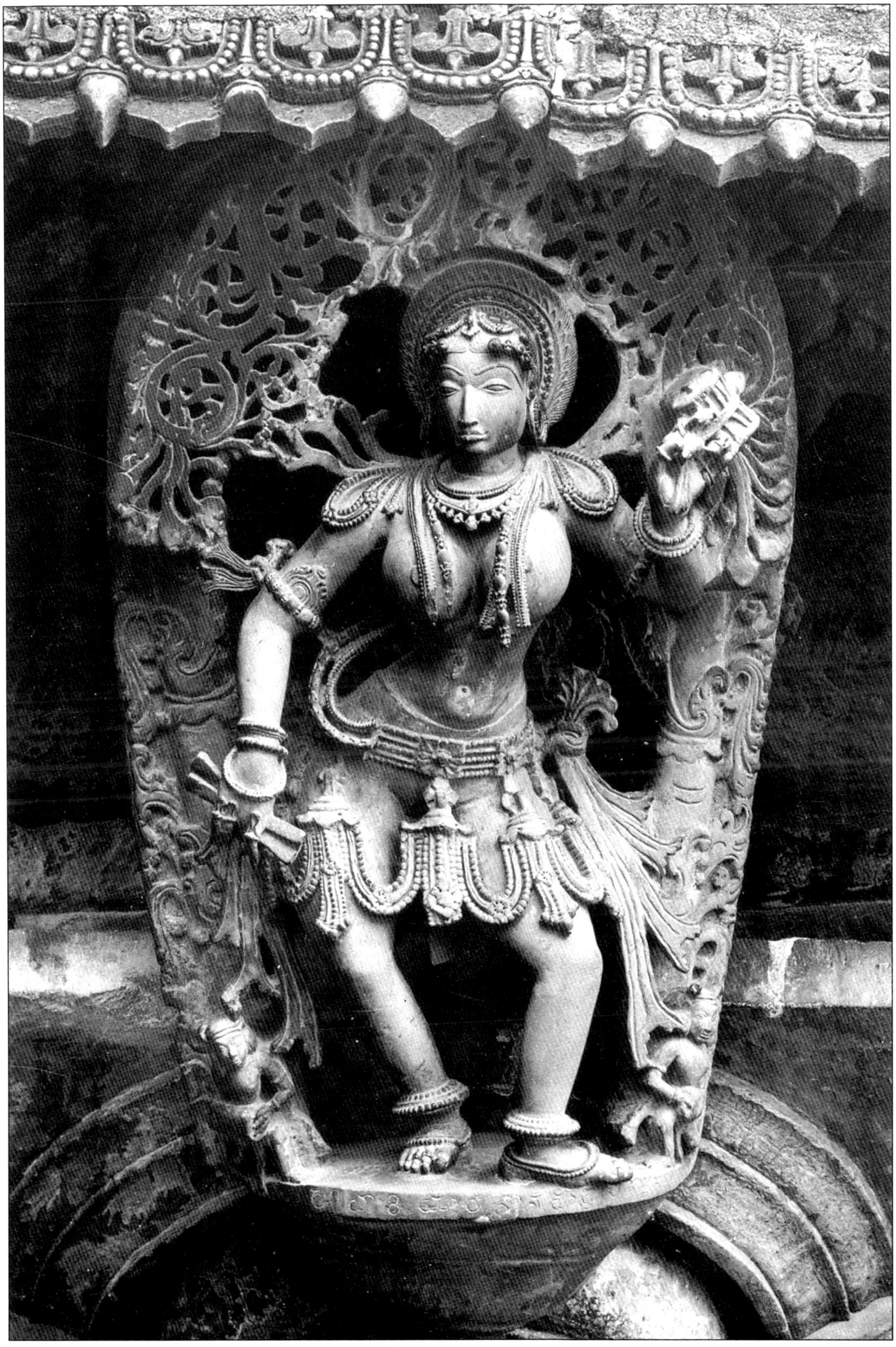

Pl. XXXIX. B.F. 33. *Apsara* playing a small percussion instrument and *Chitike tāla*

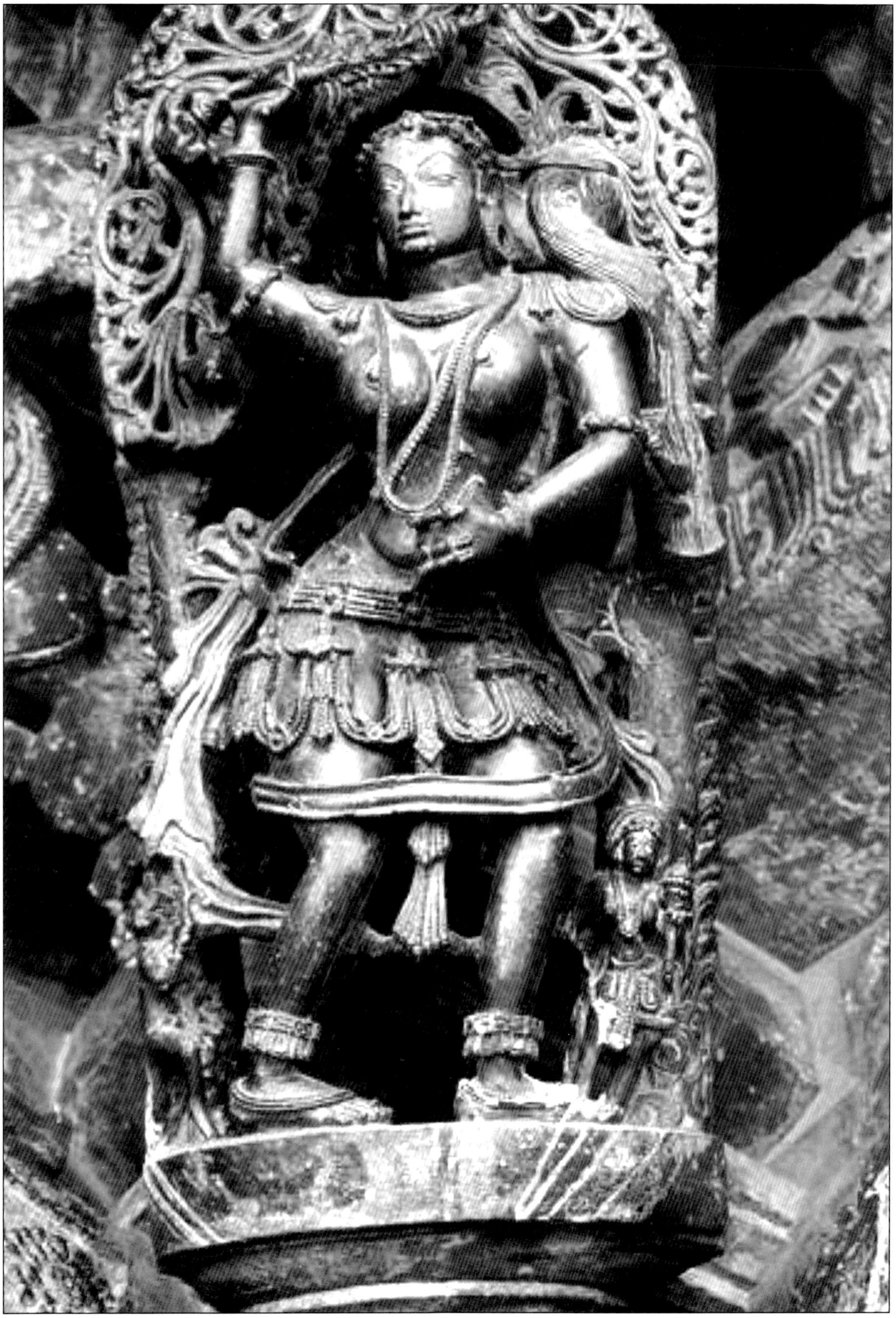

Pl. XL. B.F. 34. *Apsara*'s encounter with a monkey

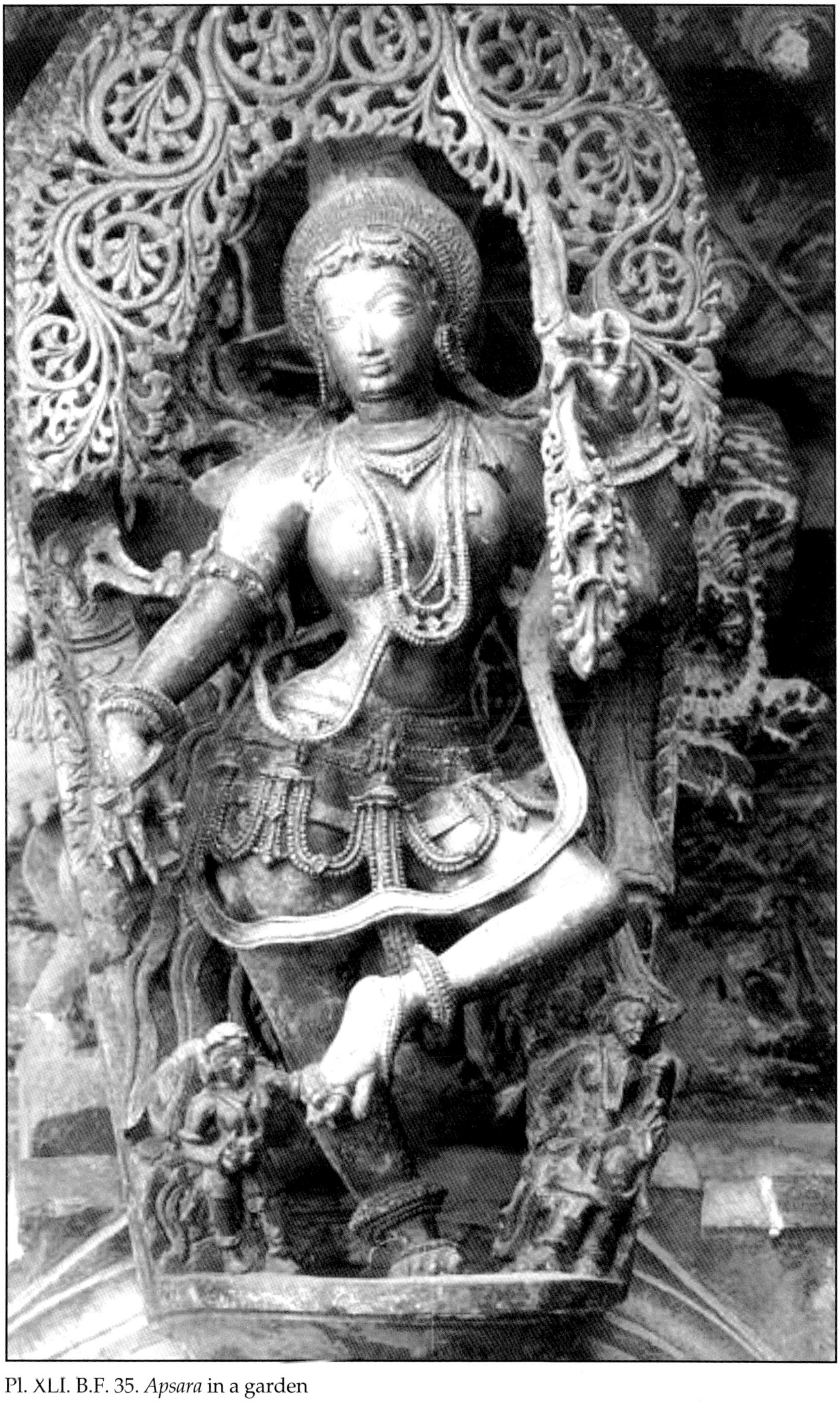

Pl. XLI. B.F. 35. *Apsara* in a garden

B.F. 36

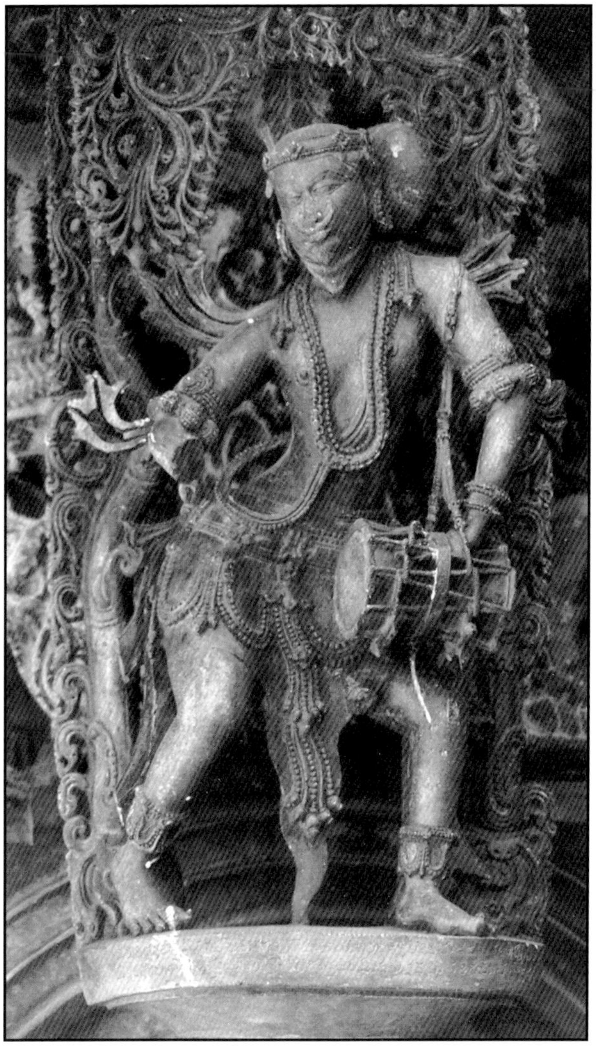

Pl. XLII. B.F. 36. A drummer (B.F. 37 – Picture not available)

B.F. 38

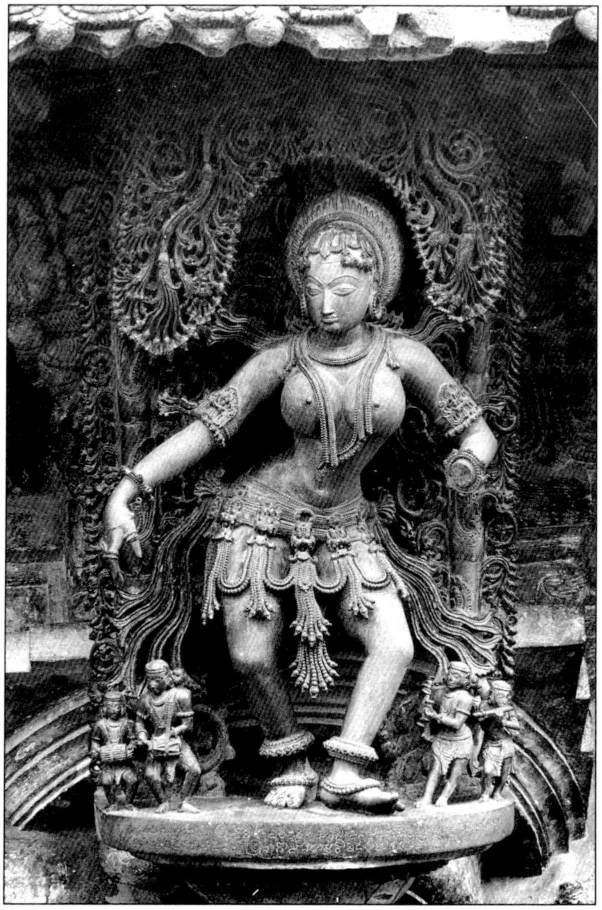

Pl. XLIII. B.F. 38. *Apsara* in a graceful dance movement

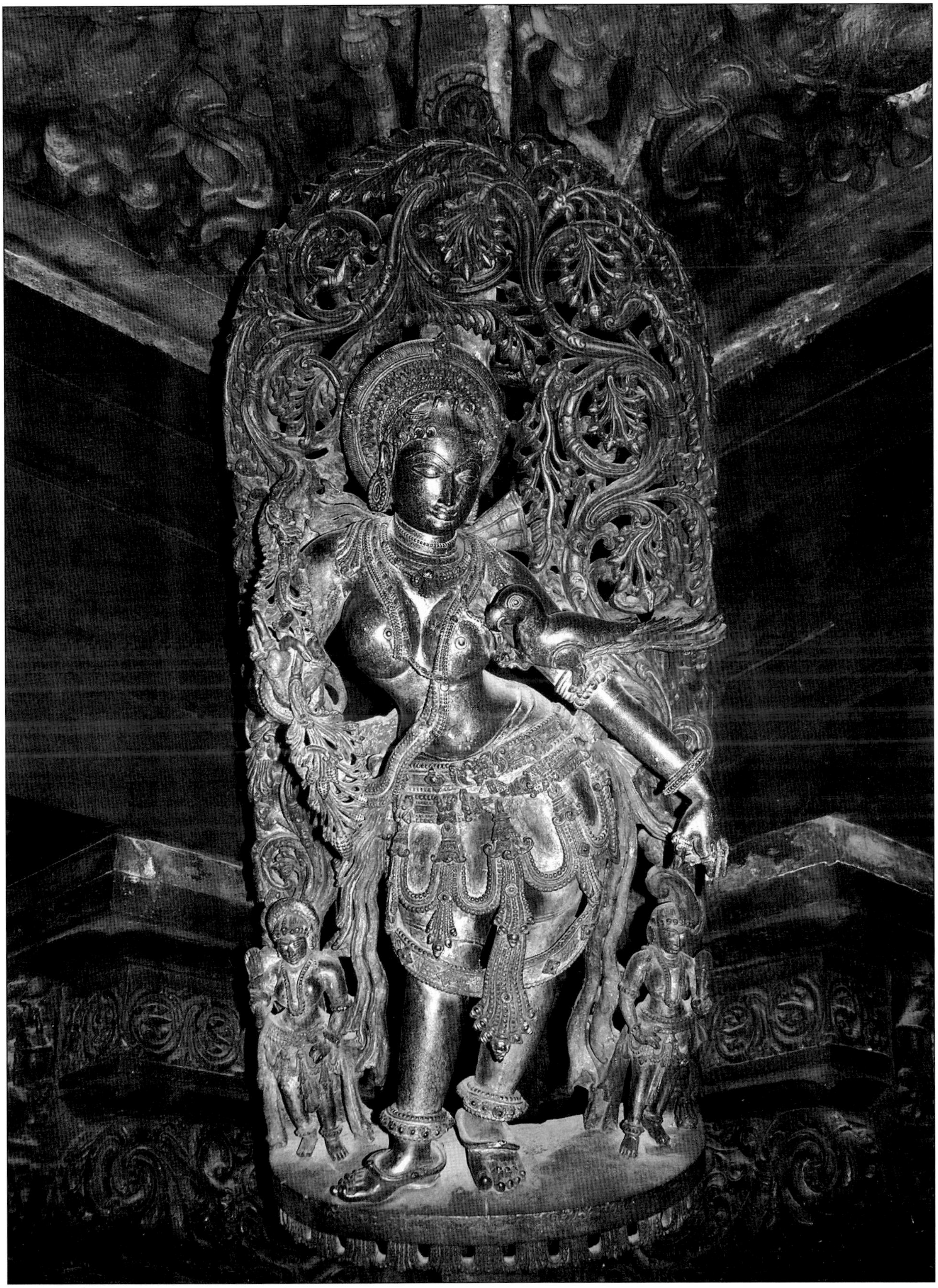

Pl. XLIV. B.F. 39. *Apsara* with a parrot (on the *Navaraṅga* pillar)

B.F. 40

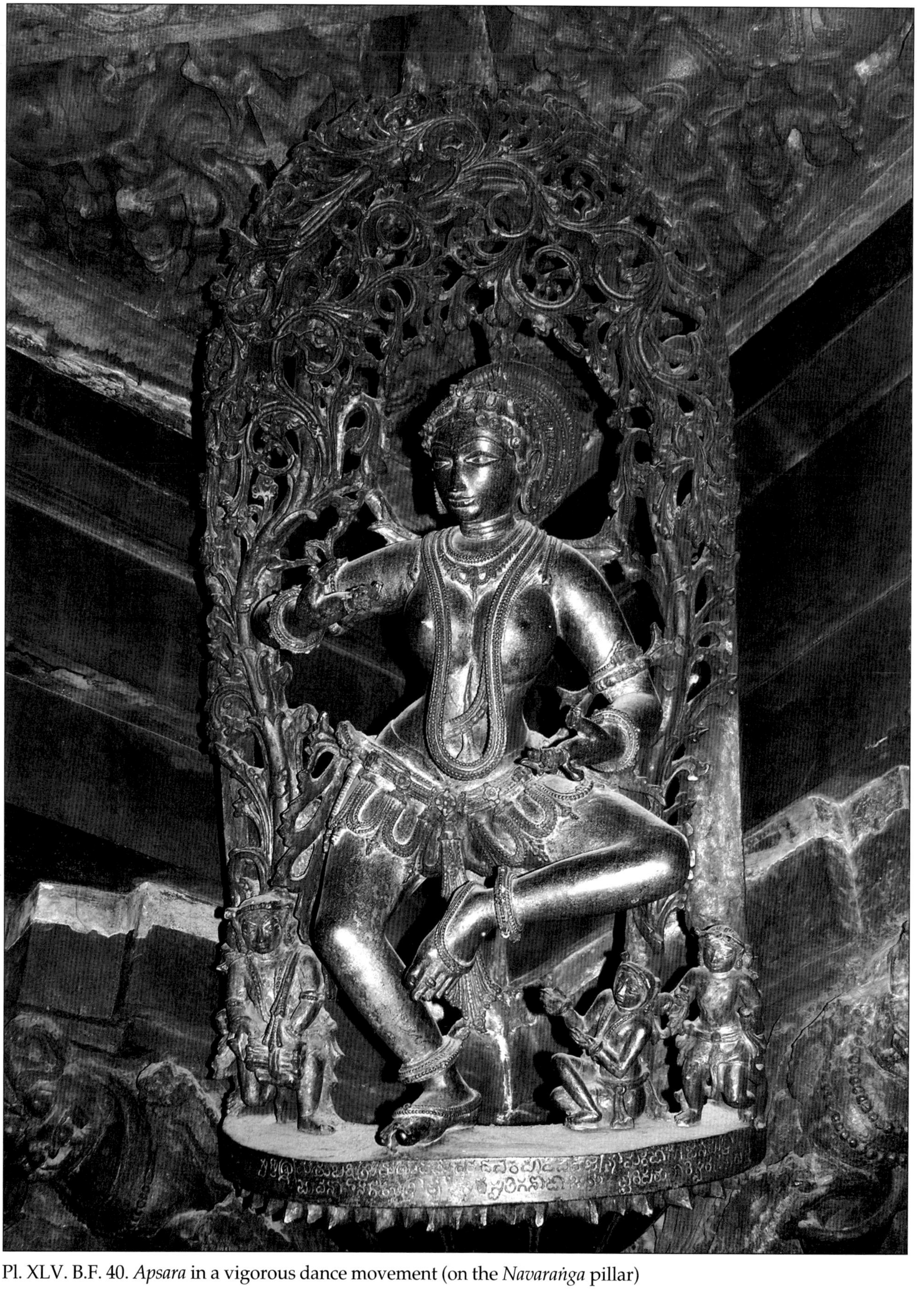

Pl. XLV. B.F. 40. *Apsara* in a vigorous dance movement (on the *Navaraṅga* pillar)

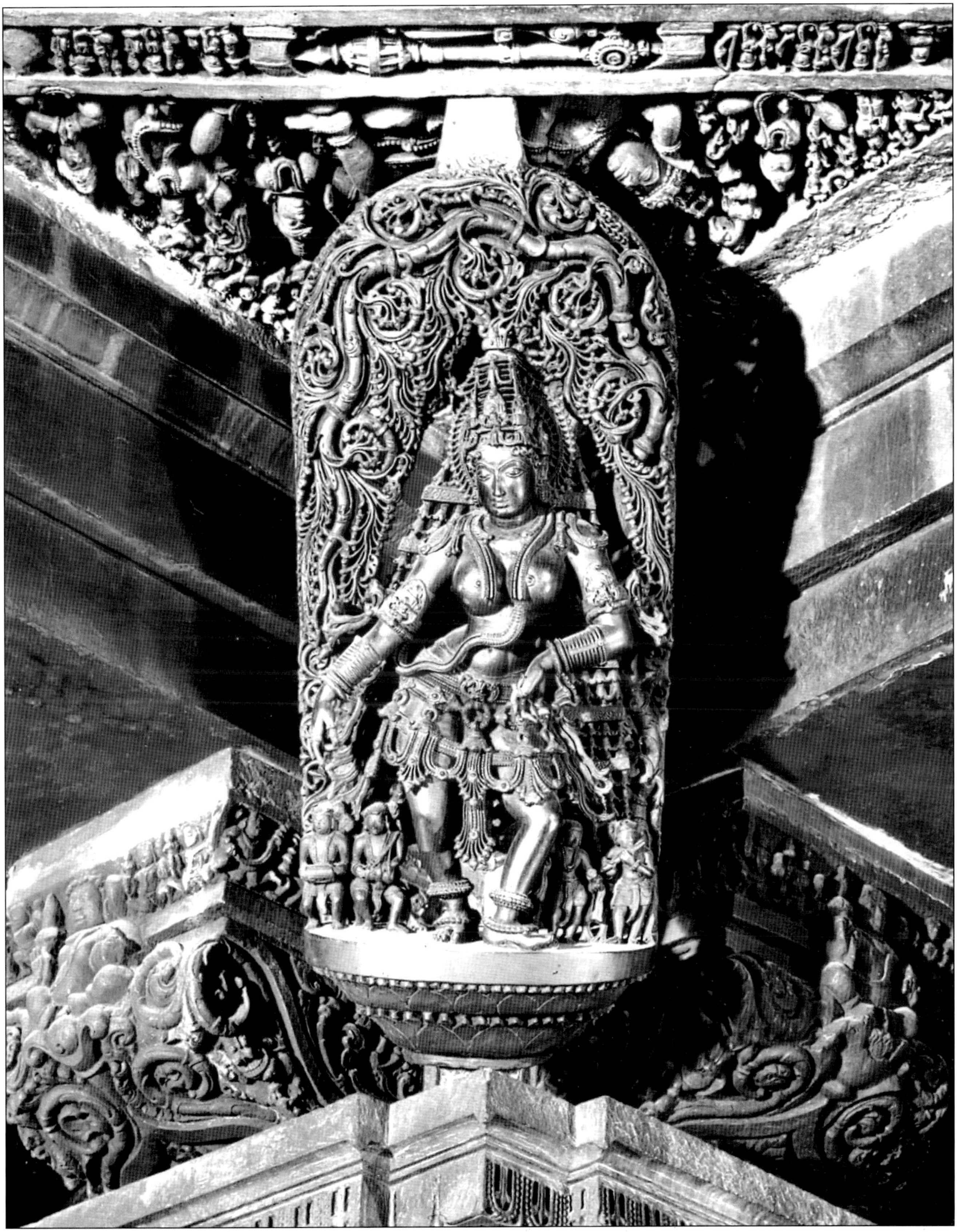

Pl. XLVI. B.F. 41. *Apsara* in a graceful dance movement (on the *Navaraṅga* pillar)

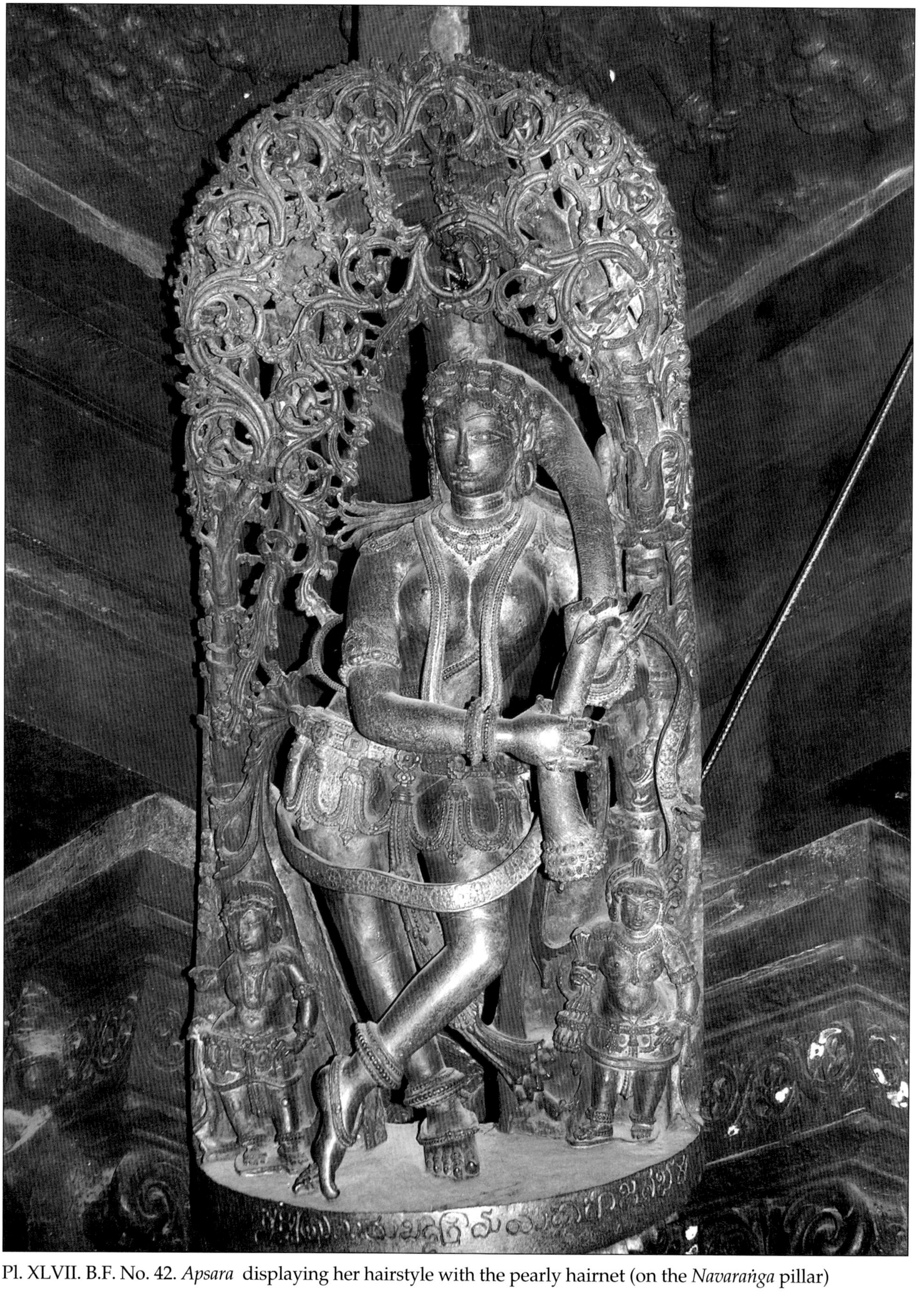

Pl. XLVII. B.F. No. 42. *Apsara* displaying her hairstyle with the pearly hairnet (on the *Navaraṅga* pillar)

Epilogue – Part II

All orthodox systems of Indian philosophy have one goal in view – the liberation of the soul through perfection, and the method is by yoga. *Apsara* is viewed here as a philosopher as she is a lover of wisdom.

The science of *Nādayoga* and *Kriyā yoga* is put before humanity through *Apsara* sculptures of Belur, a practical and scientifically worked out method of reaching the ultimate truth. The instrument of yoga is the mind. With the power of attention, when the mind is properly guided and directed towards the internal world, it illumines the facts after a phase of analysis. This is the only method of knowledge, the highest reward of which is that it has the power to take away all our misery. The theme of *Nādayoga* that is depicted in the *Apsara* sculptures is not based on any faith or belief, but the absolute practical truth which the *Apsara* finds out by herself.

The preliminary step for the attainment of total bliss, is *Kriyā yoga*, which means work or working towards yoga. Our mind is forever wandering, which gallops like a deer to a greener meadow. It means, the mind always rushes to a pleasurable site. When the rush happens often, attachment dwells on pleasures. There is no limit to a man's desires. When desires are not fulfilled, it results in pain, frustration, passion or anger. The very first step of *Nādayoga* or *Kriyā yoga* has to be the capturing of the mind and holding it firmly with the rein and not to let it wander the way it likes, or else the mind becomes a spoilt child. The next stage of *Kriyā yoga* is study. Study does not mean getting involved with light reading, but it has to be that work which guides towards the liberation of the soul. It should be strong enough to train the intellect because intellect, by itself, is a weak instrument that gives us knowledge, limited by the senses. Through the study of scriptures, a yogi has to go beyond the senses.

Further, a yogi has to meditate upon the knowledge gained or else the waves of passion that reside at subconscious level, will surface out and gain an upper hand. It is through meditation that a yogi can successfully get hold on the waves of passion and subdue them, before they become gross. Meditation is thus the means by which the obstacles for yoga can be destroyed, and the soul is guided towards renunciation or *vairāgya*. It is only on attainment of *vairāgya*, a yogi can devote himself to God which is *bhakti* or devotion, that gives the depth of understanding.

The next step is surrendering the fruit of knowledge or work to God. This is a state of total absence of ego or self-reference.

Rajoguṇ avasthā which the *Apsara* depicts has attachments, dwelling on sensual pleasures. This is discussed in Ch. I / 4. *Apsara* in *Jāgrut avasthā*. The first step of *Nādayoga* or *Kriyā yoga* – the *yoga* of technique where *Apsara* is seen with a captured deer in reins, is seen in B.F. 6, Ch. II/2 – *Apsara* in *Svapna avasthā*, which is suggestive of the wandering mind that has been captured.

The second step of *Kriyā yoga*, the study of scriptures, is discussed in *svādhyaya*, B.F. 28. The third step, where the *Apsara* is meditating on *nāda*, is clearly seen in sculptures, where she is with stringed instruments, percussion instruments and in graceful dance movements. The fourth step where *Apsara* is surrendering the fruit of knowledge is seen in B.F. 12 and 20, which is discussed in the IV stage of *Nādayoga – Vaikharī*.

Nādayoga leads to spirituality, a journey to the explorations of spiritual entity of things when reached to a pure core stage. By concentrating the powers of mind and turning them inwards, a yogi seeks to know what is happening inside. Concentration within is called *Antardhyāna*, which helps the mind to reach absolute truths, which are not anchored to the external conditions of life. In *Nādayoga*, it can be defined as *Antarmukhi gāna* or singing whose face is turned inwards giving away to *Antardarśan* to a continuous unfolding of an inner vision. This inner vision connects to *Anāhata nāda*, the unheard sound with the heard or *Āhata nāda*. In *Nādayoga*, if one is prepared with the mind, tuned to melody and rhythm, the meditation happens by itself. The steps in *Nādayoga* will help remove the obstructions to the final stage of meditation, when the soul is clear, leading to an eternal meditation. Thus, *Nādayoga* is both a physiotherapy and psychotherapy. Psychologically, *Nādayoga* initially activates the dormant centres in the brain and later higher areas of brain are activated.

Nādayoga is also a psychotherapy of act, based on the idea that all humans are endowed with the activity to unleash, examine and transform their emotions through creative endeavour of singing or dancing. The focus in *Nādayoga* is not embodied by a finished work of art. It is the process of articulation, self-awareness, exploration and improvisation that is more of a healing process. *Nādayoga* gives a unique opportunity of self-discovery, listening to the inner voice and relieving the psyche of its accumulations. As said by Aristotle, it is a pleasurable release of emotions to effect the healing and purifying of the soul. Seeing, appraising and assimilating the art of others also are the movements in the pursuit of art. (These are indicated in the *Apsara* sculptures through the male figures playing on the instruments.) *Nādayoga* provides focus on the process, rather than results. A constant exploration and assimilation of ideas positively acts as a self-mending process.

The goal of *Nādayoga*, whether it is from an inward journey of *Anāhata* or an outward journey with *Āhata*, is to reach a blissful state. *Nādayoga* definitely leads a yogi to a state of *samādhi* through a process of awakening a subject that is continuous and calls for a dedicated practice which leads the *Sādhaka* from one dimension to the other, till yoga (union) is achieved. At this level of yoga, *samādhi* can only be an experience rather than a discussion.

Glossary of Sanskrit Terms for Part I

Abhilāṣa	Longing for
Adbhuta	Marvellous
Adhōgata	Bent downwards
Āgama	Study of ancient scriptures or *śāstras*
Ahaṅkāra	Ego
Āhārya	Extra accessories
Aindra	A type of leg posture in dance
Ālambana	The root cause of a sentiment
Ālīḍha	A type of leg posture in dance
Aṅgada	Arm band
Āṅgika Abhinaya	Expression through movement of limbs
Antarāla	Vestibule
Anubhāva	The mode of expression
Apsara	Celestial beauty, represented as a celestial dancer on the outer wall of the temple
Avahittha	Standing posture
Avanaddha	Percussion
Āvaraṇa Devata	Surrounding divinities
Āyata	Standing posture
Āyōga	Appointment, accepting each other
Bhairavī	Goddess Durgā
Bhāva	The feeling
Bhavyata	To experience
Bhayānaka	Fear; the terrible
Bībhatsa	Disgust
Cārī	Leg movements
Cittānanda	Consciousness; bliss
Chandana	Sandal
Chouri	Fan
Cūḍāmaṇi	Head decoration worn on centre of head
Dāsī	Female servant
Daśarūpaka	A text on translation of Sanskrit treatise on dramaturgy by Dhananjayan and Dhanika (10th century AD)
Deśa	Place

Devalā	Goddess
Dhārāgṛha	A room with water jets
Dhātrēyī	Step-sister
Dīptī	Radiance
Dūtī	Female attendants, a messenger
Gaṇa	A troop of demi-gods; attendants of Lord Śiva
Gandharva	Gods who are proficient in music
Gaṇeśa	God of *gaṇas*
Garbhagṛha	Sanctum sanctorum
Ghana	Made of metal
Gōpura	Tower
Harṣaka	Snake-shaped neck chain
Hāsya	The comic
Hāva	Change of movements of eyes, eyebrows, neck
Helā	Graceful body movements
Jagati	Spacious platform
Kāla	Time
Kadaga	Large bangle
Kalā	Art
Kanchi	Girdle with 1 string
Kānti	Charm
Karaṇās	Basic dance units
Kārū	A servant who does menial jobs
Karuṇa	Pathetic
Kharjūrakā	Bracelet
Kiṅkiṇi	Small bell or tinkling ornament
Kinnarī	Mythical being with human figure and head of horse
Kride	Sport, Pastime, play
Kṛṣṇa	Epithet of Viṣṇu, born in his eighth incarnation
Kuṇḍalas	Large ear-rings
Kuśīlava	A male attendant who is good at playing musical instruments
Lajjānvita	Shy
Lakṣaṇas	Salient features
Lakṣmī	Goddess of wealth
Lalitā	Beautiful
Liṅginī	An attendant who is literate
Latāgṛha	A shady enclosure, surrounded with creepers
Mādhurya	Sweet, delicate
Mahābhārata	Epic
Malnad	Hilly region of western ghats
Maṇḍala	Round, circular, a standing posture, in dance
Maṇḍapa	Hall
Mēkhalā	Girdle band with 8 strings
Mocaka	Ear pendant
Mudrāṅgulīya	Finger rings with different motifs
Muktāvalī	Pearl necklace
Nartakī	A female dancer, singing girl or actress

Nāṭaka	A play or drama
Nāṭakīya	Pertaining to drama
Naṭī	An actress (regarded as the wife of Sutradhara)
Nāṭyaśāstra	A treatise on dramaturgy
Navaraṅga	Pillared hall
Nūpura	Tiny bells
Pārvatī	Epithet of Durgī; Daughter of Parvatarāja
Piṇḍipatra	Decoration on head looking like a petal arrangement
Panīyaja	A hunting game played near water
Pradakṣiṇa Patha	Circumambulatory passage
Prātiveśika	A neighbour
Purāṇa	Ancient sacred literary works
Rāmāyaṇa	Epic
Ramya	Beautiful
Rasāna	Girdle with 16 strings
Rasas	Sentiments
Rati	Permanent mood of erotism
Ratnajālaka	Broad anklet
Ratnamālā	Chain with precious stones
Ratnāvalī	Necklace with precious stones
Raudra	Furious
Ṛṣi	Saints
Sakhī	Female companion
Śakti	Power
Śālabhañjikā	Emerging through the 'sāla' evergreen tree
Sambhoga	Union
Sarasvatī	Goddess of learning
Śāstramāna	Rules laid out for measurement in sculpturing
Sattva	Full of virtues
Śānta	Bliss
Sechana	Sprinkling
Śikhara	Tower
Śikhājāla	Hair-net with pearls
Śikhāvyāla	Hair-net looking like a snake hood
Śikhāpāśa	Hair-net
Śilpaśāstra	Art of sculpturing
Śilpinī	An attendant who is skilled in art forms
Śloka	Hymn
Śōbhā	Beauty
Sochitika	A type of bracelet
Śṛṅgāra	Erotic sentiment
Sthānaka	Standing posture
Sthāyibhāva	The durable or permanent effect of a sentiment
Strīsthānaka	Resting posture of a lady
Suṣira	Wind instrument
Sutraka	3-4 stringed neck chains
Svayam	Self

Svastika	To keep limbs in cross position
Tāla	Measurement of time or metre; also called rhythm
Tala	Measure of space in sculptures, approximately 12 aṅgulas
Talāka	Network of pearls worn on hips
Tata	Stringed instrument
Tilaka	Toe ring, a mark
Tribhaṅga	The bodyline deflection at three places, viz., hip, torso and neck
Uddīpana	The promoters of a sentiment
Upadēśa	Advice
Vādya	Instrument
Vaiśākha	A standing posture
Valaya	Arm ring
Vana	Garden, forest
Vēṇīguccha	Flowery ornament on braided hair
Vēṣa	Dress
Vetika	Golden ring
Vibhāva	Any condition which depicts a state of mind
Vidyādhārī	A special type of hair decoration, where hair is tied into a topknot and decorated with jewels
Vijayanārāyaṇa	Epiteth of Lord Viṣṇu
Vikāsa	To bloom
Vikṣēpa	Out burst
Vikṣōbha	To make anything turbid
Viprayoga	Separated
Vīra	Heroic
Vistāra	To swell
Yaduvaṃśa	Descendants of Yaduva dynasty
Yajñōpavīta	Sacred thread worn across the shoulder
Yakṣa	A class of demi-gods
Yakṣī	Celestial beauty when associated with a tree
Yogins	Angels with transcendental power

Glossary of Sanskrit Terms for Part II

Āhata	Struck, sound created by beating of two objects
Ājñā chakra	The sixth *chakra* situated between the eyebrows of the subtle body. At this *chakra*, the consciousness goes transpersonal
Ākāśa	Region of etheric space; pure consciousness
Anāhata	The unstruck sound; the heart *chakra* in the subtle body
Ānanda	Transcendent bliss, spiritual ecstasy
Annamaya kośa	The food formed sheath of the gross body, made up of the five elements – earth, water, fire, air and ether – which resolves to initial state after death
Antar	Being in the inside
Apāna	Breathing out, the wind that goes down
Ātmā	The self
Avidyā	Ignorance
Bhāva	The feeling
Bhupura	The square courtyard of the *yantra*, with four gateways
Bindu	Metaphysical point; the compact mass of *Śakti*
Brahman	The absolute reality
Bṛhat kinnarī	A stringed instrument with two big gourds
Buddhi	Intellect
Chanchala	Fluctuating, unsteady
Chinchinī nāda	The feeble sound of silver bells
Citta	Consciousness
Dhāraṇa	Concentration
Dhyasita	Sustained concentration, contemplation
Gettu vādya	A type of stringed instrument, where bamboo blades are used to strike the strings
Granthi	Psychic knots. The *chakras* are associated with Brahmā, Viṣṇu and Sadaśiva *granthis*
Guṇas	The quality of a material
Guru	A teacher, a spiritual preceptor
Icchā śakti	The power of will
Indriyās	The senses
Jāgrut	The first state of *jīva* – a wakeful state
Japa	A constant repetition of mantra either silently or audibly
Jnana śakti	The power of knowledge

Jñāna yoga	The union with the self through knowledge – A path of yoga which seeks self-realization through the pursuit of philosophical knowledge
Jñānendriya	The five senses of knowledge in the physical body; the organs through which knowledge is perceived
Kālī	The divine *Śakti*, symbolic of the dynamic power of eternal time (*Kāla*)
Kapāla	The skull bowl
Karmēndriya	The organs of action
Khatvānga	A sort of club made up of forearm bone and the skull of human.
Kōṇa	The curved stick used to beat the drum
Kośa	Sheath
Kriyā śakti	The power of action
Kuṇḍalinī	The cosmic female energy – that is located in the individual
Laghu kinnarī	A stringed instrument with two small gourds
Lāsya	The graceful form of dance
Laya	Rhythm
Maddala	A type of percussion instrument
Maṇḍala	The circular mystical diagram with specific symbols of divinities.
Madhyama	Cosmic sound in a gross form, prior to its manifestation
Manana	To remember repeatedly what is learnt
Maṇīpura chakra	The third *chakra*, psychic centre that is called the gem city
Manō nigraha	Control of the mind, which is wandering
Manōnmani	The mind is in *unmani* state, the highest state of consciousness; a secret name of Goddess Durgā
Manōnmayā kośa	The sheath of discriminatory process between *māyā* the illusion, and reality
Māyā	Illusion; the veiling of reality
Mṛdaṅga	A percussion instrument made of (*mrun*) mud or wood
Mukta	Liberated, free
Mūlādhāra	The first or root *chakra*, at the base of the spine in the subtle body
Murujā	A type of small drum, percussion instrument
Nādayoga	Union of the human soul with the supreme soul through the path of *nāda* oneness with *nāda*
Nādānusandhāna	Movement of the mind exploring the melody of mystic sounds
Nāḍīs	The channels of the subtle body through which the vital and *praṇic* currents flow
Nādōpāsana	Meditation on sound vibrations
Nṛtya	Pure dance, which is devoid of *abhinaya*
Pakhāvaz	A big percussion instrument
Paṇava	A type of ancient percussion instrument
Paravāṇī	The divine voice, the highest manifestation of sound energy, which is beyond the reach of ordinary consciousness
Paramātmā	The supreme soul
Pārvatī	Consort of Lord Śiva
Paśyanti	Second stage of the divine descent of cosmic sound, which is visually experienced. It is like seeing or observing sound, emerging towards audibility
Pratyāhāra	Withdrawal, restraining the organs
Prāṇa	The vital air of the inner body; the life force
Prāṇamaya kośa	The sheath through which vital energy circulates in the subtle body.

Prēyas	That which is pleasant immediately
Purāṇa	Ancient scriptures
Rāga	Colour, passion, amorous or sexual feelings
Rājasik	The phase of activity
Rajoguṇa	The state or quality, which is full of activity, both physical and mental
Ṛgveda	Knowledge. Veda of verses consisting of lyrics, mainly in praise of different gods
Rudra vīṇā	The long tabular stringed instrument; Lord Śiva was the inventor of this instrument
Rudra granthi	The psychic knot at *Ājñāchakra*, which is located in-between the brows of the subtle body
Rūpa	The form
Śabda Brahman	*Śakti* as the ultimate reality, in the form of primal sound energy
Sahasrara chakra	Thousand petalled, the seventh and the highest psychic centre – the dwelling place of Śiva
Śakti	Force, divine energy of Śiva
Sāmaveda	The third veda; the knowledge that is appealing
Samādhi	Deep meditation; a trans-like state in which the fluctuation of the mind ceases
Saṅgīta	Sung in chorus; singing accompanied by instrumental music and dancing, a triple symphony
Saṅkīrtan	Music sung expressing gratitude for God, in chorus
Surasvatī	Goddess of knowledge
Satchakra Nirūpaṇa	Defining the seven *chakras* – the psychic knots of the subtle body
Satya lōka	The abode of Brahman, the uppermost *lōka*, the world of truth
Śiva	Hindu God Śiva is pure consciousness
Sparśa	The sense of touch
Śraddhā	Faith, backed up by effort, sincerity and devotion
Śravaṇa	Hearing; to listen from a Guru
Śrēyas	That which is pleasant in the long run
Sukṣma Śarīra	The subtle body, which is invested by the grosser material
Suṣupti	The state of deep sleep, where the soul is withdrawn from the agitation of body and mind
Svādhyaya	Study of scriptures
Svādistāna	The second *chakra* in one's own abode
Swaramaṇḍal	A stringed instrument
Tāla	Rhythm; measurement of time or metre
Tala	Unit of measurement of space, approximately 12 angulas
Tambura	A stringed instrument used as a drone
Tāṇḍava	The vigorous and forceful presentation of dance movements
Tantra	The secret doctrine, that explains the knowledge of *tattvas*
Tapōlōka	In the world of meditation, one of the seven worlds
Tattva	The material elements of the universe like fire, earth, water, ether and air
Turīya	A state of the self uniting with the supreme self; oneness with God
Vādya	Musical instrument
Vaikharī	The fourth stage of sound, gross physical sound or vibrations
Vāk	Speech

Valaya	The netted concentric circles of a *maṇḍala*
Vāsanā	Impressions, unconsciously left on the mind by past good or bad actions, resulting in pleasure or pain
Vāyu	Air – god of winds
Vijñānamaya kośa	The fourth sheath of intelligence in the subtle body
Vikruta puruṣa	Changed person, affected by emotions of anger
Vikṣepa	Outburst
Vikṣoba	To make anything turbid
Viśuddha	The fifth *chakra* in the throat region, that is pure
Yogi	A student of yoga with transcendental power
Yantra	An instrument for holding several diagrams of meditative practices

Bibliography

Ali, Sheikh (ed.), *Hoysala Dynasty* (with special reference to an article by Settar S. 'Salabhanjikas' with special reference to Belur), Prasaranga University of Mysore, Mysore, 1972.

Chinmayananda, Swami, *Meditation and Life*, Chinmaya Publications and Central Chinmaya Mission Trust, 1992, Reprint June 2004, Mumbai.

——, *The Holy Geeta* (Commentary), Central Chinmaya Mission Trust, Reprint 2002, Mumbai.

Collyer, Kelleson, *The Hoysala Artists: their Identity and Styles*, Directorate of Archaeology and Museums, Mysore.

Encyclopedia of Indian Temple Architecture, South India upper Dravida Desha – Later Phase, American Institute of Indian Studies.

Ghosh, Manmohan (ed.), *Nāṭyaśāstra*, Vol. 1 and 2, Calcutta.

——, *Nandikesvaras Abhinaya Darpanam* (A Manual of Gesture and Posture used in Ancient Indian Dance and Drama), The Manisha Granthalaya Pvt. Ltd., Calcutta.

Gondekar, S.G.K., *Manasollasa* (Abhilasitartha Chintamani, Part III), Somesvara, O.R.I. Baroda, 1939.

Hardy, Adam, *Indian Temple Architecture: Form and Transformation*, Indira Gandhi National Centre for the Arts, New Delhi.

Kamath, Jyotsna K., 'Social Life in Medieval Karnataka', New Delhi, 1980.

Khan, Hazrat Inayat, 'The Mysticism of Music, Sound and Word', *The Sufi Message*, Vol. II, Motilal Banarsidass, 1988, Reprint 2004, Delhi.

Kalaburgi, *Mānasōllāsa* (Kannada trans.), Prasaranga, Karnatak University, Dharvad.

Nagaraj, Nalini, 'Art Series - 3, Belur', Art Publishers of India, Bangalore.

Narasimhachar, L., *A Guide to Belur Chennakeshava Temple*, Directorate of Archaeology and Museums, Government of Karnataka.

Rangacharya, Adya, *Nāṭyaśāstra* (Kannada), Akshara Prakashan, Sagar, Karnataka for Ninasam Theatre Institute, Heggodu.

Rao, H.S. Gopala, *Kalyana Calukya Devalayagalu: A Cultural Study* (in Kannada), Karnataka.

Rao, Rekha, *Therapeutics in Indian Sculptures*, Aryan Books International, New Delhi, 2006.

Sivananda, Swami, *Tantra Yoga, Nada Yoga and Kriya Yoga*, A Divine Life Society Publication, U.P. Himalayas, India, 2000.

Subbanna, K.V., *Dasharoopaka* (Kannada), translation of the Sanskrit treatise on dramaturgy by Dhananjaya and Commentary by Dhanika (Both 10th cent. AD) with detailed introduction and notes, Ninasam Theatre Institute, Akshara Prakashan, Heggodu.

Subrahmanyan, Padma, 'Bharatas Art Then and Now' (Lecture by Padma Subrahmanyam), Bhulabhai Memorial Institute, Bombay.

Tarlekar, G.H., *Studies in the Nāṭyaśāstra* (with special reference to the Sanskrit drama in performance), Motilal Banarsidass, Delhi.

Vadya Darshan (An exhibition of Indian Musical Instruments), Lalitkala Galleries, Ravindra Bhavan, New Delhi, Sangeet Natak Academy, National Academy of Music, Dance and Drama, New Delhi.

Index